EIGHT MEN OUT

The Black Sox and the 1919 World Series

ELIOT ASINOF

An Owl Book

Henry Holt and Company
New York

Henry Holt and Company, LLC
Publishers since 1866
115 West 18th Street
New York, New York 10011

Henry Holt® is a registered trademark
of Henry Holt and Company, LLC.

Published in Canada by Fitzhenry & Whiteside Ltd.,
195 Allstate Parkway, Markham, Ontario L3R 4T8.

Library of Congress Cataloging-in-Publication Data
Asinof, Eliot.
Eight men out.
"An Owl book."
ISBN 0-8050-6537-7
1. Chicago, Baseball club (American League)
2. World Series (Baseball)   I. Title

Henry Holt books are available for special promotions and
premiums. For details contact: Director, Special Markets.

First published in hardcover by
Holt, Rinehart and Winston in 1963.

First Owl Books Edition 1987

Designed by Ernst Reichl

Printed in the United States of America

30   29   28   27   26   25   24   23

Grateful acknowledgment is made to the following authors
and publishers for permission to reprint excerpts from their
copyrighted works:

Charles Scribner's Sons for permission to quote from
The Great Gatsby by F. Scott Fitzgerald.

Russell & Volkening, Inc., and to Nelson Algren for permission
to reprint scattered lines from *Swede Is a Hard Guy*,
copyright 1942 by the Southern Review, Inc.

A. S. Barnes & Company, Inc., for permission to reprint extracts
from *My Baseball Diary* by James Farrell.

To John Sayles and Maggie Renzi

CONTENTS

PREFACE

The 1919 World Series sellout and its dramatic aftermath has long remained in the public eye. The Black Sox Scandal, as it came to be called, was reported in its day on the front pages of every major newspaper in the country, then revived in a score of magazine articles and described in histories of modern baseball. But the accounts, at the time and since, have inevitably been fragmentary. No one delved into the scandal's causes and morality, exploded its myths and distortions. The complete story, shrouded in complexity and silence, remained untold. Apparently, the real truth was lying hidden beneath the weight of all the reports and speculations.

The question was, how to uncover it?

Obviously, there were too many diverse ingredients to be uncovered from any one source. No one person could possibly know all the factors. Many of the participants never met each other nor even knew of each other's existence. Top-level gamblers who controlled the action remained hidden from the small-time gamblers who operated on their own. The actions of the eight ballplayers remained unknown to the fixers. And, as revealed in their confessions, much of what each of the players did was a mystery even to their co-conspirators.

My problem, then, was one of weaving together a multitude of obscure, seemingly unrelated threads. A dozen leading newspapers around the country gave a daily, play-by-play account of the series. Columns by noted writers like Hugh Fullerton of the Chicago *Herald and Examiner* and the New York *Evening World,* Dan Daniel of the New York *Sun,* James Isaminger of the Philadelphia *North American,* Jim Cruisenberry and Irving Vaughn of the Chicago *Tribune,* Warren Brown of the Chicago *American,* and the syndicated Damon Runyan and Ring Lardner all contributed important leads and invaluable insights. The coverage in baseball's national weekly, *The Sporting News,* published in St. Louis by Taylor Spink, was extensive after the scandal broke. The monthly *Baseball Magazine* was persistently rich with interviews and stories about leading baseball personalities.

As the years went by since that fateful world series, references to its leading participants inescapably kept the scandal in the news. Each of these reports added something to the whole picture. A word here, an action there. For example: Attorney Raymond J. Cannon precipitates an angry flurry in a 1924 Milwaukee courtroom while trying to recoup Shoeless Joe Jackson's unpaid back salary, and suddenly uncovers a vital secret of the 1919 mystery. Arnold Rothstein is murdered in 1928 and the FBI discovers in his files a number of pertinent references to his involvement. John Lardner, son of Ring who reported the series, writes an article in 1938 exposing a previously unreported detail that immediately places another in proper focus. Rothstein's partner, Nat Evans, dies in 1959 permitting Abe Attell, another ex-Rothstein associate, to reveal his participation in the fix. A Chicago Judge, Hugo Friend, who presided at the 1921 Black Sox trial, reveals a hitherto unexposed legal point and throws a fresh light on the devious political machinations surrounding the trial.

Little by little, in this fashion, the story gets pieced together. Hanging over all this research, however, were two severely limiting factors: first, the official documents relating to the scandal had disappeared; and second, most of the participants had died without talking, while those who survive continue to maintain silence.

As for the missing documents, their disappearance is an intriguing story in itself, the main details of which are covered in this book. Three of the eight ballplayers signed confessions, but they were stolen from the Illinois State's Attorney's office before the trial. The last reference to their whereabouts dates back to 1924. Somewhat the same story applies to the voluminous testimony of the turbulent 1920 Grand Jury investigations of gambling in baseball. No one with whom I came in contact had ever seen the transcripts nor had they any idea where they might be found. Fortunately, most of the important testimony, including the confessions, was leaked to the battery of hungry reporters who crowded the hallways outside the Grand Jury room. As for the records of the 1921 trial, with the co-operation of John Stamos, Assistant Illinois State's Attorney in 1960, a thorough search of the basement archives in the Criminal Courts Building was made. It revealed only a despairing recollection from an aging clerk that "someone else was hunting for them a dozen or so years ago," but they were not to be found, then or now. Once again, this leaves newspaper accounts as the principal source. Since the news of the trial dominated front pages throughout the country, the coverage was adequate.

The silence of the participants presented another formidable obstacle. I covered several thousand miles tracing down a number of surviving members of that great 1919 Chicago ball club. They were aging men, most of them living quietly in retirement. During lengthy meetings with them and members of their families, I found them willing, even eager, to recount the pleasures and frustrations of their baseball careers. But they immediately turned away at the first suggestions of talk about the 1919 world series.

This was generally true not only of the Black Sox, but also of their innocent teammates. Their recollections of the series were guarded, as if the shame of the scandal was to be shared by them all.

On top of this there was a residue of fear. The tradition of silence sprang from a deeply imbedded awareness of the vindictive power of the 1920's gambling-gangster world with which they had all come in contact. I was told by more than one ballplayer that it was safer to keep one's mouth shut about this whole affair.

For all the reticence, however, there are usually leaks with so many people involved. The uncovering of the scandal was as dramatic an experience as this writer has ever had. A persistent siege on the stronghold of secrecy inevitably reveals an opening. In time, there were many. Many of the sources spoke in complete privacy and choose to remain anonymous. Many dialogues and incidents recounted in the book are the result of invaluable reminiscenses of these men.

Wherever possible, it seemed appropriate to reconstruct the story of the Black Sox in the jargon of the participants. Based on all that has been written about the players and on the additional information I have gathered, I have sought to recapture the turmoil of their experience. Many of the incidents reported in the book inevitably represent a composite of sources. Newspaper accounts of the games and confessions indicated, for instance, how the players actually threw the Series. The book, then, stands as a reconstruction of the Black Sox scandal drawn from a rich variety of sources and from research into all the scattered written material concerning it.

I am indebted to many for their assistance. For those passages relating to the history of baseball, I relied on the excellent works of Robert Smith and Dr. Harold Seymour. In Cooperstown, N.Y., baseball's historian, Lee Allen, generously offered his knowledge and the documents of the Hall of Fame's excellent library. In Chicago, the staff of the Historical Society Library was more than co-operative. The New York Public Library and its newspaper annex were invaluable sources.

My appreciation also goes to Mervin Block of the Chicago *American,* and Bill Surface, formerly associated with the Chicago *Tribune.* I am especially grateful to the noted Chicagoan, James T. Farrell, who supplied a fund of names, events, and dates from his amazing memory. Many of these names led to others. Much of his data opened doors to previously unexplored areas. Above all, he encouraged me to pursue a central theme that gave the work its real reason for being: the story of the 1919 World Series scandal must be centered around the lives of those eight men. Why did they do it? What were the pressures of the baseball world, of America in 1919 itself, that would turn decent, normal, talented men to engage in such a betrayal?

—E.A.

INTRODUCTION

In *The Godfather, Part II*, gambler Hyman Roth laments that the real movers and shakers of society—kings and princes of the underworld—do not receive their proper public acclaim. He suggests that, above all, a statue should be erected to Arnold Rothstein for his brilliant and audacious job of fixing the 1919 World Series. In his lyrical novel *Shoeless Joe*, W. P. Kinsella tells the story of Ray, an Iowa farmer who, seated one spring evening on his porch, hears a voice stating, "If you build it, he will come." Ray somehow knows that the unnamed man could only be Shoeless Joe Jackson, and that if Ray builds a ballpark in his cornfield, Jackson will come to play.

These tales, from such disparate men and sources, illustrate the continuing hold that the Black Sox Scandal has upon the hearts and minds of baseball fans and, more widely, upon anyone fascinated with American history or human drama at its best. The "eight men out" of Asinof's wonderful book—eight players of the Chicago White Sox, banned for life from baseball for their roles in dumping the 1919 World Series to the Cincinnati Reds—do not represent an isolated incident in an otherwise unblemished history of baseball. Links between players and gamblers, and the subsequent fixing of games, had become a scarcely concealed sore that threatened to wreck professional baseball in its youth during a difficult period of declining attendance and waning public confidence. Bill James pays homage to this book (in his *Historical Baseball Abstract*) by titling his discussion of game fixing during the teens and twenties "22 men out"—to show how many more beyond the Black Sox were accused. The others included such greats as Ty Cobb, Tris Speaker, and Smokey Joe Wood, but no plot was so sensational, no resolution so fierce as the Black Sox Scandal. The "eight men out" of the Black Sox embody what can only be called baseball's most important and gripping incident.

If we ask why this story so interests us more than half a century later, I would venture three basic sets of reasons:

First, so many aspects of the scandal are intimately bound—in interestingly ambiguous rather than cut-and-dried ways—with our most basic feelings about fairness and unfairness. We bleed for these men, banned forever from a game that provided both material and personal sustenance for their lives. They were not naïve kids, tricked by some slick-talking mobsters, but seasoned veterans, embittered and disillu-sioned by a sport that had promised much, but had sucked them dry. We feel that, whatever they did, they were treated unfairly both before and after. Sox owner Charles Comiskey was not only the meanest skinflint in baseball, but a man who could cruelly flaunt his wealth, while treating those who brought it to him as peons. Later, when the Black Sox had been acquitted in court, the brass of baseball, behind their first commissioner Kennesaw Mountain Landis, continued their ban nonetheless. On the other side, whatever the justice of their bitterness, the Black Sox did throw the Series, thereby betraying both their uninvolved (and mystified) teammates and a nation of fans. The oldest of all Black Sox legends, the story of the boy who tugged at Jackson's sleeve as he left the courtroom and begged "Say it ain't so, Joe," still has poignancy.

Second, history's appeal for us lies largely in the fuel it provides for the ever-fascinating game of "what if?" How would the subsequent history of baseball have differed if the 1919 World Series had been honest, or if other men and teams had been involved? We can focus on many themes, from the persistence of the Reserve Clause and the failure of players' organization (until recently) to the continuing power of the Commissioner of Baseball, an office set up in direct response to the Black Sox Scandal. But consider only one personal item, perhaps the saddest result of all. Most of the Black Sox were fine players; pitcher Eddie Cicotte (29–7 with an ERA of 1.82 in 1919) might have made the Hall of Fame. But one man, Shoeless Joe Jackson, stands among the greatest players the game has ever known—and his involvement in the scandal wiped out an unparalleled career. His lifetime batting average of .356 is third highest (behind Cobb and Hornsby) in modern baseball, and the few who remember say that they did not see such a hitting machine again until Ted Williams arrived. He turned thirty-three in 1920 (while batting .382), his last year of play. If age had begun to creep upon him, the records give no indication. Moreover, batting averages increased dramatically in 1920 and stayed high for twenty years, so Jackson's unplayed 5–10 seasons might not have decreased this career record. Not that I can vote, and not that it matters, and not that this old issue will ever be settled—but Joseph Jefferson Jackson is the first man out whom I would put in the Hall of Fame. His sin is so old, the beauty of his play so enduring.

Third, putting emotion and speculation aside, the Black Sox Scandal had as enormous and enduring an impact on the nature of baseball as any event since Cartwright, or Doubleday, or Ms. Rounders, or whomever you choose, first laid out the base paths.

A few years ago, and for a different reason (yet another attempt to explain the disappearance of .400 hitters), I began to study the statistics of batting averages through time. Ever since the professional game began in 1876, league averages for regular players have hovered about .260. This equilibrium has been broken several times, but always quickly readjusted by judicious changes in rules. (For example, averages soared in 1894 when the pitcher's mound was moved back to its current sixty feet, six inches, but they equilibrated within two years thereafter. Falling averages in the 1960s, culminating in Yaz's league leading .301 in 1968, led to a lower pitcher's mound and a smaller strike zone—and averages quickly rose to their conventional .260 level.)

But one exception to this equilibrium stands out for its impact and endurance. Starting in 1920, league averages rose into the .270s and .280s and remained there for twenty years (the *average* hitter in the National League exceeded .300 in 1930). This rise signaled the most profound change that baseball has ever undergone. Scrappy, one-run, slap-hit, grab-a-base-at-a-time play retreated and home run power became the name of the game.

Babe Ruth was the primary agent of this transformation. His twenty-nine homers in 1919 served as a harbinger of things to come, but his fifty-four in 1920—more by himself than almost any entire team had ever hit before in a season—sparked a revolution. Fans have long assumed that this mayhem was potentiated by introduction of a "lively ball" in 1920, but Bill James has summarized the persuasive evidence against any substantial change in the design of baseballs (see his *Historical Baseball Abstract*). Rather, the banning of the spitball along with other trick pitches and, particularly, the introduction of firm and shiny new balls whenever old ones got scuffed or scratched were the primary agents based on equipment rather than people. (Before 1920, foul balls were thrown back by fans, and fielders would help their pitchers by scratching and darkening the ball whenever possible.)

If Ruth so destabilized the game, why didn't the brass change the rules to reequilibrate play as they always had before (and have since)? Why, in fact, did they even encourage this new trend with a changed attitude toward putting new balls into play and removing other advantages traditionally enjoyed by pitchers? The answer to this question lies squarely with the Black Sox and their aftermath.

The game had been in trouble for several years already. Attendance was in decline and rumors of fixing had caused injury before. The Black Sox Scandal seemed destined to ruin baseball as a professional sport entirely. Thus, when Ruth's style emerged and won the heart (and pocketbooks) of the public, he was viewed as salvation and permitted to instigate the greatest and long-lasting change in the history of the game. Bill James puts the issue well in writing: "Under those unique circumstances [the Black Sox Scandal and its sequelae], the owners did not do what they quite certainly would have done at almost any other time, which would have been to take some action to control this obscene burst of offensive productivity, and keep Ruth from making a mockery of the game. Instead they gave Ruth his rein and allowed him to pull the game wherever it wanted to go."

Educator and historian Jacques Barzun wrote, in a statement often quoted, that "whoever wants to know the heart and mind of America had better learn baseball." If baseball's appeal, beyond the immediacy of the game itself, lies in its history and its mythology, then the Black Sox Scandal represents a pivotal moment. For this incident sparked changes in all these areas: in the character of the game itself (see above), in the history of baseball's links to American society at large, and in mythology, by dispelling forever the cardinal legend of innocence. Innocence is precious, but truth is better. Babe Ruth visited sick kids in hospitals, but he also did more than his share of drinking and whoring—and his play didn't seem to suffer. Do we not all prefer *Ball Four* to the cardboard biographies of baseball heroes that were *de rigueur* before Bouton published his exposé? We must also understand the Black Sox if we ever hope to comprehend baseball. With sympathy, and with a tear.

—Stephen Jay Gould

"Who is he anyhow, an actor?"

"No."

"A dentist?"

". . . No, he's a gambler." Gatsby hesitated, then added coolly: "He's the man who fixed the World Series back in 1919."

"Fixed the World Series?" I repeated.

The idea staggered me. I remembered, of course, that the World Series had been fixed in 1919, but if I had thought of it at all I would have thought of it as a thing that merely *happened,* the end of some inevitable chain. It never occurred to me that one man could start to play with the faith of fifty million people—with the singlemindedness of a burglar blowing a safe.

"How did he happen to do that?" I asked after a minute.

"He just saw the opportunity."

"Why isn't he in jail?"

"They can't get him, old sport. He's a smart man."

F. Scott Fitzgerald
THE GREAT GATSBY

I THE FIX

"Arnold Rothstein is a man who waits
in doorways . . . a mouse, waiting in
the doorway for his cheese."

—*William J. Fallon*

1

On the morning of October 1, 1919, the sun rose in a clear blue sky over the city of Cincinnati. The temperature would climb to a sultry 83° by midafternoon. It was almost too good to be true, for the forecast had been ominous. From early morning, the sidewalks were jammed. A brightly clad band marched through the streets playing "There'll be a hot time in the old town tonight." Stores were open but business came to a standstill. There was only one thing on everybody's lips: The World Series.

Cincinnati had never been host to a World Series before. Nor did its citizens dream, at the start of the season, that the Reds would do much better than last year's weak third in the National League. Somehow the Reds had worked a miracle, which is exactly what the fans called their triumph. For winning the pennant, Manager Pat Moran was known as the "Miracle Man."

"Cincinnati is nuts with baseball!" wrote syndicated columnist Bugs Baer. "They ought to call this town Cincin*nutty!*"

The first two games of the Series were to be played here and every seat had long since been sold. Ticket scalpers were getting the phenomenal price of $50 a pair. Every hotel room was taken; visitors found themselves jammed three and four to a room, thankful to have a bed. In private homes, families crowded into one room and hung hastily made signs ROOMS FOR RENT on their front doors. City officials, recognizing the extraordinary conditions, announced that the public parks would be available to those who could not secure accommodations. Visitors slept on wooden benches, officially assured that added police patrols would protect them from thieves.

The center of all this activity was the Sinton, Cincinnati's leading hotel, which appeared to be bursting at the seams. The huge lobby was barely large enough for the throngs who used it as a meeting

place. Through it went such notables as Senator Warren G. Harding,
entertainer and songwriter George M. Cohan, former star pitcher
Christy Mathewson, brilliant young writer Ring Lardner. The restaurant and coffee shop were constantly overcrowded. The management
had the foresight to triple its food purchases, reaching a staggering
sum of $5,000 a day. The bakery boasted a daily production of seven
thousand rolls.

To the hard-nosed New York newspaperman, Damon Runyon,
the big day started like this:

"The crowds coagulate at hotel entrances. Soft hats predominate.
It's a mid-Western, semi-Southern town. Hard-boiled derbys mark
the Easterners. The streets of old Cincy have been packed for hours.
People get up before breakfast in these parts. The thoroughfares
leading to Redland Field have been echoing to the tramp of feet, the
honk of auto horns since daylight. It is said that some people kept
watch and ward at the ballpark all night long. Might as well stay there
as any place in this town. They would have had the same amount of
excitement. Flocks of jitneys go squeaking through the streets. This is
the heart of the jitney belt. A jitney is the easiest thing obtainable in
Cincy. A drink is next. . . . Cincy is a dry town—as dry as the Atlantic Ocean."

The excitement of the Series was prevalent throughout the country. The games would be telegraphed to every major city in America.
Halls were hired to which Western Union would relay the action,
play by play. Fans would experience the curious sensation of cheering a third strike or a base hit in a smoke-filled room a thousand miles
from the scene. Over 100,000 miles of wire were to be used for this
purpose, servicing 10,000 scoreboards in 250 cities, from Winnipeg,
Canada, to Havana, Cuba.

This was the climax of baseball, 1919, the first sporting classic
to be played since the end of the World War in Europe.

On this Wednesday morning, 30,511 people paid their way into
Redland Park. To the Cincinnati fans, there was a throbbing nervous
excitement and a secret foreboding. For all their enthusiasm, few could
realistically anticipate a World's Championship. Deep down inside,
they foresaw the adversary walking all over them. Not even Miracle

Men could be expected to stop the all-powerful colossus from the West.

For they were the Chicago White Sox, a mighty ball club with a history of triumphs. It was said that Chicago fans did not come to see them win: they came to see *how*. They would watch the great Eddie Cicotte, a pitcher with a season's record of 29 victories against only 7 defeats, who would tease the Reds with his knuckle ball that came dancing unpredictably toward the hitter. They would see Ray Schalk behind the plate, a small bundle of TNT, smart, always hollering. They would see the finest defensive infield in baseball, "Buck" Weaver, like a cat at third base, inching ever closer to the batter, defying him to hit one by him, always laughing. And "Swede" Risberg on shortstop, a big, rangy man who could move to his left almost with the pitch when he sensed a hit through the middle of the diamond. On second, Eddie Collins, the smooth one, the greatest infielder of his time; he made plays that left White Sox fans gasping. And "Chick" Gandil on first, the giant with hands like iron. They would wait for "Shoeless" Joe Jackson, the left fielder, to knock down fences with the power of his big black bat. They would laugh at "Happy" Felsch in center, since anything that was hit out there was a sure out. And "Shano" Collins in right; he could run, hit, and throw with any ball club in the league. There was a growing mythology about this great team; the public had placed a stamp of invincibility on it. To Cincinnati fans who had never seen the White Sox play the image seemed frightening. These were the big-city boys coming down to show the small-towners how the game should be played. There was no other way for any real fan to see it.

There was, however, one incredible circumstance that would have a bearing on the outcome: eight members of the Chicago White Sox had agreed to throw the World Series.

2

Of all the big league cities one
Is easy to get lost in.
I hardly need to tell you that
The one I mean is Boston.

Ring Lardner

Exactly three weeks before the World Series was to begin, a tall, beefy, red-faced man in a white suit and bright bow tie stepped out of a taxi and walked into Boston's Hotel Buckminster. His name was Joseph "Sport" Sullivan. His occupation: bookmaker and gambler.

He moved through the musty lobby to the front desk, picked up the house phone, and asked to be connected with Mr. Arnold "Chick" Gandil. As he waited, he surveyed the subdued, conservative, old-lady atmosphere. Although he had lived in Boston all the forty-four years of his life, he could not remember when he had been here last. In his profession, he seldom did business with subdued, conservative old ladies. There was something ludicrous about the Chicago White Sox Baseball Club staying here instead of at the Somerset or the Buckingham, more commercially centered and alive. Sullivan knew the reason for the change. He made it his business to know everything about the club.

During an earlier visit to Boston, there had been some trouble. These White Sox boys were an especially volatile, spirited bunch, a club loaded with bitterness and tension. There had been an excessive amount of drinking one night, and before the party was over, they had made wrecks of the funiture. Chairs, lamps, tables, even beds had been dumped out of the windows into the courtyard below. The hotel management thereupon had advised the Chicago organization that its patronage was no longer solicited. Harry Grabiner, Secretary of the Club, decided that a more subdued atmosphere might influence the boys. The Hotel Buckminster was the result. . . .

Sullivan's ear was suddenly jarred by Gandil's loud greeting. Having identified himself to the ballplayer, Sullivan was immediately asked to come up. He had sensed that something special was in the air when they had spoken earlier in the day. Now the tension in Gandil's voice confirmed his hunch. Sullivan liked to rely on his ear. It was said of him that he could tell what a man was about to say by the first few seconds of his speech. That Gandil had called him was in itself certainly not surprising. He had known the first baseman for eight or nine years and, as a result, knew all about him:

Chick Gandil was as tough as they come. He was thirty-one years old. He stood six feet, two inches tall; a broad, powerful 197 pounds. This was his fourteenth year in baseball. He had started at the age of seventeen after running away from home in St. Paul, Minnesota. He had hopped a freight bound for Amarillo, Texas, where he'd heard he could get a job playing semipro ball. Later, he caught on with an outlaw team in Cananea, Mexico, just across the Arizona border. Cananea was a wide-open mining town, congenial to his wild, rough temperament. Gandil not only played ball; he became a heavyweight fighter, taking in $150 a fight, far more money than he had ever seen before. In the off season, he worked as a boilermaker in the local copper mines. Back in Texas, at nineteen, he met the girl who became his wife. If the marriage had gratified him, it was because he was permitted to remain a roughhouse character.

He played minor-league ball until 1910 when he was picked up by the Chicago White Sox. He was sold to the Washington Senators, then to Cleveland in 1916, then back to Chicago. He was a reliable .280 hitter and an exceptionally strong first baseman, whose extraordinary hands were his greatest asset. It was said that he was the only first baseman around who didn't need a glove.

It was while Gandil was with Washington that Sullivan met him at a Boston pool hall. In typically gracious manner, he made friends with the big ballplayer immediately, buying him drinks, handing him good cigars. And also, before long, he found a way to profit by the friendship. Gandil would give him tips on ball games. "How is the great Walter Johnson feeling today? . . . Is there any reason why he might not be effective this afternoon?" This sort of innocent-sounding information gradually led to a more advanced procedure. When the Washington Senators were not in Boston, a timely long-distance phone call might elicit a piece of news that would alter the balance of the odds . . . like an unexpected change in pitching plans. If Sul-

livan alone had such a tip, he could use it to great advantage. His
office would immediately get busy on the several long-distance hook-
ups to various gambling centers and place bets accordingly. His resulting success baffled others, gaining him a reputation as something
of an expert on baseball. A number of prominent sporting people
began to commission him to bet for them, granting him a profit of
20 per cent on the winnings.

While there was nothing actually illegal about such manipulations,
their effectiveness was limited. This was the problem that Sullivan,
like all gamblers, had to contend with. Baseball was a complicated
game. It was extremely difficult to dope out the probabilities on any
one afternoon. There were simply too many variables. While this
might well present a challenge to the shrewder among them, its un-
predictabilty often left them frustrated. Constantly seeking to minimize the margin of doubt, they kept their ears open and waited for an
opportunity. Sullivan, however, did more than wait. Having found
Gandil, he went to work on him. He quickly saw that the big, tough,
unschooled rube, literally from the Wild West, glowed in the company
of successful men in big cities. Gandil liked the slick, prominent urban types. To be welcomed among them was, he felt, a mark of his
own rising status in the world. Sullivan the Bookmaker could boast
of an intimate acquaintance with V.I.P.'s like millionaire Harry Sinclair and George M. Cohan, and he made sure that Gandil met them.
Gandil was thrilled. They were all pleasant, friendly guys.

Today Gandil was in his hotel room alone. Sullivan greeted him
with his usual friendliness. In less than three minutes of small talk
the dour ballplayer got down to business, remarking to the gambler
that he had a proposition for him.

Sullivan kept his normally big mouth shut. When Gandil started
to talk about the coming World Series, Sullivan sensed what was in
the air.

Gandil was saying, "I think we can put it in the bag!"

His proposition was simple enough. He would guarantee to in-
volve a sufficient number of ballplayers to insure the defeat of the
highly favored White Sox. He wanted $80,000 cash as payment for
their implication. He had come to Sullivan because he knew no one
else who could raise that kind of money.

Sullivan listening, maintaining a cool façade. He acknowledged that such a scheme had possibilities, and told Gandil he would think it over. But when he left that hotel room, he knew only one thing: the biggest gambling bonanza in the history of baseball was being dropped magnificently into his lap like manna from heaven. Here was the big pay-off for all his efforts, the return for all those beers, the pool games, the fifty-cent cigars. He was the persistent salesman who'd finally made a big sale, bigger by far than he'd ever dreamed.

The fact that this was a shatteringly dishonest venture did not escape him. Curiously enough, he found the immorality of the scheme momentarily more troublesome than any fear of its consequences. It barely occurred to him that he was in any way vulnerable to the law, even assuming that something should happen to expose the fix. He could take this position not out of ignorance, but out of precedent. He knew of no case in which a gambler had gotten into serious difficulty for this kind of manipulation. Sullivan had always laughed at the workings of law and politics, for he had all the connections he needed to stay out of trouble.

Yet he had to admit that fixing a World Series was something else again. It was a very special American event. To tamper with it seemed treacherous, almost like sacrilege. On the other hand, this very circumstance could also make the deal fantastically rewarding—which, of course, was the determining factor.

But Sullivan was worried. For all his blustering, he never really considered himself either powerful or adept enough to assume control over a project as mighty as this one. It was not the kind of thing he would initiate. However, it had been brought to him; the problem was to whom he, himself, could take it.

In the last analysis, Sullivan would make peace with the fix readily enough. He would go with it wherever it led him and play it strictly by ear. He would keep the escape channels open in case he found himself in over his head.

There was always the chance that he could pull it off.

3

Baseball and betting were allied from the beginning. In the pre-Civil War years, the game was played in private clubs as an upper-class recreation, a polite competition in the tradition of British cricket. The gentlemen who played, as well as those who watched, saw in baseball a fine vehicle for a wager. And wagering was always an unofficial national pastime indulged in by all classes of American society. The very terms used in the first ball games were those of the gambler: runs were called "aces," and turns at bat were "hands."

To the bettors of the 1860's, a ball game had definite advantages. It was more intriguing than a horse race, more civilized than a boxing bout or a cockfight. It afforded a pleasant, even exciting afternoon in the sunlight, an event to which a gentleman could take his lady—and bet.

As long as the game remained amateur, wagering seemed only a pleasant diversion. But as the quantity of the bets increased, so did the desire to win. After the Civil War, the game really began to change for the better—or, if you will, for the bettor. The quality of the play improved. It was to win bets that inspired more and more clubs to hire ballplayers. (A star would be hired as a company clerk for $40 a week, a job that normally paid $6.) With the formation of the National Association of Baseball Players in 1871, followed by the National League in 1876, baseball became fully organized: admissions were charged, ballplayers were paid.

And with that, the professional gamblers moved in.

Baseball lost its gentlemanliness. It was quickly learned that a boy from the coal mines or the lumber mills could hit, run, and throw as well, if not better, than the son of the rich merchant. Pay him, and he would play harder, certainly be more tolerant of broken fingers (there were no gloves in those days) and vicious spike wounds (there was no end to them).

Though rising in popularity, baseball became corrupted with almost incredible rapidity. There was hardly a game in which some wild, disruptive incident did not occur to alter the outcome. An outfielder, settling under a crucial fly ball, would find himself stoned by a nearby spectator, who might win a few hundred dollars if the ball was dropped. On one occasion, a gambler actually ran out on the field and tackled a ballplayer. On another, a marksman prevented a fielder from chasing a long hit by peppering the ground around his feet with bullets. The victims had no chance to appeal: there was nothing in the rules to cover such behavior.

There were, of course, more subtle techniques for controlling ball games. Bribery became a common weapon, more widespread than baseball historians are wont to acknowledge. In 1878, just two years after the founding of the National League, the St. Louis weekly, *The Spirit of the Times* reported:

"Baseball, as a professional pastime, has seen its best days in St. Louis. The amount of crooked work is indeed startling, and the game will undoubtedly meet the same fate elsewhere unless some extra strong means are taken to prevent it."

The Buffalo *Express* indignantly suggested that the local club should "fold up if they can't play a square game."

So widespread were these ruinous practices, it seemed impossible to contain them. A famous attempt was made by President William Hulbert, founder of the National League:

In 1876, the Louisville Club had the pennant all but clinched. They moved eastward for a final six-game series with Hartford, a team that had been no real competition all season. The series was played in Brooklyn, on neutral grounds, and much to everyone's amazement, the great Louisville Club seemed to fall apart. Four players made innumerable errors in game after game. So staggering were these defeats that Louisville's President, Charles Chase, began an investigation. Struck by the numerous telegrams that one player, Al Nichols, was receiving daily, he demanded a written authorization to open them.

The messages were coded, but the repeated appearance of one word "sash" provided the key. "Sash" was the code for a fixed game. Chase shrewdly questioned his suspects. One of them was Jim Devlin, a star pitcher who had won 35 games. Another was George Hall, star outfielder and home-run hitter. Chase, playing one off against the other, got them to break down and confess. President Hulbert had them thrown out of baseball for life.

Curiously, perhaps, few seemed to take the expulsion seriously. Hulbert, however, did not relent—even though Hall was said to have appeared in the President's office some months later, with his toes exposed through torn boots, begging for a chance to earn bread for his wife and baby.

Significantly—though seldom noted—the four players who had accepted bribes (no more than $100 or so each) had done so because the Louisville Club had not gotten around to paying them their salaries!

In time, organized baseball grew up. Corruption dwindled as the status of the game rose in the public mind. Like the freewheeling roughhouse morality of the American frontier, excessive drinking, wildness, brawling, and contempt for umpires came to be ruled out. Baseball became a highly organized, respectable institution.

It was also becoming big business; in fact, by 1917, it was the biggest entertainment business in America. It could be said that its bigness rendered it blind. A consequence of its bigness was the inevitable appeal to all the promoters and opportunists who gathered like leeches to feed on its success. One promotion scheme was the baseball pool, which was a kind of lottery. Tickets would be printed each week on which anyone, with ten cents or more, could bet on a team to score the most runs per inning or game, the most victories per week, and so on. A typically famous pool, known as the Keystone, distributed over 165,000 such tickets each week. It employed 50 agents who, in turn, had 300 subagents. Since this kind of gambling was frowned upon in many communities, it was necessary to pay police protection that totaled $17,000 per week. Yet the Keystone Pool could boast a weekly profit of over $50,000.

The baseball owners had been informed of these practices—or malpractices. They did not really object, for all their public protestations. For one thing, because of the pay-offs, the pools had strong political backing. For another, the owners believed that they generated an even greater interest in big-league ball, especially among the children.

America's entrance into the World War in 1917 brought about

notable changes. When the Government shut down the race tracks for the duration (baseball was permitted to continue), gamblers and bookies who lived by the horses were left in limbo. They needed a place to hang out, some sport to talk about, an outlet for their need to bet. They simply converted their vast machinery of operation from horses to baseball. They applied themselves to doping ball games with the same diligence they'd used in handicapping horses.

In the process, they intruded themselves into the most intimate circles of the baseball world. The lobbies of major-league hotels were full of Sport Sullivans, operating around-the-clock schedules. Nice guys, one and all; friendly guys, ready with the warm hello and the funny yarn. They got to know the ballplayers well. The biggest of the gamblers had long since moved into higher social circles; many of them had become intimate even with the owners.

Inevitably this led to tampering with the outcome of games. Artfully, gamblers would find the likely players—preferably pitchers, the key men in any ball game. Who was getting on in years? Who was bitter about his dwindling paycheck? Who was getting along badly with his wife or with his manager? Such situations might be exploited by a little tasty extracurricular procurement while on the road. Gamblers were masters in the use of women and whisky: they seemed to have an endless supply of the choicest of both. Was there something "messy" in a ballplayer's life that could be held over his head? Then, finally, there was always the threat of violence to fall back on. . . .

By 1919, gamblers openly boasted that they could control ball games as readily as they controlled horse races. They even went so far as to put a few choice players on weekly salaries. Exploiting their own talents, bribed players learned to become adept at throwing games. A shortstop might twist his body to make a simple stop seem like a brilliant one, then make his throw a bare split second too late to get the runner. An outfielder might "short-leg" a chase for a fly ball, then desperately dive for it, only to see it skid by him for extra bases. Such maneuvers were almost impossible for the baseball fan— even for the most sophisticated sportswriter—to detect.

Only the ballplayers would know—sometimes. It was their profession and they weren't entirely blind. There were many who hated the corruption, but it soon became apparent that there was nothing they could do to prevent it. For one thing, how could anyone prove it? Even an honest, courageous newspaperman, tipped off to some specific sellout, could do nothing. Newspapers had to be careful because of libel laws.

But mostly, the cloak of secrecy was maintained by the power of the owners themselves. They knew, as all baseball men came to know. They knew, but pretended they didn't. Terrified of exposing dishonest practices in major-league ball games, their solution was no solution at all. It was simply an evasion. Whenever there was talk of some fresh incident, they would combine to hush it up. The probing sportswriter would be instructed—or paid off—to stop his digging. Ballplayers would be thanked for their information—and disregarded. Always, the owners claimed, for the good of baseball. Their greatest fear was that the American fan might suspect there was something crooked about the National Pastime. Who, then, would pay good money to see a game?

The official, if unspoken, policy was to let the rottenness grow rather than risk the dangers involved in exposure and cleanup. So all the investigations were squashed. This was business, pure and simple, for all the pious phrases about the nobility of the game and its inspirational value for American youth. In fact, that, too, was part of the business.

The story of Hal Chase illustrates the temper of the times. Chase was a superb first baseman, a dangerous hitter, an incorrigible troublemaker. He enjoyed the company of gamblers, if not for pleasure, then certainly for business. An enterprising man, he quickly learned that he needn't wait for gamblers to approach him before selling out a ball game. He'd arrange it himself and bet accordingly. He became adept at making faulty plays around first base so that everyone looked bad but himself. In the process, the outcome of the game would be altered.

He also tried to bribe his teammates, and one such incident eventually worked toward his undoing: In 1917, while Chase was playing with Cincinnati, a young pitcher, Jimmy Ring, was called in from the bull pen to save a game. The score was tied, two runners on base. As Ring was warming up, Chase walked over from first base and with incredible gall told him, "I've got some money bet on this game, kid. There's something in it for you if you lose." Ring snubbed him, but ended up losing anyway. The following morning, Chase found him seated in the lobby and deftly slipped him $50 without saying a word. Ring reported this to the new Red's manager, Christy Mathewson, formerly the great right-handed pitcher of the New York Giants. Matty immediately brought it to John Heydler, President of the National League. A hearing was held and Chase was conveniently acquitted. The evidence, according to Heydler, was insufficient.

Mathewson, a man of principle and a real lover of baseball, was disgusted. He wanted nothing more to do with Chase and got rid of him. But John McGraw of the New York Giants was not so touchy. By 1919, Chase had merely changed his base of operations to New York.

And so it went, incident after incident, year after year. If a man can sin with impunity, he will continue to sin—especially if he gets paid for it.

4

Chick Gandil had been thinking about the coming World Series for a long time. It could be said that he'd been thinking of little else. His problems would be manifold, and he was thoroughly aware of them all. How many ball players were necessary to insure the fix? Five? Six? And more significant than the number—who? First, pitchers. Impossible to fix the Series without them. He had to start lining up pitchers.

In July, the first door opened for him: the White Sox almost went on strike.

During the 1918 season, the war had cut into baseball's attendance figures. Wary of another financially difficult year after the war ended, the club owners had agreed to cut the ballplayers' salaries to the bone, despite the fact that they extended the season. Charles Comiskey, owner of the White Sox, had been especially loyal to the agreement. His ballplayers were the best and were paid as poorly as the worst. By mid-July, however, it became startlingly clear that the fears of the owners had been completely unfounded. Baseball attendance topped all expectations, especially at Comiskey Park.

Aware of simple arithmetic, the White Sox ballplayers griped. In the face of higher attendance, the lowered salaries angered them. They were winning ball games, burning up the American League. Their brilliance on the ball field added fuel to the fire. It was time to make demands.

There was an angry clubhouse meeting, and it was agreed that action should be taken. William "Kid" Gleason, serving his first year as manager, was to take their plea to Comiskey. Gleason could be trusted as sympathetic: the year before he'd had a salary dispute with Comiskey and had refused to accept terms. It had been Gleason's first season out of baseball since he'd broken in in 1888.

On the following day, Gleason returned empty-handed. Comiskey had refused even to discuss salaries!

The ballplayers heard this while dressing for a game. Enraged, they threatened to strike, but Gleason talked them out of it, promising to persuade Comiskey to give them bonuses. However, Gandil had noted one ballplayer who was so furious that Gleason thought better of playing him that afternoon.

He was Chicago's number one pitcher, Eddie Cicotte.

The more Gandil thought of him, the more he sensed he was ripe for plucking. Cicotte was thirty-five years old. He had pitched big-league ball for fourteen seasons. In 1917, he had won an incredible 28 games, leading his team to a pennant and world's championship. In 1919, he was on his way toward winning 29 games. Yet Comiskey saw fit to pay him less than $6,000! Many players of less stature got almost twice as much on other teams. Cicotte was not the type to show his bitterness, but he knew full well he would be dumped after his first poor season. Old men, it was said, don't make comebacks.

By mid-August, Gandil was openly talking "fix" to him. He posed as a fellow conspirator; together they would hatch a brilliant plot. But Cicotte wasn't buying. He had no arguments against the proposal: just scruples. Gandil kept after him, day after day, baiting the hook with the one bait that could overshadow a man's conscience: money. Cicotte was the type who always worried about money. He had bought a farm in Michigan and saddled himself with a stiff mortgage. He had tried to give his family a social status commensurate with his professional reputation, but his salary never justified it. There would be no pension waiting for him, only memories of his greatness. Memories, Gandil reminded him, didn't pay mortgages. He could promise Cicotte a tremendous sum of money. Cicotte could even name his own figure! He could make more in one week than he made all year.

But Cicotte remained adamant. He wanted no part of it. And as the weeks went by, it seemed to Gandil that his efforts were fruitless; it frustrated him terribly, since it had been clear from the start that he could not begin to operate without Cicotte.

Then, one night on a Pullman heading for Boston, Cicotte sat down next to him. Inexplicably, he mumbled his change of heart: "I'll do it for ten thousand dollars. Cash. *Before* the Series begins!"

That was all he said.

Immediately Gandil was off and running. With Cicotte aboard, he knew he could get others. Second on the list—there would be no trouble here—was shortstop "Swede" Risberg. He had already mentioned to Risberg the possibility of "fixing" the Series. Once too often, in fact. They had discussed it briefly in the locker room, not knowing that another ballplayer was lying on a bench behind a set of lockers. Utility infielder Fred McMullin, a friend of Risberg's, overheard and wanted in. There was no way to exclude him.

Gandil needed another pitcher. Cicotte would pitch two, maybe three games. The 1919 World Series was to run five out of nine. Gandil went after Claude "Lefty" Williams.

It was in New York, after a ball game against the Yankees. Gandil stood outside their hotel, the Ansonia, on Broadway and 74th Street, waiting for Williams to return from dinner. He pulled the great left-hander aside, and broached the matter to him. Williams was baffled, refusing at first to believe that such a wild scheme would be attempted. But Gandil was persistent and persuasive. Though Williams shied away, he didn't close the door behind him. He wanted to think it over.

That was enough for Gandil. He said that he'd already lined up the whole deal and that they were going ahead with it regardless of what Williams decided to do. So, if he was smart, he might as well get in on the take.

Williams was flustered. "Cicotte, too?"

Gandil nodded. He knew he had Williams now.

All he needed to complete the roster were a few of the big hitters. He set out after Chicago's big three, the 3rd, 4th, and 5th hitters. They were George "Buck" Weaver, "Shoeless" Joe Jackson, and Oscar "Happy" Felsch. Somehow Gandil got them all to a meeting on the following night.

That Gandil had selected a powerful combination, there was no doubt; it was also a convenient one. The White Sox had spent the season split into two cliques, and Gandil's eight ballplayers made up one of them. Unknown even to loyal Chicago fans, this was a ball club ridden with dissension. The rival group was led by the brilliant team captain, Eddie Collins, recently of Columbia University, New York City bred, high-salaried. (Collins had been smart enough to have his $14,500 Philadelphia salary written into his contract when Comiskey bought him from the A's in 1915. This was more than double the salary of any of his teammates.) Risberg hated this great second baseman, resenting his income and his background. Though they played side by side, the Swede refused to talk to him. So did Gandil. Collins could legitimately complain that there were times when he didn't get a chance to feel the ball unless Ray Schalk threw it to him.

Schalk, a fiery little catcher, was another whom Gandil hated. Schalk was hardly the sociable type: he had no trouble despising them back. Schalk and Collins, pitchers Urban "Red" Faber and rookie Dickie Kerr were constant companions. The two groups seemed like strangers.

Not all of the reasons for the animosity are known, or even explicable. Much of the conflict stemmed from clashes of temperament that grew to serious rifts. Some of it sprang from sectional prejudices: Jackson, an illiterate Southerner, found affinity with Lefty Williams, another Southerner. He also seemed to feel at home with the undisciplined toughness of Gandil and Risberg, both from the wilds of California. Felsch was a smiling, easygoing, badly educated boy from Milwaukee, constantly seeking raucous pleasure and adventure. This group was alive with it. Collins and his clique seemed somber and subdued.

To anyone who knew this ball club intimately, it was incredible that, with all the bitterness and dissension, they could continue to win ball games. That they did was, perhaps, the greatest possible testimonial to their baseball abilities.

On September 21, the eight ballplayers assembled after dinner in Chick Gandil's room at the Ansonia. In the history of American sport, it would be difficult to find another meeting that led to events so shattering. The ballplayers, however, appeared to have treated it all lightly. There was none of the conspiratorial somberness that might normally be attached to such occasions. Several of them made a joke out of it all, suggesting special bonuses to the guys who could make the most errors or leave the most men on bases. Happy Felsch lapped it up: he recalled—aptly—that when he was a kid, he used to get hit on the head by fly balls that seemed to slip through his glove.

Gandil, however, made sure that the terms were clearly specified. He recounted how he had demanded $80,000—in advance—at his meeting with Sport Sullivan, who had agreed to get it. The ballplayers would be paid off in full before the opening game. Details on how the games were to be thrown would be worked out with Sullivan and his backers, depending on how they wished to manipulate the odds— and how Kid Gleason chose to work the pitchers.

With hindsight, this meeting looms as a macabre opening to a tragedy. No doubt a wiser man than any of these eight players would have known it then and there. Here were eight men at the peak of their careers, playing on a pennant-winning club that might well be rated as one of the great teams in baseball history. They were idols to millions of fans, especially in Chicago, perhaps the best baseball town in America. With the exception of Cicotte, they could look forward to six to ten years of continuing triumphs and rising incomes. Instead, they chose to risk all this for a sleazy promise of dirty money.

Here was Shoeless Joe Jackson, commonly rated as the greatest natural hitter the game had ever seen. At thirty, he had passed ten sensational years in big-league ball, compiling a remarkable batting average of .356. His tremendous skill as a hitter kept improving with each passing year. He was a superb outfielder with a rifle for an arm.

Here was George "Buck" Weaver, smiling, boyish, not quite thirty, already heralded as the classiest third baseman in the game. Agile as a cat, defiant of all hitters, the only man Ty Cobb refused to bunt against. He had become a steady .300 hitter, climbing each year. He was an indomitable lover of baseball.

Here was Charles "Swede" Risberg, twenty-five years old, and in his third season in the majors. A big, rangy, brilliant shortstop, who could throw bullets to first base, who played ball like a man on fire.

Here was Oscar "Happy" Felsch, a warm, smiling, fast-moving outfielder, also under thirty. He was rapidly becoming a leading power hitter. As a centerfielder, he was among the best.

Here was Claude "Lefty" Williams, number two pitcher for the Sox. A quiet, soft-spoken Southerner with a highly skilled left arm. He had won 23 games, could boast of the finest control in baseball. On the mound, he always knew exactly what he was doing.

Then why . . . ?

Or, perhaps more significantly, why not?

It never entered their minds that they could not get away with their plan. There was almost no discussion of its dangers. They didn't even care about the men who would back it. The only security measure they ever took was to leave the hotel room one or two at a time.

For this was the world of baseball in 1919. Every one of them knew of thrown ball games. Two years before, they had participated in a strange manipulation that helped them win the American League pennant: almost the entire club had been openly assessed $45 each, ostensibly to reward two Detroit Tiger pitchers for beating Boston in a crucial series, but actually to bribe them to throw a double header to the Sox. Their own experience, as well as the existing corruption in baseball, made their participation in the fix all too easy.

Money was the goal, to be leaped at from a springboard of bitterness. These were eight bitter man with a common enemy: Charles Albert Comiskey. Whatever his stature in professional baseball, however many his notable contributions to its turbulent history, to his employees he was a cheap, stingy tyrant. All baseball salaries suffered in 1919, as noted, but even before that a skimpy paycheck was nothing new to a Chicago White Sox ballplayer. Joe Jackson, one of the greatest sluggers of his time, had never earned more than $6,000. Buck Weaver, the same. Gandil and Felsch were paid $4,000. Lefty Williams and Swede Risberg got less than $3,000. No players of comparable talent on other teams were paid as little. Compared with their

1919 World Series rivals from Cincinnati, these figures seemed piti-
ful. Outfielder Edd Roush, leading Reds hitter, though some 40 or 50
percentage points below Jackson, made $10,000. Heinie Groh, at
third base, topped Weaver's salary by almost $2,000. First baseman
Jake Daubert, recently acquired from Brooklyn, earned $9,000. It
was the same all around the leagues. Many second-rate ballplayers
on second-division ball clubs made more than the White Sox. It had
been that way for years.

The White Sox would receive their annual contracts and stare
glumly at the figures. In the face of Comiskey's famous intransigeance,
their protests were always feeble. Harry Grabiner, who, as club secretary, handled the contracts, would repeat the timeworn threat: Take
it or leave it! The threat had absolute impact, backed by the rules and
contracts of professional baseball itself. For each of them was owned
by the club, totally and incontrovertibly. If they refused to accept the
terms offered them, they could not play baseball anywhere else in
the professional world. No one could hire them. This was the famous
reserve clause, included in every contract, the rock upon which professional baseball rested. It said, in effect, that the club owner would
employ the player's services for one year, holding in reserve the right
to renew his contract the following year. And so on, in perpetuity.

But there was more to their grievances. Comiskey's penuriousness
went beyond their salaries. It was his habit to squeeze them in petty
ways as well. They resented his $3-a-day meal allowance while on the
road. It was a kind of joke among other clubs, almost all of whom
received a minimum of $4. Even the poorer clubs that finished in the
second division did not cut such corners. This was all the more an irritant since Comiskey seemed inordinately concerned about the newspapermen who hung around. For them, he had a special room in
Comiskey Park, with a huge table laden with succulent roasts and
salads, a chef to serve them, and a bottomless supply of fine bourbon
to liven their spirits. His generosity here was unmatched. Yet his great
ball club might run out on the field in the filthiest uniforms the fans
had ever seen: Comiskey had given orders to cut down on the clean-
ing bills.

There were betrayals, too. Like Comiskey's promise to give Cicotte a $10,000-bonus in 1917 if he won 30 games. When the great
pitcher threatened to reach that figure, it was said that Comiskey

had him benched. The excuse, of course, was to rest him for the World Series. There had also been talk that Comiskey had promised all the players a bonus if they won the 1917 pennant. They won it—and the world's championship. The bonus was a case of champagne at the victory celebration.

A monetary frustration hung over them all. If the public looked up to them, admired them, chased after them, this very prominence served to exacerbate their sense of helplessness. Their taste of fame whetted their appetites, but there was no meat and potatoes to satisfy them. All they'd been eating was Charles Comiskey's garbage. They wanted to shout to everyone: "Look, it's not the way you think it is!" The obvious outlet for their complaints was cut off from them, for newspapermen were Comiskey's boys. Their bread was buttered on the other side. They rode in the Pullmans as guests of the club owner, all expenses paid and then some. Officially they were on the staff of their respective papers, but Comiskey always made them feel as if they were working for him. And in the process, he made the ball-players feel like dirt.

It was foreboding that Gandil's meeting broke up without any real resolution. The players could rationalize that the next move was not theirs anyway: it was up to Sport Sullivan to come up with the money. Even now Lefty Williams didn't particularly go for the idea. Happy Felsch covered a growing uneasiness.

They would all wait and see.

5

The "spirit" of the coming World Series was not confined to Chick Gandil and company. It also bit the sweaty palm of one William Thomas Burns, known among his old baseball colleagues as "Sleepy Bill." Burns was a former ballplayer, a third-rate pitcher with a record of five unsuccessful years in the majors. (He won 29 games, lost 55.) His nickname was derived from his somnolent personality as well as his habits: it was said that he used to fall asleep on the bench during the ball games. It was also said that he was a little odd about riding on trains. He claimed to have witnessed, as a boy in Texas, many daring train robberies. As a man, he could not free himself from his fears of brigands, and often placed a giant revolver under the pillow in his berth. Any unusual sound was a cue for him to level the shiny iron at the passer-by. It became customary for his teammates to move with extreme caution in Burns's car.

Burns retired from baseball in 1917, and went into the oil business, a logical outgrowth of a lifelong ambition to get rich quick. Incredibly, he did. And by the late summer of 1919, he was ready to head back north to do a little business with some oil leases and a little boasting on the side.

It was perhaps coincidence that he arrived in New York at the time the White Sox were there. But when he started hearing some talk, it was no coincidence that he bumped into his old baseball buddy, Eddie Cicotte, in the lobby of the Ansonia. As pitchers in rival clubs, they had talked baseball many times. Immediately Burns asked: was it true? Was there a plan to fix the Series? Cicotte laughed and replied there was always that kind of talk floating around.

But Burns had a very low kindling point, and Cicotte's whole attitude indicated something was up. It was all Burns needed. He decided that he was the perfect man for the organization job: clean record, well liked by the ballplayers, quick-witted and clever enough, and above all, eager. He pumped Cicotte for details. And in time, the great pitcher admitted that there was a plan; it was just a matter of getting up the money to finance it.

Burns begged Cicotte not to make any commitments. At least not yet. He promised to work fast. It was the kind of operation that needed an associate, but the best Burns could come up with was a third-rate character named Billy Maharg, an ex-fighter now living in Philadelphia. Burns wired him to come to New York immediately.

Maharg obediently hopped a train to New York and the two thrashed out the possibilities. If Maharg found it all vague and far-fetched, his skepticism did not stop him from joining Burns and Cicotte at the Ansonia on the following day. Cicotte, this time, was accompanied by Gandil, who finally laid it on the line. Gandil was no piker. This competition for his services delighted him. Now he could up the ante. He told Burns they would arrange to throw the Series for $100,000!

Like Sport Sullivan, Burns had to go scouting for the money. He was due in Montreal on the following day, ostensibly on oil business. He would, however, spend some time on both projects. Meanwhile, he sent Billy Maharg back to Philadelphia with instructions to contact every big-time gambler and money-man in town. On such a magnificent proposition, surely somebody would come through for him!

Between them, they didn't raise a dollar. Maharg returned only with some advice: they should try the number one gambler-sportsman in America, the man most likely to accede.

His name was Arnold Rothstein.

Arnold Rothstein was an extremely well-heeled man. How rich, nobody really knew except Rothstein himself. He was referred to as a sportsman by the newspapers, as a professional gambler by the Broadway crowd, and as a hoodlum by his father. The truth was, he was all of these things, though he saw himself merely as a man who wanted money. He recognized the corruption in American society and made it his own. Whatever could be turned into money, he used. He applied his genius only for making money.

A psychiatrist might attribute this to his rebellion against his father. Abraham Rothstein had been a devout man. He had wrestled with the poverty of New York's Lower East Side, and quit school to support his mother, brother, sisters. He had worked in a clothing factory, later operated a dry-goods store, then had gone into the cotton-converting business. In time, he became prosperous. But always he was loved and respected for his piety. In 1919, a testimonial dinner was held to praise his arbitration of a garment-industry dispute. Alfred E. Smith, Governor of New York, and Louis D. Brandeis, Justice of the United States Supreme Court, were there to honor him. "Abe the Just," they all called him.

They called his son, Arnold, "The Big Bankroll."

The father had never understood the son. When Arnold was barely three, his father, awakened by a strange noise, had gone to the boy's room to find Arnold standing over his older brother Harry, a knife poised in his hand, "I hate him," Arnold cried. Harry was a bright, cheerful, well-liked, all-around boy. Arnold was not. "You hate me, but you all love Harry!" he cried and retreated from his father, into a dark closet.

He was a poor student, except in arithmetic. He was not stupid, just deliberately indifferent. He began cutting school, found his way into street crap games. The more the pious father objected, the more the son gambled. At fourteen, he was gambling seriously. He was good at it. He understood about odds and was calculating enough never to bet against percentages. All he needed was a decent bank roll and he could break any game.

His father, unwittingly, supplied it for him. Every Friday night, the orthodox Jew empties his pockets of money and jewelry and goes to Temple for prayer. Arnold would help himself to the cash and pawn the old man's gold watch to supplement his own growing bank roll. He could gamble with this for twenty-four hours, until Shabbos ended on Saturday evening. He always got the cash and the watch back on time.

Gradually, always taking his time, never pushing his luck, he amassed a few thousand dollars. He found he could make that work for him in different ways. He used money to make money. He began lending it—at 25 per cent interest. If he had any trouble collecting, he got Monk Eastman, a moronic brute whom he met through political contacts, to get it back for him. He was still a kid when Big Tim Sullivan of Tammany Hall took a liking to him. It was Arnold's first real contact with political life. Immediately, he sensed its benefits; he never let go.

He hung around pool rooms a lot, especially one owned by John McGraw, manager and part owner of the New York Giants. He liked it there because it was a meeting place for several great men of the sporting world. Stan Ketchel, a champion fighter. Ted Sloan, a big-time jockey. Arnold wanted to be like them, to be known as the best.

But only money would give him status. He saved. He lived frugally. He got a job selling cigars wholesale. He never spent money on girls. By their nature, gamblers tend to be celibate, and the young Rothstein was no exception.

And all the time, he stayed clear of his father.

Arnold Rothstein, the man, was wiser, richer, and just as ambitious. He had amassed a fortune at two gambling dens in the West Forties, artfully protected by Tammany police. He was ready for bigger games. Saratoga, New York, the summer home of the Eastern wealthy, was where the horses ran in the afternoon and the roulette wheels spun all night. Rothstein bought a mansion there, spent $100,000 converting it to a luxurious gambling house, cabaret, restaurant. It was the talk of the millionaire sporting crowd. The finest foods were served to its fabulous guests, without any prices listed. They paid—especially at the gambling tables. Joshua Cosden, oil magnate, dropped $300,000 in one night, $20,000 the next. Harry F. Sinclair, another oil king, was a liberal contributor. Millionaire Charles Stoneham, owner of race horses and the New York Giants . . . Sam Rosoff . . . Nick Dandolis, known as Nick the Greek . . . a host of others. By the end of summer, 1919, Rothstein could have retired and lived like a king. He need never place another bet.

But it was not in him to stop.

On the afternoon of September 23, 1919, Rothstein was enjoying a routine session at the Jamaica Race Track. Sometime after the third race, two strangers worked their way to his box.

Billy Maharg presented a message of introduction from a mutual acquaintance in Philadelphia. He then introduced his partner, Bill Burns. Rothstein nodded politely, asked what they wished of him. Maharg indicated he had a proposition he thought Rothstein would find interesting. But the gambler sloughed them off. He was busy, he told them. He had some careful betting he wanted to attend to. He suggested they wait in the track restaurant. Perhaps he could get to them later.

The two visitors swallowed their eagerness and left for the restaurant. There was nothing else for them to do.

In Rothstein's entourage, there was a unique little man. Raised in San Francisco, with the name of Albert Knoehr, he later changed it to Abe Attell. For twelve years, this little man had held the featherweight championship of the world. His reputation as a fighter had been unmatched in his time. He fought 365 professional fights, was beaten only 6 times. He was never knocked out. He weighed no more than 116 pounds, yet he defeated first-rate fighters in heavier divisions. The Little Champ, they called him. He had a right to be proud of the title.

Attell was, in fact, so great a fighter that when he failed to win quickly, there was reason to believe he was holding up his rival past a certain predetermined round. And when he lost, it was said that Attell was "doing business." In his later years, he grew careless. More than one boxing commission made charges against him. In January, 1912, he fought K.O. Brown at the National Sporting Club of New York—and lost. The fight looked so shady, the New York Boxing Commission held a hearing which resulted in Attell's suspension.

A few months later, he lost the championship to Johnny Kilbane and finally quit the ring.

Attell had met Rothstein back in 1905. Rothstein, the big sportsman, appreciated a real pro in any field, and the two became friends. When Attell was through as a fighter, he started seeing a lot of Rothstein. They'd meet at the popular hangout for the sporting-gambling-theater crowd, the Metropole Hotel on Times Square, home of some of the biggest crap games in New York history.

Attell spent his time making contacts. He was cheerful and willing to do favors. He dressed nattily, in the finest tradition of the Broadway crowd. He wanted to be liked and went out of his way to achieve this, especially with important people. He was quick to see the rising power of a man like Rothstein, and carefully cultivated his friendship.

As for Rothstein, he liked Abe, and it flattered his ego to have a champion as a hanger-on. Besides, he always had use for a man like Attell.

After the fourth race, Rothstein asked the Little Champ to find out what Maharg and Burns had in mind. Attell dutifully left for the track restaurant, delivered Rothstein's message and waited for a reply. This wasn't the way Burns wanted it to work out. But again, it appeared that they had no choice.

Burns outlined the proposition: eight ballplayers on the Chicago White Sox were willing to throw the World Series. They wanted $100,000 cash. Rothstein was the only man around with that kind of money.

Attell made no comment. He told them he would relay this to Rothstein and get back to them. Burns said he could be reached at the Ansonia Hotel.

Attell returned to his thirty-seven-year-old mentor but thought better of discussing the matter in the presence of others. He arranged to meet with Rothstein that night.

Reuben's Restaurant, in 1919, was located on Broadway at 74th street, directly across from the Ansonia. It was a convenient eatery for Rothstein who lived on Riverside Drive and 84th street. It was his custom to dine around seven, in a small back room, away from the noisy crowd out front. On this night, Attell was there waiting for him. Assured of privacy, Attell recounted Burns's proposition.

Rothstein listened as he ate, and was quick with his reply. He didn't think it could work.

When Attell passed this negative piece of information on to Burns, the ex-pitcher had no reason to doubt its reliability. He did, however, question its finality. This was too big a proposition to give up on. He would simply expand his operation and make new contacts.

Enter now, Hal Chase, that noted master of the fixed ball game. Burns had no trouble finding him (or was it the other way around?) since the Hotel Ansonia was a popular gathering place for the New York baseball crowd. Chase, as it turned out, had ears every bit as long as Burns's and had heard the fix rumors from their inception. Burns was not surprised: after all, this was Chase's chosen profession.

The great first baseman of the New York Giants was highly encouraging. He assured Burns that the whole scheme was a solid one, and who in the history of baseball knew better than Chase? Chase advised him to pursue Rothstein personally. The famous gambler would be at the Astor Hotel in Times Square later that night. Burns should confront him there.

Burns thanked him, then asked Chase what he wanted out of this deal. Chase grinned with typical pleasantness. He didn't want anything—except the right to bet.

The sleepy Texan rounded up his partner, Billy Maharg, and sat down in the Astor lobby to wait. When Rothstein entered, accompanied by a friend, Val O'Farrell, head of a detective agency, Burns approached him with typical brashness. Did Mr. Rothstein have a minute to spare?

Rothstein nodded, recognizing him from the race track that afternoon. Burns told him that he believed his proposition to be much too promising to be abandoned. He knew those ballplayers. They were close friends, even. They would go through with this if the money was available to back it.

But Rothstein shook his head. In his opinion, "whatever that was worth," he added modestly, Burns ought to forget it.

That seemed the end of it. Maharg returned to Philadelphia, and Burns went about his oil business, trying to forget this pipe dream.

Not so, Attell.

The Little Champ had not been in Rothstein's company for all these years without soaking up some of his *modus operandi*. One ingredient always stood out: guts. The ex-fighter could admire that most of all. Rothstein could size up a proposition, and if it seemed promising, he would plunge in as if it were a sure thing. Attell speculated: maybe this time A.R. had doped it out wrong. What was so impossible about such a fix? Why was he so certain it would not work? With eight ballplayers working for you? Hadn't A.R. once told him that anything could be fixed, from a checker game to a World War!

The thought began to prey on him, keeping him awake nights. Assuming that it was feasible to fix the Series with Rothstein's backing, why couldn't it be fixed without him? And if Rothstein refused to participate, why should Attell have to kick away a possible gold mine? And, most significantly of all, if it was Rothstein's backing they needed so badly, why shouldn't Attell merely pretend that he had it?

One night the Little Champ summoned the guts that had made him a champion, propelled his agile body out of bed, and made for the telephone. He hoped that sleepy-eyed fellow from Texas was still in town. . . .

Bill Burns waited in the huge Ansonia lobby, and when the dapper little man arrived, immediately escorted him upstairs.

Attell told him that Arnold had changed his mind. He now wanted to go through with it. Burns asked about the money, and Attell assured him that Rothstein would put up a hundred grand. But, he added, A.R. wanted his name kept out of it and didn't want to see or hear from Burns or Maharg again. Attell would do the handling for him.

Burns got the picture. It made sense. All he cared about was getting the cash for the ballplayers. Attell was sure he would.

With only three days before the Series began, Burns dropped everything and went to work. He phoned Cicotte in Chicago, but Cicotte was noncommittal. That, however, was all right with the fired-up Texan. Confidently, he wired Maharg in Philadelphia:

ARNOLD R HAS GONE THROUGH WITH EVERYTHING. GOT EIGHT IN. LEAVING FOR CINCINNATI AT 4:30. BILL BURNS.

The wheels of deceit began to turn, the first in a chain of lies and betrayals that would twist the World Series of 1919 into a nightmare.

On the evening of September 26, Arnold Rothstein received a call at his home on Riverside Drive from Sport Sullivan. Sullivan was coming to New York on the following day and wanted to talk with him. Would Rothstein consent to see him?

A.R. knew of Sullivan. He had heard the name mentioned favorably a number of times over the years. He was, therefore, favorably disposed and told the Boston gambler so.

Sullivan stood in the awe of the young New Yorker. Compared with Rothstein, he thought of himself as a penny-ante punk from the back woods. Encouraged by Rothstein's friendliness, he told the whole story of his experiences with Gandil, emphasizing how strongly he felt that the ballplayers were committed to the fix and were eager to go through with it. All that was necessary to cement the deal was the substantial amount of cash.

A.R. believed this man. He had no comparable respect for Burns and Maharg, neither of whom lived in his world. Sullivan did. The fact that two rival factions were working the same street did not bother him. This was presumably true of most promising setups. Deciding that it would not hurt to pursue this whole project further—if only on an exploratory basis—he told Sullivan he would think about it and let him know.

A.R. discussed the scheme with one of his partners, a man named Nat Evans. There were obvious objections to it, the principal one being the number of people who must already be aware of it. This would make secrecy impossible. On the other hand, Rothstein reasoned, it might serve as a blessing. "If nine guys go to bed with a girl, she'll have a tough time proving the tenth is the father!"

He suggested that Evans go to Chicago with Sullivan, meet with the players to appraise the entire project, and call back as soon as possible, since time was running short. Then he advised him to use another name while on this project, a common procedure which Evans well understood. Later, if there should be trouble—and Rothstein always anticipated trouble—a little confusion about names would be a valuable asset. It would serve to complicate the story.

Evans agreed and it was decided that he would be known simply as "Brown."

6

When the Chicago White Sox returned from the Eastern trip during which they clinched the pennant, their city was waiting for them. Thousands turned out to give them a rousing welcome, much more spirited than the pennant victory greeting of 1917 when the war had dampened their joy. The great ball club was Chicago's special pride. They had swept through the season, winners all the way. There was no doubt but that they would repeat in the World Series. Shoeless Joe's slugging, the amazing shine ball of Eddie Cicotte, the magnificent all-around play of Eddie Collins, the fiery personality of little Ray Schalk, the flashiness and color of the incredible Buck Weaver—these were what Chicagoans were talking about in late September, 1919.

It was, in effect, just what 2,700,000 Chicagoans needed. It provided a soothing relief from the turmoil just past, and a wonderful escape from the turbulent problems of the day. Last year, lick the bloody Hun. This year, lick the Cincinnati Reds. This was better. You could really feel this one, and there was no pain attached to the struggle, no sacrifice, no hardship. You didn't even have to go to the ball park to feel the guts of it. It was all over town, on every street, in every place of business. In the papers, the problems of President Wilson and his League of Nations took second place to the series. People who had never seen a ball game knew all about Shoeless Joe.

Chicagoans could forget the ominous steelworkers' strike in their own backyard, and the coal miners' strike that had followed it. They could blot out the horrible week of the summer just passed when a seventeen-year-old Negro boy was stoned into drowning at a Chicago beach because he inadvertently floated across that imaginary line separating white swimmers from black. A savage race riot had resulted in which scores were killed and hundreds injured.

The city itself was something of a mess. Michigan Avenue, the main street, a narrow one lined with old brownstone houses, was in a constant snarl of traffic. Streets were paved with brick, and provided no traction when wet. After a rain, horses slipped and fell, compounding the problems. There were more wagons than trucks, but hardly any buggies left. Cars were much in evidence, especially, of course, among the well-to-do. Most people, however, got to work in streetcars and El trains.

The first motor coach had begun operating two years before; for most Chicagoans, it provided the first ride in such a vehicle and many paid their fare just for the thrill of it. They would cross the river on the old Rush Street Bridge after a wait of five to fifteen minutes in confused traffic. Then they would plunge into smelly, filthy, teeming markets on the South Side. The city, described in the *Atlantic Monthly* of the period, was "the ugliest in the world . . . an idiot child of cities."

William Wrigley, the sudden chewing-gum millionaire, began construction of a shining white building on the Chicago River. Visitors were told it was to be insulated with chewing gum. Some of them believed it.

Chicagoans, like the rest of America, in September, 1919, wanted to be carefree. Hadn't they earned that right? With the end of the war, they expected the end of all responsibility. They were fed up with humanitarianism, liberalism, do-goodism. The word was out: have fun! So they went to see Charlie Chaplin in "Shoulder Arms"; Douglas Fairbanks in "His Majesty, the American"; Will Rogers in "Almost a Husband"; Mary Pickford in "The Hoodlum." City youths were in rebellion, led by those who had been in Europe and tasted the uninhibited atmosphere of the war-torn continent. Disillusioned with America on their return, and wanting a good time, they protested the old Victorian morality of their upbringing. They rode around recklessly in automobiles which, with the moral and sexual freedom that opened the 1920's, came to be called "houses of prostitution on wheels." Young people danced a wild new dance called the shimmy-and-cootie crawl. Women wore hobble skirts and immense hats and wound their long hair in buns. Soon hemlines would rise and the hair would be cut short. Tabloids became popular. American life began to seem like a three-ring circus of sport, crime, and sex. Everything was changing and changing fast.

There were immediate problems for everybody. A kid in knicker-bockers, high shoes, and cap faced them as he watched penny candy double in price. Sugar went up to 11 cents a pound, steak to 32, and everyone hated the high cost of living. Over 1,000,000 Americans were on strike. From overseas, the headlines screamed about each new Bolshevik threat. Europe was in a turmoil. In England, a member of Parliament warned that Germany would conquer Poland and dominate Europe unless we all combined to contain her. . . .

Chicago was ready for the World Series.

Only the ballplayers were not. At least, not those eight members of the White Sox who had met in New York's Ansonia Hotel ten days earlier. They were still hanging up in the air. Gandil tried to convince them that everything was set; Sullivan was rounding up the money, that was all. The others shrugged and tried to forget about the fix. It had never generated any real enthusiasm among them anyway.

Gandil, meanwhile, burned at Sullivan's evasiveness, having repeatedly failed to make any contact with him. It was the same with Cicotte: he had only promises from Sleepy Bill Burns. But again: where was the money?

Then suddenly, as the World Series fever began to rise, the action began. On September 29, the day before the players were to leave for Cincinnati and the opening of the Series, Sullivan arrived in Chicago with a New Yorker named Brown. He called Gandil at once, and it was hastily decided they would all meet at the Warner Hotel. It was an inconspicuous meeting ground: several of the players stayed there.

Sullivan introduced Brown as the man who would back them with cash. He was here in Chicago to be assured that the ballplayers were ready to go through with this. It was an understandable precaution: after all, a lot of money was going to change hands in the next ten days.

The ballplayers were not averse to his caution; they merely wanted to see the color of his money. They'd been promised $80,000, payable in advance. Wasn't that the proposition? Brown, however, was reluctant to show any of it. After all, he argued, what guarantee could they offer him that the Series would be thrown? Gandil replied that they'd give their word. Sure . . . Sullivan would vouch for that. Brown only smiled and shook his head. "In my book, that's not much collateral for eighty grand!"

Nobody could dispute that.

The conference ended, however, on a more encouraging note. Brown indicated that he'd been impressed by the tone of the meeting and would consult with his associates. He would get back to them through Sullivan as soon as possible. He assured them that something could be worked out. Then he left with Sullivan.

Gandil was nervous. He saw himself having trouble from all sides, not the least of which would be the ballplayers. Here was Lefty Williams saying he didn't want anything to do with the deal. Gandil told him he was a sucker: they were going ahead with it regardless. And when he cornered Jackson, the big Southerner insisted on getting $20,000 for his participation. Since Gandil needed him, he was forced to agree to it. And what was going on in Buck Weaver's head?

In New York, Arnold Rothstein, by this time, had gotten wind of Attell's devious manipulations. This could hardly have amused him, but there was nothing he chose to do about it at the moment. He would take care of Attell when the time came. He knew the Little Champ would be unable to raise any substantial capital with or without using Rothstein's name. It was also probably true that Attell had no intention of trying to. By the time Nat Evans, alias Brown, called to report, A.R. had already decided to go ahead with the fix. He told Evans to take $40,000 and turn it over to Sullivan to take care of the players. This would insure the action. In typically business-like fashion, A.R. arranged for the second payment of $40,000 to be placed in the safe at the Hotel Congress in Chicago. If the Series went according to plan, that, too, would be given to Sullivan for the players. If not, it would be returned to Nat Evans.

Evans approved the plan, then went about his real business: starting, as quickly and quietly as possible, to get their money down on the Cincinnati Reds. He anticipated no trouble doing that in Chicago.

A.R., meanwhile, began to operate from New York. He got on the phone and called his friend Harry F. Sinclair, multimillionaire oil baron and fellow horse enthusiast. Ostensibly the call was about horses, but in the course of conversation, he asked Sinclair whom he liked in the coming World Series. Sinclair, like any other baseball fan, replied, "Chicago." Rothstein found it easy to seduce him into a $90,000 bet. He even managed to get decent odds.

He went on down his list, and before he was through, he'd gotten $270,000 down. He stopped at this figure, not for any lack of suckers, but because he did not choose to go further; he simply did not have enough faith in the project to splurge. At least, not yet.

In the foyer, meanwhile, a visitor was waiting—one Rothstein was always glad to see. It was Nick Dandolis, known as Nick the Greek. He was a gambler who would go for broke, and Rothstein had succeeded in breaking him on more than one occasion. A year before, he had taken Nick for $250,000 in a series of poker and crap games. The Greek kept coming back for more.

On this occasion, however, he had not come to gamble, but to borrow. He'd spent a disastrous summer at Saratoga where the horses and dice had run badly for him. He was hoping that A.R. would stake him.

Rothstein did more than that. He peeled $25,000 from his everpresent bank roll and told Nick to put it on the Cincinnati Reds.

In the meantime, Gandil's apprehensions were growing. Nothing was moving smoothly. There seemed to be little solidity to the plans and even less cash. The strain of the past two weeks began to tell on him. He started to feel annoying stomach pains, not at all typical of him. To top it all, on the night before the team was to leave for Cincinnati, there was an ominous phone call.

"Gandil? This is Jake Lingle."

He knew Lingle, a Chicago newspaperman.

"Yeah, what is it, Lingle?"

Lingle was brief. "The word is out that the Series is in the bag!"

Gandil roared into the phone: "Where'd you ever hear that rot!" and slammed the receiver on its cradle.

Before long, a lot of people would hear it.

Sport Sullivan was surprised when Nat Evans handed him $40,000. Despite the fact that he was supposed to be organizing the scheme, Sullivan had never actually believed it would reach this point. He had pursued it with an attitude of skepticism; though he had spoken the words of a man convinced, he had never been wholly sure of its efficacy. That a smart man like Arnold Rothstein believed in it seemed incredible.

But the forty crisp $1,000 bills in his hand brought about a complete reappraisal of his talents. His broad, beefy smile, so often a posture for others, could now come spontaneously. There was nothing he couldn't do.

This fresh wave of confidence induced a concomitant wave of greed. Sullivan didn't care about the ballplayers for whom the cash was earmarked; they would have to wait. He had more important things to do with the sudden wealth.

To a gambler, money in the pocket has only one real function—to be wagered—and, in this case, time was of the essence. He was well aware that Rothstein must have a day's head start in getting his money down on the Series. If the odds on the White Sox to win had started at 8–5, they must already have begun to drop. Sullivan's problem was to get his bets made while the odds were still favorable.

This would not be easy, for he did not want to move in the usual gambling circles. Those boys were too smart. Big Sullivan money on Cincinnati would raise too many eyebrows. Well, that was inevitable. But he must go where he could get the best odds—which would be here, in Chicago, where even the wealthy had pride in their ball club.

He put $10,000 aside as an opening payment to the ballplayers. He needed the other $30,000 to bet. Where he was going, he'd need cash.

There was a new Sullivan axiom: play it big. He hopped a taxi for Chicago's Board of Trade section, arbitrarily choosing a large brokerage firm. He knew he would find money people there. It figured that some of them would be White Sox fans.

The important brokers were too busy to see him, but he managed to corner a young assistant named Harry Long.

To prove that he was a betting man, Sullivan peeled off $10,000 to place on the Cincinnati Reds. The going odds, he added cautiously, were 7–5.

Long, knowing there was always a commission for the man who places the bets, took the $10,000 and went off to some inner office.

Fifteen minutes later, he returned and told Sullivan he could get his money down, but not at 7–5. The odds, apparently, had dropped to even money.

So quickly? This angered Sullivan. He asked permission to use a phone and called his office in Boston and a contact in Pittsburgh. Within the last few hours, the odds had shifted there as well. To Sullivan, it was clear what had happened: Rothstein had beaten him to the punch. Here he was, the man who made all the contacts, the man among gamblers who deserved the first rewards—and he couldn't even get in on the ground floor of his own deal!

Sullivan put down $29,000 at even money.

Sullivan had to face Gandil relatively empty-handed, a prospect that far from delighted him. If he felt guilty about his misuse of Rothstein's money, he showed Gandil only an angry arrogance. He handed over the $10,000 as if he were doing the ballplayer a big favor. "You're lucky to get it!" He scowled. "Brown is plenty sore. The odds have dropped already. He said one of your players has leaked it out!" Then, drawing on a recent rumor: "Are you guys working with someone else?"

If the question threw Gandil, he didn't show it. He was much too absorbed with the inadequacy of the payment in his hand. He knew every dime of this would have to go to Cicotte. It would leave nothing but promises for the rest.

Gandil's frustration at the whole business began to overwhelm him. He reminded Sullivan of his pledge: $80,000 cash. What was he going to tell the others? But he pocketed the money and Sullivan, watching, knew he had won this round. "Tell 'em to keep their mouths shut!" he snapped.

Gandil blew up. He accused Sullivan of bad faith, and Sullivan returned in kind. They stood there blasting at each other, the two partners in betrayal. They came near to blows.

Then wisdom, inspired by greed, got the upper hand. They subsided. They even apologized for their anger. Sullivan assured Gandil that there was no cause for worry. He never went back on his word. He would see that Gandil got his money in short order. Gandil had to accept this. There was simply nothing else he could do. But as he packed his suitcase for the trip to Cincinnati, he was still steaming with resentment. The $10,000 was staring at him, a reminder that he really was hooked. There was no turning back now.

This was September 29. The World Series would open on the first of October.

Cicotte found the $10,000 in his room, carefully hidden under his pillow. He immediately sewed the bills securely into the lining of his jacket.

II **THE SERIES**

"To me, baseball is as honorable as any other business. It has to be, or it would not last out a season. . . . Crookedness and baseball do not mix. . . . This year, 1919, is the greatest season of them all!"

Charles A. Comiskey, to his biographer, G. W. Axelson

1

Early in the morning, on the day before the Series opener, the White Sox checked into the Hotel Sinton, having taken the sleeper from Chicago. They paraded into the lobby past hundreds of gaping Cincinnati fans who wanted a first look at this awesome American League powerhouse. Fashionably dressed Eddie Cicotte was prominent among them—a new pearl-gray kelly on his head, pearl-gray spats to match, and a bright pink shirt. Someone, of course, had to ask Joe Jackson how come he was wearing shoes. Buck Weaver picked up a copy of the Cincinnati *Post* and laughed at the picture of himself and his wife on the front page: the caption said it was Heinie Groh, the Red's third baseman, and his missus. They were a colorful gang, wisecracking and cocky, with the style and manner of professionals who had come to show off their professionalism. The hotel manager offered his own gold pen for them to sign a fresh page on the register. Except for the bottom line, their names consumed the entire page. There was a mad scrimmage among other arriving guests for the privilege of filling this space.

The players were followed shortly by another check-in, vitally important to the Series, but relatively unnoticed—Abe Attell.

He had moved east from Chicago a half day after the ballplayers, and had been begging, borrowing, conniving for every dollar he could get his hands on, getting it down on Cincinnati. Like Sport Sullivan, he had little trouble finding Chicago money, though the odds were no longer to his liking. Among his suckers was a young Midwestern manufacturer's agent, Sammy Pass, a loyal fan who knew and loved the White Sox. Pass figured a Chicago victory was worth a $3,000 investment. Neither man had ever bet with a greater feeling of security.

Also at the Sinton were a few acquaintances of Attell's from some years back, a group of businessmen-gamblers from St. Louis

and Des Moines: David Zelser; Carl Zork; Harry Redmon; and the
Levi brothers, Ben and Lou. Zelser, a man with his ear close to the
ground, had already picked up rumors. He was quick to go to the
Little Champ. Attell, who needed capital, was more than willing to
cut him in. Zelser, reacting warily as a matter of policy, employed the
Rothstein tactic of changing one's name for the duration. Henceforth, he would be called "Bennett." The choice of name was Attell's idea: he had a partner in New York, Curly Bennett. Two Ben-
netts, in two distant cities, could properly muddy up the trail.

Attell, a garrulous type, riding high and aglow with a sense of
power, could not keep quiet when he suddenly found himself in position to do some important people a favor. In the dining room of the
Sinton he spotted Rothstein's friend, Nat Evans, working on George
M. Cohan. Even from a distance, that much was clear. He waited
until Evans left, then confronted the great song and dance man. Had
Cohan placed a bet on the Series?

Cohan nodded. "Thirty grand. I got even money—on Chicago!"

Attell shook his head. "Take a tip from the Little Champ: switch
sides." He advised Cohan that the Series was fixed.

Cohan was jolted. It didn't seem possible—but he knew that
Attell was an inside man. He also knew that there was nothing that
would stop someone like Nat Evans from separating him from a bank
roll, even on a swindle. When the shock wore off, Cohan agreed to
play it safe. He thanked Attell and left to call his partner, Sam Harris,
in New York. Sam would hedge the bet, and maybe put a little extra
on Cincinnati.

It did not bother Attell that it was Nat Evans whom he was
jeopardizing or that it was Rothstein's money he was cutting into.
In fact, he could enjoy the thought of the latter, since Rothstein had
left him out. So he executed the same devious maneuver when he saw
Evans with Monte Tennes, a big Chicago gambler. Attell figured you
never knew when you could get a favor in return.

The trouble was, however, that the word was spreading. It had
swept through the gambling centers of America in as little time as it
took to make a phone call or send a wire. Cincinnati became alive
with it. In New York, Jack Doyle's betting establishment had witnessed a sudden sweep of Cincinnati money that had jolted the odds
from 7–10 to 5–6. In Wall Street, big money was being laid at even

money. Bets of $5,000 were reported. The influx of National League supporters was so heavy that odds-makers were of the opinion that the clubs would go to bat at 9–10.

The New York *Times* reported this as a strange phenomenon. "Until yesterday, it seemed that so far as New York was concerned, the Reds could carry little except moral support. But late yesterday afternoon, the situation underwent a sudden and surprising change that was little short of startling."

It was the same in Boston, Pittsburgh, Los Angeles. The smart money had abandoned the White Sox. The excuse given for this— or so it was rumored—was a report that Cicotte's arm was sore. Gamblers knew this was nothing more than a cover-up for the fix.

Gandil, meanwhile, wanted to get his own money down. His trouble, however, was twofold: he didn't have much cash since Sullivan hadn't come through for him—nor was Sullivan around to take his bet for him. In the end, he had to make contact with some second-rate gambler he knew, fully aware that such a tactic only added to the possible exposure of the fix.

Swede Risberg was more cautious. He wired his friend, Joe Gedeon, second baseman for the St. Louis Browns, advising him of the pending action. But the message was jumbled so that it would make no sense to an outsider. It would barely make sense to Gedeon.

When Sleepy Bill Burns reached Cincinnati, he waited for Maharg to arrive from Philly. Together, then, they went to the Sinton to meet with Attell. Their mission was a vital one: they had to secure the fix with the ballplayers. They wanted the promised $100,000 cash.

They found Attell in a room crowded with his partners, its telephone buzzing with action. Among others, Attell introduced them to Bennett, who, he said, would be his close partner. Burns attempted to pin them down, but Attell was evasive. He said he had the money, all right, but it was all out on bets. Burns was furious. What in hell could he tell the players? Attell was ready for him: he would talk to them himself.

A meeting was held in Cicotte's room at the Sinton later that evening. Seven ballplayers were present. Jackson, alone, was missing. Burns introduced Attell as the man who was handling the affair for Arnold Rothstein in New York. Attell then told them that he had the

$100,000, but he'd been instructed not to give it to them in a lump sum, but to stagger the payments over the course of the Series, $20,000, after each game they lost. Since the Series would run five out of nine games, that would make the required total. The Little Champ was firm about this, readily noting the objections of the players. One of them asked if Rothstein was good for that much money. Attell laughed at the question: "You needn't worry about Arnold, he's a walking bank." But Attell's amusement was lost on them.

Gandil was worried. These guys would promise you everything one day, then turn around and forget it on the next. The other players shared his bitterness. All except Cicotte who had the ten grand sewed into his coat.

There was a brief discussion as to the order of games to be thrown. Attell indicated he did not care. Whatever the players chose to do was all right with him. It was decided that they would throw the first two, since Cicotte and Lefty Williams were scheduled to handle the pitching chores. But they added that they would not win for Dickie Kerr, who would pitch the third game. They'd prefer to win for Cicotte in the fourth, not for the "busher," their term for Kerr. This was fine with Cicotte, who would want the victory as a bargaining point in his 1920 contract. It was also agreed that Burns was to pick up the money for the players and bring it to the Sinton.

The meeting broke up in the same muddy indecisiveness with which it began. The ballplayers had spoken the words of their complicity, but they did not actually believe in them. There were mumblings of doubt and mistrust. Their leadership, such as it was, shared their misgivings and could not conceal it.

Gandil, practiced in a cocky look and confident manner, tried hard to pretend that everything was under control. But he failed to hold the pose for long. There were too many pressures working on him, too many needles being stuck into him. He walked to a cigar store, asked for a pack of cigarettes. The man was a total stranger, could not possibly have recognized him. But when he handed Gandil the cigarettes, he felt free to offer the latest scuttlebutt: "Well, this is gonna be one lousy Series. . . ."

Gandil perked up. "Whattaya mean by that?"

"I hear Chicago is gonna throw it!"

Gandil scowled and left. He smoked more cigarettes in the next few hours than he usually did in a week.

It followed that sleep was not easy to come by. When anxiety did not keep him awake, the telephone did. It started around 11:30 P.M.

"Hello?"

"Gandil?"

"Yeah. Who is this?"

"Never mind. . . ." The tone was threatening. "Just make sure everything goes according to plan, that's all!"

Click.

There were other calls, from the opposite side of the fence, also anonymous: "What's this I hear about the Series being fixed? Don't do it . . . don't do it!"

It was as if everyone was working to insure the defeat—if not by the fix, then by sheer mental torture.

Cicotte wasn't having it any better. He, too, could not sleep. He, too, received menacing calls. By 2 A.M., he gave up, got dressed, and went downstairs to take a walk.

But he didn't get very far: a block from the hotel, he heard a familiar voice: "Cicotte!"

He turned. It was Kid Gleason, the manager.

"What in hell are you doing out at this hour!"

Cicotte's reply was classicly simple: "I couldn't sleep, Kid."

Gleason took him back to the hotel and put him in his room.

In another room of the Sinton, one of America's leading sportswriters, Hugh Fullerton of Chicago's *Herald and Examiner,* was growing annoyed at the rumors. Honest and diligent, Fullerton resented any implications of evil-doing that would sully the reputation of the game he loved. He had written a series of syndicated articles analyzing the rival ball clubs, position by position. He had come to the conclusion that the White Sox were a much superior team and would easily defeat the Reds. He was ready to stake his reputation as a sportswriter on a White Sox victory.

In his years of experience, he had heard similar rumors at times like these. He despised the punks who circulated them, vigorously mistrusted their intentions. He preferred to think that the opposite of a frame-up was behind them, recalling the Series of 1912 to substantiate this prejudice: during that Series between the New York Giants and the Boston Red Sox, the word was out that a certain Tammany politician had fixed it for the Giants to win. The result was a foolish rush of New York sucker money, tipping the odds in favor of the Giants. An investigation showed that the gamblers who spread the stories were the very ones who were taking all the New York money and backing Boston. There never was any evidence that any Tammany politician had manipulated a fix.

At first, Fullerton believed that the same thing was happening now, but he was quickly disillusioned: this time, the smart money was all going on Cincinnati. A few phone calls to New York confirmed that. Later, he ran into Bill Burns whom he had known as a ballplayer. He liked Burns. He considered him honest enough, though an inveterate gambler. He invited Burns to have a drink at the Gibson House, across the street from the Sinton, and casually asked how he was betting. Burns replied that he was sinking it all on the Reds, and added confidentially: "Get wise, Hughie, and do the same!"

Fullerton returned to the Sinton where he ran into a Chicago sporting figure named Hines who asked him point-blank if he believed the rumors. Fullerton ducked him and hurried up to his room. There, his roommate, the former Reds manager, Christy Mathewson, was lying on the bed, reading the late papers. Back from the war, Matty had been assigned to cover the Series for the New York *World*. Fullerton told him what he'd heard, adding his own revised opinion: it was possible that something was up! To Matty, this was not without a bitter irony. He recalled his own frustrating experience of having caught Hal Chase, his first baseman, fixing ball games—only to see him whitewashed by John Heydler, President of the National League. Fullerton decided to send out a warning. He wired all papers that used his accounts of the ball games:

ADVISE ALL NOT TO BET ON THIS SERIES. UGLY RUMORS AFLOAT.

Still, Fullerton had doubts. He probed into Matty's great baseball experience, digging for every possible way in which ballplayers might throw a ball game. Matty explained the simplicity of it, describing the ultra-thin line that separated an effective pitch from a disastrous one, a beautiful fielding play from a spectacular near-miss. As for a hitter, there was simply no way of knowing how hard he was trying.

They arranged to sit together in the press box and go over every doubtful play. And just for the record, Fullerton decided he would pencil a circle on his score card around every play that was really suspect.

During this discussion, they were interrupted by a visit from Ring Lardner, noted young columnist for the Chicago *Tribune*. Lardner was another baseball buff, and a particular fan of the White Sox. He came into the room laughing, a clear sign he had uncovered some delicate vignette that piqued his misanthropic nature. In this case, it involved the Cincinnati pitcher, "Dutch" Reuther, scheduled to start on the morrow. Lardner had seen him drinking heavily just a few minutes before. Fullerton immediately called Pat Moran, Reds manager, to report this. Moran thanked him and told him of a plot he'd heard about: a few Chicago gamblers were trying to get his whole pitching staff drunk. Reuther, who was a serious drinker, had somehow eluded Moran's scouts.

Fullerton began to see the nature of this insane situation: a rival group was out to fix the Series for Cincinnati to lose!

2

Opening day, October 1, began early. When the ballplayers came downstairs for breakfast, the lobby was already teeming with action. Gamblers who had heard the rumors and believed them had spent the night getting their hands on betting money. They had hit the pawn shops at opening hour, loaded with watches, suits, jewelry, anything that was convertible into cash. In the Sinton lobby, they accosted anyone who looked like a bettor. So heavy was the Cincinnati money, an even-money bet against Chicago was considered favorable. Hugh Fullerton saw them waving $1,000 bills in the air, a sight he had never seen before.

If all this bothered the eight ballplayers, they didn't show it. If the handwriting of betrayal was on the wall, they ignored the sight of it. Betrayal was nothing new to them. It was just another part of living. They weren't going to get stirred up about the fixed ball game they were about to play, even if they got swindled out of the money. You win, you lose. You try to take a bigger slice of the pie, and maybe you get away with it . . . and maybe you don't. It wasn't a big deal either way. You just go along with it if you happen to get involved.

To Charles Albert Comiskey, this was another proud day of a long career in baseball. No club owner in the history of the sport could boast a more intensive, more dedicated, more experienced background. His colleagues were men to whom baseball was mostly a secondary interest: a hobby, perhaps; or a strictly financial investment. Comiskey, almost alone, had started at the very bottom of the baseball ladder.

It was on a hot summery day in 1876. The seventeen-year-old son of "Honest John" Comiskey, city alderman, was driving a wagonload of bricks to the site of Chicago's new City Hall—the old one had been destroyed by the great Chicago Fire of 1871. The boy stopped at the corner of Jackson and Laflin Streets, hearing the jubilant noises of a ball game. From the driver's seat, he noticed that the Liberty Club's pitcher was having the life hammered out of him. He dropped the reins, hopped down and performed a remarkable job of relief pitching.

Two miles away there were impatient calls for bricks. It was several hours later that the father found the son in the process of striking out the side. Honest John indignantly leaped into the empty driver's seat and hurriedly departed. Young Comiskey watched him go with a sense of uneasiness. He realized this would generate a crisis: Was it going to be baseball or bricks?

"At the family counsel that night," writes G. W. Axelson in his biography of COMMY, "the world lost an indifferent teamster but gained a great baseball man."

Comiskey was a tall rangy youth, over six feet, and very well co-ordinated. His first real paying job was in Dubuque, Iowa, less than two years later. He was paid $50 a month to play ball and supply travelers on the Illinois Central Railroad with magazines and candy. Four years later, at the age of twenty-three, he joined the St. Louis Browns of the National Association, where his salary was $90 a month. A year later, he was appointed playing manager. Before he left that club, he led it to four successive pennants and two world's championships. His salary rose to $8,000 a season.

Comiskey was one of the first imaginative and creative minds in professional baseball. As first baseman, he developed the idea of playing deep and away from the bag, thereby covering much more territory. He trained his infielders to shift positions for different hitters, to back up throws, to play in to cut off runs, to execute double plays, to defend against bunts. He gave the game a new look, which, because it won pennants, became part of baseball for all time.

He was fair hitter (lifetime average .269) and a brilliant glove man. In the World Series of 1886, he led the Browns to a surprising 4 games to 2 championship over the National League Chicago White Stockings, led by Albert Spalding and his great stars, Cap Anson and King Kelly. The stakes had been unique: $15,000, winner take all. In a Series typically marred by 63 errors (in those days, there were always more errors than runs), Comiskey played errorless ball.

During these years, professional baseball was rocked by turbulent upheavals and internecine warfare. By 1889, the sport and its athletes were in the vicelike grip of severe, uncompromising businessmen like Arthur Soden of Boston, Albert Spalding of Chicago, and John T. Brush of Indianapolis. These men instigated the reserve clause, imposed a salary limit of $2,000 a year, and heaped a multitude of abuses on the players—including, in some cases, an outright refusal to pay salaries. This, despite the fact that baseball was making good money for its club owners. There was even talk in the big cities of raising the admission charge from 25¢ to 50¢—to keep out the roughnecks, and increase the take. But there was no talk of increasing salaries. The National Brotherhood of Professional Baseball Players was formed to deal effectively with the owners. The owners, after all, had operated collectively right along. The Brotherhood statement of purpose included this indignant explanation:

"There was a time when the [National] League stood for integrity and fair dealing. Today it stands for dollars and cents. Once it looked to the elevation of the game and an honest exhibtion of the sport; today its eyes are on the turnstiles. Men have come into the business for no other motive than to exploit it for every dollar in sight. . . ."

In 1890, an entirely new league (Players League) was organized in protest against the highhandedness of Spalding and Brush, with the Brotherhood players forming its nucleus. Comiskey gave up his managership of the St. Louis Browns and cast his lot with them, taking a substantial cut in salary as a club manager. His move must be appraised as a sacrificial one: "I couldn't do anything else and still play square with the boys!"

Eleven years later, at the formation of the American League in 1901, Comiskey returned to his home city, Chicago, organizing a new club called the White Stockings—later changed to the White Sox, out of deference to newspaper headlines. He put together a makeshift team of minor leaguers, set up a makeshift ball park, but pulled his team to the first American League pennant to the accolades of a huge number of spectators.

For Comiskey, then forty-two, it was the last year as a bench manager, after twenty-five years in uniform. Henceforth he would run the front office while Clark Griffith took over. It could be said, however, that he never really relinquished the reins. His need to win was as compelling as ever. Every manager he hired had to be as hungry for victory as he was. A story, perhaps apocryphal, illustrates this drive: Comiskey, dining at a seafood restaurant, was brought a giant lobster with only one claw. "Where's the other claw?" he demanded. The waiter explained that lobsters were known to be fighters. Apparently this one got in a tussle and lost a claw. Comiskey picked up the huge platter and handed it back. "Bring me the winner!" he exclaimed.

By 1909, Comiskey had become a rich man with his ball club. Chicago's Southside, he discovered, offered the finest baseball fans in America. "A winning ballclub in New York, say, will wear out the turnstiles, but their average crowd would not be up to standard if the team were a loser. In Chicago, my team has played to 12–15,000 fans on a weekday with the club in the second division. *That* is the test of loyalty."

As a token of his faith, Comiskey plowed $500,000 of his profits back into the rebuilding of the ball park. In 1910, a new

Comiskey Park, seating 33,000, was opened. Magnanimously, he dedicated it to the people of Chicago, who had paid for it. He turned it over to them without charge for special events. He let them use it for everything: church festivals, community barbecues, free-lance games, meets, picnics. There were even auto polo games (exasperating to the groundskeepers). He built a huge and beautiful lounge at the front entrance, opened it up for a select group of some 200 loyal White Sox rooters, who called themselves the Woodland Bards. For them (and the gentlemen of the press), there was always open house, including huge roasts, carved especially for each of them, and bolstered by Comiskey's unlimited supply of drinks.

Then he began the difficult—and expensive—process of putting together a ball club worthy of the new stadium. Up to 1915, Comiskey had spent a fortune for a quantity of minor-league players (hoping to pick up promising young players cheap). Few made good. Then he decided to go for the best. He started by buying Eddie Collins from Connie Mack and the Philadelphia A's for $65,000. Then he sent Harry Grabiner to Cleveland with a blank check. "Bring me back this fellow Jackson!" Jackson cost him another $65,000. For $12,000 he picked up Happy Felsch from Milwaukee. By 1917, he finally had his pennant—and the World's Championship. He suffered a setback in 1918 during the war, but his tremendous pride in his club was justified again in 1919. "It's a wonderful combination —the greatest team I ever had. . . . It's the best bunch of fighters I ever saw. With them, no game is lost until the last man is out."

The 1919 pennant was a glorious topping to Comiskey's sixtieth birthday.

"Why not run for mayor of Chicago?" he was asked by a V.I.P. who knew exactly how possible this was. Comiskey's objection was indicative of his real ambitions: "I'd rather win a pennant than an election!"

But now, on the morning of October 1, Comiskey had heard the disquieting rumors. While he didn't believe them for a minute, somehow they had given him a restless night. It worried him that he was even worried at all, setting off a kind of chain reaction; strange, since he was convinced it was all based on nothing. Wasn't there a report from the gamblers in New York that the odds had shifted because Eddie Cicotte supposedly had a sore arm?

After breakfast, Comiskey left the Sinton Hotel dining room for the ball park, attributing his bad night to a routine pre-game nervousness.

3

In the dugout, the manager of the Chicago White Sox watched his ballplayers warm up for the game. He was William Gleason, known for years as "The Kid." Although he was almost fifty-three years old, it still seemed an apt nickname. Small, open-faced, simple, direct, Gleason was a youngish type. He wore his cap slanted on the left side of his head and his emotions on his baseball sleeve. On this dramatic morning, his frown betrayed his anxiety. Gleason, in the past twenty-four hours, had heard enough to choke a horse.

As he looked from one to another of his ballplayers, he could not believe the rumors. He had convinced himself that after a year as wonderful as this one, they just didn't make sense.

But he couldn't deny everything he had heard. Aside from the innate ludicrousness of any scheme to throw the Series, Gleason had instincts that had always guided him. Any good baseball man knows how much they are part of the game. A manager can play the so-called percentages, make dope sheets, analyze till his brains ache. But his decisions, likely as not, will be conditioned by some irrational component. A hunch. Leave a pitcher in, or take him out? Try a bunt? Try a hit-and-run? Change the batting order? A dozen decisions a day. Reasoning was fine, but instinct won ball games.

Gleason had spent his entire life in baseball. As a big-league pitcher, he had won 129 games and lost the same number. Then, for fourteen more years, he played second base, a total of twenty years as a major-leaguer. Six years more as a White Sox coach, helping out where he could, nursing sore arms, teaching rookies, settling disputes, assuaging tempers. He was tough, single-minded, always fair. The ballplayers had to respect him, whether they liked him or not. No one ever spoke harshly about him; they knew no one would believe them if they did.

When Cincinnati took its turn on the field, Gleason went back to his dressing room. It disturbed him to note he was not alone: the newspaperman, Ring Lardner, was sitting there, a pencil between his teeth. Gleason liked Lardner, though he was a little afraid of him. Lardner was a bright young guy, a real writer, not like a lot of these bums who covered baseball. Lardner loved the game as much as Gleason did. He had the same deep respect for talent, got the same glow from a brilliantly pitched game or the sight of a great hitter having a great day. Lardner gave baseball class, just by being part of its world.

But Gleason didn't want to see him now: he dreaded what Lardner might be asking. . . .

"Hello, Kid," Lardner offered.

"Hya," Gleason returned.

He moved to his locker, fumbling through his gear for a lighter sweatshirt. It had gotten real hot out there. He felt Lardner's eyes on him, but nothing was said for a long moment.

Then Lardner spoke: "Just came to wish you luck, Kid. That's all."

The words cut into Gleason like nine little darts: Lardner's tone was funereal.

To Happy Felsch, pre-game warm-up could be more fun than the ball game. In batting practice he smashed into those fat pitches as if they all had his name written on them. Then he'd cruise around the outfield chasing fly balls fungoed far across the vast expanse of the stadium, a hundred feet from him and then some. He'd dig his cleats into the soft green turf and leg it with the joy of a kid racing down the street to a candy store. The little white pellet soaring through the air was the world itself: he had to catch it before it hit the ground and maybe crumbled.

Felsch had been called "Happy" since he was a kid. He was born laughing, his father had told him. Laughter was part of his face, and no adversity could rub it off. His father was a tough, hard-working factory laborer with his roots in the old country. Along with immigrant German friends, he had settled in Milwaukee and raised twelve kids.

Happy got as far as the sixth grade, then quit. He got a factory job paying $10 a week, which he'd bring home to his father, who'd give him back a quarter to play around with. The old man would say it was a rotten thing for a boy to have to work like that; in America it should be different. He'd been working all his life and he had nothing to show for it. Now his kids had to start the same rotten grind all over again.

On Sundays, "Hap" played ball. When he got to be good enough, he also played twilight ball when the plant closed. There were dozens of factory teams around Milwaukee. First he was an infielder; later he found his real spot in the outfield. He was good. He had a lot of power. At twenty-one, they took him on Milwaukee in the American Association. Ray Schalk was the catcher. Jimmy Callahan, who managed the White Sox, would come to Milwaukee to see Schalk play, and he saw Felsch, too. In 1916, the White Sox brought him to the big town at $2,500 a year. He sent his money home and laughed through the long season that was never long enough for him. On the road, he enjoyed his whisky and the fun of strange big cities. He could go on a rampage and tear up a hotel with the wildest of them. He had showed them that in Boston, back in July.

Now Felsch was twenty-eight. Back home in Milwaukee, everyone treated him like a big shot. He liked that, until he thought about his low salary. The big thing about the World Series was not the glory but the extra money. In the 1917 Series, he made more in one week than he made all season. And this Series would be even better.

Joseph Jefferson Jackson stood lackadaisically in the outfield, catching an occasional fly ball hit his way. He had come a long way in ten short years of ballplaying. He was born on a broken-down plantation run by an eccentric old fire-eater, who drove his tenants to a fury. Joe's father had eked out a mere subsistence from the barren and rocky South Carolina land. It was a county of corn whiskey and ignorance. If a man learned to read or write, he was looked on as a freak.

The Jacksons moved to the environs of Greenville, South Carolina, living in one of the little mill towns that were the mark of Northern ownership of Southern cotton. The town was called Brandon Mill. Beginning at the age of thirteen, Joe worked in the mill, along with his father, six brothers, and two sisters. The hours were from six to six.

The work was unwholesome, even dangerous, but his father told him it was a lot better than the plantation.

The Brandon Mill, like all the others, promoted a baseball team. Among its eight hundred mill hands, young Jackson registered big, right from the start. Even at thirteen, he had something extra special as a ballplayer. He was told to catch because none of the others wanted to risk it. He carried a scar all his life from that experience: a big mill hand let one go so rapidly, Joe didn't have the strength to stop it. It drove his hands back, smashed into his mask so deeply that a metal band cut into his forehead.

He shifted to pitcher, since he had a strong throwing arm. He threw one so hard, he broke his catcher's arm. Both catcher and pitcher quit their posts. Jackson moved out to the outfield.

Joe's brother, Dave, also showed promise as a ballplayer, but life in the mill destroyed his chances. One day he was caught in the whirring machinery and was carried to the roof on a revolving belt. His arm and leg were broken and never properly set. Dave spent the rest of his life bent and malformed.

In 1907, when Joe was nineteen, he was playing against a mill team in Greer, South Carolina. The opposing second baseman was Tom Stouch, an old ballplayer with one fast trip to the major leagues. Stouch recorded his first confrontation with Jackson's ability: ". . . This tall skinny-looking kid stepped up to the plate, he didn't appear to have much in him, but he drove the ball on a line to a spot where I was standing, like a bullet out of a gun. I thought to myself, if this rube hits 'em like that every time, he must be some whale. He was. He hit three times that game, twice for extra bases, and when he hit, he left a trail of blue flame behind them as they shot through the air. We played five games in all with that outfit, and he kept hitting 'em. The last time, he hit the ball at the pitcher's head. The pitcher looked at the ball for a 100th of a second then ducked as if he were facing a shell out of a Krupp mortar.

" 'Did you discover his weakness?' I asked him.

" 'No, but he discovered mine!' "

When Stouch became manager at Greenville, he hired Jackson at $75 a month, almost double what he was making at the mill.

At Greenville, playing every day, he began to realize his true potential as a ballplayer. And there, he also picked up his nickname:

Jackson had bought a new pair of spikes, and they'd raised a few
blisters. He wanted to sit out the next day's game, but his club turned
up short an outfielder, and he had to play. He put on his old shoes,
but the soreness made it impossible to wear them. In desperation, he
went out to play in his stocking feet. Nobody seemed to notice until
the seventh inning when he blasted a long drive to right center and
had to leg it hard. As he pulled into third, a leather-lunged voice from
the opponent's bleachers blasted at him: "You shoeless bastard, you!"

The crowd laughed and picked it up. They started calling him
"Shoeless" Joe around the league, and it stuck.

Toward the end of the season, Tom Stouch called his friend Con-
nie Mack in Philadelphia to say that he had a few good prospects
Mack might want. Mack sent a scout down to Greenville and bought
Jackson, along with two others. The price for Shoeless Joe was $325.

But Jackson was timid. He actually seemed unhappy about going
to the big leagues. "I hardly know as how I'd like it in those big
Northern cities," he told Stouch. The manager reassured him, not believing what he'd heard.

Stouch took the trouble of escorting Jackson on the trip to
Philly, fed him supper on the train, and even put him in his berth. But
when the train arrived in the morning, Jackson was not on it. He had
slipped off at Richmond and caught the first train back to Greenville.
A telegram reached Philly that explained everything—and nothing:

AM UNABLE TO COME TO PHILADELPHIA AT THIS TIME. JOE JACKSON.

Mack was flustered by this kind of conduct. Stouch explained
that Jackson just didn't want to leave home, that big cities frightened
him. Mack turned to Socks Seybold, a coach: "Go down to Greenville and get this fellow's brothers and sisters and whole family to
come with you if necessary . . . but bring him back!"

This time, Jackson came all the way. He played in the game the
day he arrived and got two hits. Then, it began to rain. . . . By the
time the rain stopped a few days later, Jackson had sneaked home
again. His teammates had been ribbing his illiteracy unmercifully.

In 1909, Connie Mack farmed him to Savannah. Jackson hit a
powerful .358 and, perhaps more significantly, met his wife there.
Late in the season, he was recalled to Philadelphia and she went with

him. But again he didn't like it. He didn't know how to conduct himself. His ignorance made him the butt of everyone's jokes. He became sullen, difficult, irresponsible. One afternoon, on his way to the ball park, he passed a burlesque show. He had never seen one, so he hopped off the streetcar and spent the afternoon in the theater. Connie Mack jumped all over him for that. One day in Detroit, perched on third base after a tremendous triple, a raucous fan jeered at him: "Hey, Jackson, can you spell 'cat'?" The crowd laughed derisively as Jackson glared back, squirted a stream of tobacco juice to indicate his contempt, and roared, "Hey mister, can you spell 'shit'?"

Mack tried to get close to the boy. He offered to get him a companion who would teach him to read and write, but Jackson was stubborn and stuck to his ways. Mack eventually gave up on him, sold him to Cleveland.

Jackson came up with the Indians in midseason after spending the early months in New Orleans. In 20 big-league games, he hit .387. In 1911, his first full season, he hit .408, losing the batting title to Ty Cobb's .420. By 1912, he had begun to adjust to big-league life. Perhaps too well. The glamour of the cities lured him into new and exciting dissipations. The rube had opened his eyes. Fortunately, his ballplaying wasn't affected. Jackson had too much natural talent and too much drive for that. Washington pitcher, Walter Johnson, said, "I consider Joe Jackson the greatest natural ballplayer I've ever seen."

In 1915, Comiskey bought him for $65,000. Jackson moved to Chicago and had to struggle to make friends once again. His hitting suffered with the change.

Meanwhile, he had grown accustomed to the feel of money, larger sums than he had ever imagined he would have. He became a slick dresser, very conscious of his clothes. He liked the feel of shiny new shoes and bought more than he needed. Hungry for more money, he tried to set up businesses over the winter. He bought a fine pool room in Greenville which, with the enormous prestige of his name, should have been successful. But his partner, who managed it for him, ran it into the ground. Jackson also bought a farm near Greenville: that, too, was mismanaged, and cost him money. The following year, he bought the best house in Brandon Mill, and gave it to his parents. He, himself, went to live in Savannah with his wife.

In Brandon Mill, people spoke affectionately of his nature, but sourly of his chances. "Wait five years or so," an old mill hand commented. "Then Joe will go through all his money and he'll be back here working for $1.25 a day again."

An old friend from Greenville said, "Joe's record is the best example I ever saw of what a man may accomplish in this world wholly without brains."

Meanwhile, Jackson played ball seriously and dedicated himself to his talent. He had learned a big lesson from Connie Mack's relentless drive. He worked on his fielding, improved the accuracy of his powerful throwing arm. He conceived a unique eye exercise that helped his vision: he would place a small, lighted candle on a table in a dark room. He would sit before it, cover one eye, and stare at the light until blinded. Then he would repeat the process with the other eye. At other times, he would strengthen his arms and wrists by holding his famous big black bat ("Black Betsy") at the handle with one arm outstretched. He would hold the position for as long as he could, then shift to the other.

He'd had another great year in 1919, once again hitting over .350. He was fully convinced he had not yet realized his full potential, that there were far greater years ahead. But on this day of the Series opener, there was no joy in him. Nervously, he fingered the hairpins in his back pocket in a superstitious groping for security. (A dozen years before, a little girl in Brandon Mill had given him a hairpin for good luck and he'd had a good day. Subsequently, he told himself that if he let a hairpin lie on the ground, wherever he was, he would go hitless. Since then, he seldom played without hairpins in his pocket.) He watched Happy Felsch toss a practice ball into the bleachers and laugh when it was tossed back to him, an action that was repeated to everyone's amusement. Jackson, however, could not free himself of the pressures of the fix. He was caught in its vortex, but could not understand what he was doing in it; it fed his persistent feelings of inferiority. He was the dumb one. Gandil, Cicotte, and his friend Lefty Williams, were the smart ones, hungering for the big fat dollar. He had quietly gone along with them, but now it had begun to hurt. He turned from the laughing Felsch and made his way back to the bench. There, he sat sullenly and apart, waiting for Kid Gleason to spot him.

Jackson returned the manager's curious stare, and offered that he did not feel good. "I don't wanna play!" he added.

Gleason wheeled. "What!"

"I said I don't wanna play." Then he added, much too loudly, "You can tell the boss, too!" He wanted Comiskey to know this.

Gleason stared at him for a long moment, not knowing what to say. When he rallied, finally, he moved closer to the great slugger and murmured in his ear, "You'll play, Jackson. You'll play!"

It was not a prediction; it was a threat.

A half hour before game time, the stadium was almost completely filled. The head usher, a young man named Alfred Bauer, was perspiring freely with the heat and the intensity of his job. Actually, he was a medical student as well as a baseball fan. At med school he had had no trouble rounding up an extra thirty ushers to help seat the tremendous crowd. It amused him that none of his friends had bothered to ask how much they would be paid. Most of them didn't even expect any money; all they wanted was to see the game.

A wave of angry cries greeted Eddie Cicotte as he went to the warm-up rubber. The Cincinnati fans drowned out the few Chicagoans who were there to cheer.

"There's the bum from Chicago!"

"Sore arm, Cicotte!"

"Old man Cicotte!"

Cicotte's record of 29 wins and 7 losses gave them the right to be afraid of him. But their derisive cries hit a sensitive spot when they called him an old man. Cicotte was thirty-five. "Baseball player in the twilight years," the reporters described him. Husband. Father of two. Respected by teammates. Very likable, pleasant personality, full of pranks and jokes. But how long would Cicotte last? After thirty, one bad year and a pitcher was marked lousy. The previous season, Cicotte had looked bad: 12 wins, 19 losses. His arm had given him trouble. So, he stated, had his paltry $4,500 salary: thirteen years in the majors and he was still earning less than $5,000 a year! In 1917, he had won 28 games, but Comiskey had only offered him $4,500. "There's a war on!" Comiskey had snapped. "Baseball, like everything else, will have to pull in its belt!" Comiskey had them marching close-order drill before gametime with a baseball bat at right shoulder arms, a daily reminder of the national emergency that justified his penuriousness. Then in 1919, when the war was over, Cicotte had asked for more money. Comiskey, worried about Cicotte's sore arm and the bad year behind him, would give him no more than $5,500. His cagey right arm had snapped out 29 wins and helped capture the American League pennant. His best year in baseball. Only $5,500 for the finest pitching record of the year. Cicotte was fully aware that Cincinnati pitcher, Dutch Reuther, at twenty-six, after two years in the majors, was getting almost double that figure!

As a kid, twenty years earlier, Cicotte had been pitching semi-pro ball in Northern Michigan mining towns. He weighed no more than 135 pounds, but he had to throw nine innings, sometimes three times a week, snapping off curve balls, bearing down savagely on every pitch. His arm would tire and hurt, but he would never quit. A kid who wanted to go up couldn't hurt, couldn't quit. A kid had to stay for nine and maybe throw something extra in the last couple of innings to hold on to a lead.

Now he was at the top. Major-leaguer, pennant winner, World Series choice number-one pitcher. He still had a fast ball that could move. He had his good stuff today, but he wasn't going to use it. It was a painful thing to cope with.

Later, he would ask himself, over and over: Why had he gotten into this mess? The answer was a jumbled-up set of facts and emotions. The $10,000 in $1,000 bills first placed under his pillow, then sewed into the lining of his coat. He had a sore left thumb to prove it; the needle had jabbed him unmercifully.

Someplace off to the side, an unseen band was blaring a sticky version of "I'm Forever Blowing Bubbles." It echoed throughout the park.

In a box behind the Cincinnati dugout, Governor Cox of Ohio and his party were early arrivals. He sat graciously for photographers and quoted Pat Moran to a reporter: " 'Governor,' Moran said to me, 'we are absolutely certain to win the series. There's not a possible chance that we won't. If Cicotte pitches the first game, our boys will knock him out of the box!' " He smiled for another picture, then added, "That's what I came to see!"

In New York City, Arnold Rothstein walked through the lobby of the Ansonia Hotel. In the Green Room, set up for a telegraphed system to relay the World Series, play by play, several hundred chairs were already occupied; it was smoke-filled, noisy. Rothstein entered, glancing at his watch. One minute to three. He walked to the rear, a few feet from the door, and stood against the wall, waiting. The reports would be read aloud, pitch by pitch, in a manner attempting to recapture the spirit of the game. A diamond-shaped chart on the wall would move the players from base to base a few seconds later. Those who had seen this fascinating new procedure at work would testify to its excitement. It was almost like being there, they said.

Rothstein didn't intend to stay for more than the first inning. He wanted to hear how Cicotte pitched to Maurice Rath, lead-off man for the Reds. Rothstein had given instructions that Cicotte was to hit him with the pitch. A token of his compliance with the deal.

Outside the Cincinnati ball park, a number of apartment buildings overlooked the outfield stands. Two or three sets of binoculars peered out from every window. The nearby roofs were dangerously crowded. Overhanging the barrier in left field, three boys were clinging to a telegraph pole, their legs precariously straddling the upper crosspiece. They were joined, occasionally, by a few passing pigeons who needed a rest. Then, too, there was a crack in the right-field cement wall, sufficient to allow one adept eye to focus on a limited field of vision. The boy who had discovered it had been bought off. The buyer, it turned out, was forced to use his fists to protect his squatter's rights. Eventually a policeman chased them all away.

The Little Champ, Abe Attell, had a fine box seat behind third base. The hot sun beat down on his taut little body, but never disturbed his impeccably tailored clothes. He could tell you: he'd done his sweating in the ring for over a dozen years.

Attell had known sporting crowds from his boxing days. They hollered like fury. One day they liked you, the next day they didn't. The one thing he had learned was that they were stupid. He could always fool a crowd. Not once had they ever known he was carrying some punk an extra five rounds because he owed someone a favor.

The band suddenly blared forth "The Star Spangled Banner" and Attell immediately rose and started to sing with the others. The words always wrought a great transformation in him. Singing, he felt a strong surge of patriotism. Baseball, after all, was a great American game.

In the press box, the sound of clicking typewriters suddenly stopped as Cincinnati's Dutch Reuther got set to throw the first ball. Newspaperman Hugh Fullerton had seen thousands of ball games in every major-league city in America, but this opening moment always excited him. Like any lover of baseball, he felt the tight knot in the pit of his stomach. He heard talk of theater people who boasted of something like it in that quiet hush just before the curtain went up. But baseball was something special. You could look forward to nine innings in which any number of things might happen, and no one knew what they might be. No other game could match it.

Today, however, there was something extra, something baffling, added to it. Was it or was it not going to be an honest ball game? He reminded Christy Mathewson of his plan to circle any play that looked suspicious, and Matty again consented to advise him.

Then Dutch Reuther reared back and blazed a high, fast ball to the plate. Lead-off man John "Shano" Collins watched it go by.

Black-suited John Rigler raised his left arm. "Ball one!"

The crowd shouted and the game was on.

A moment later, Collins lashed a single to center, and Fullerton smiled. "Well, here we go!" he said to Matty.

Around them, the crowd groaned in anticipation of White Sox power. It seemed like an ominous beginning.

The great Eddie Collins stepped to the plate. Fullerton turned to Matty. Would Gleason have him bunt and play for one run? With all that power coming up? Matty commented that it all depended on whether the manager had complete confidence in Cicotte. If so, one run could be the big one.

Fullerton nodded, respecting Matty's superior judgment. He wanted Eddie Collins to bunt now, if for no other reason than to confirm his faith in this ball club. Collins turned on the pitch, obviously prepared to bunt. It went foul, but Fullerton was pleased.

So was Chick Gandil. Especially on the next pitch. For Collins bunted badly, right to Reuther who wheeled, threw to second in time to force Shano Collins. Gandil's hatred of Eddie Collins was no secret around the dugout. That the great captain should fail to execute a simple bunt play delighted Gandil. Doubly so under the circumstance.

Buck Weaver stepped up to the plate. Weaver worried Gandil. He was the smiling type, all-American, loved his wife, loved the fans, the umpires, everybody. But most of all, he loved baseball. Gandil doubted that he could trust Weaver. Ever since the first fix meeting he had wondered whether Weaver was just being shrewd, ready to share the take, but not to play to lose.

Then Gandil had a sweet surprise. Eddie Collins, number-one American League base stealer, was thrown out trying to steal second —to make up for his failure to sacrifice bunt. Instead of a man on second with one out, there was nobody on and two out.

Weaver hit a hard shot to left center that looked good for extra bases, but Roush made a fine running catch that ended the inning. Gandil jogged out to his position, cursing, trying to catch Weaver's eye. Weaver could paste that ball when he wanted to.

Whatever complicity Weaver had indicated by his presence at meetings, on the diamond he was incapable of committing himself to anything but his best efforts. There was no bitterness, no hatred, no frustration powerful enough to corrupt his love for baseball. He played ball with the purity and dedication of a child. And though he had fully understood the motivations for the scheme, even allowed himself to participate in the evolution of it, he could not perform accordingly when he put on spikes.

Weaver became a ferocious bulldog to the Cincinnati Reds. If Gandil saw him as the enemy, Weaver didn't care: he was there to play ball.

Raymond William Schalk assumed his squatting position behind the plate and got set to receive Cicotte's first pitch. At twenty-seven, he was an old pro. Since 1914, he had been the regular catcher for the White Sox, including the 1917 World Series victory against the Giants. In fact, Cicotte had pitched the opener, just like today, and won it, 2–1. Schalk was called "Cracker," a name derived from his whiplike manner. He was a little man, five feet, eight inches tall, weighing less than 150 pounds. But there was nobody that size who made a bigger impact on a ball game.

Schalk barked at Cicotte, impatient to get going. His signal to the pitcher was a fast ball. He figured Rath to be taking the first pitch. He was right. The ball crossed the plate, letter high. Rigler grunted, "Steerike one!"

But Schalk didn't like the pitch. Too high. He had called for it lower. Much lower. Rath liked them up high. Schalk reared back and snapped the return throw with deliberate viciousness, aiming it low, at Cicotte's knees. It was Schalk's way of telling Cicotte what he wanted.

Cicotte bent over to make the catch. He could see the Cracker's glaring eyes through the iron slits of the mask. He turned back to the rubber and set himself for the next pitch. Rath, a fair .260 hitter, stood up there as if he would beg for a base hit. Cicotte could see the pattern clearly enough: curve him, low. A foul strike, maybe. Strike two. Knuckle ball. If it was in there, Rath would pop it up. Cicotte's fast ball was jumping today. On a day like this, he could go down the entire order that way. One, two, three; one, two, three. To Cicotte, there wouldn't be a dangerous man on that club. He'd been around enough to know. He'd sat behind the screen during batting practice, watching them hit.

Cicotte set himself and picked up the Cracker's sign. Curve ball. The Cracker knew the pattern, too. Sooner or later, Cicotte was sure Schalk would get on to him.

He wound up and reared back to throw. This was one pitch he had to put something special on. He let it go hard. It spun in rapidly, exactly the way he wanted it to.

It hit Rath squarely in the back. Right between the shoulder blades.

Arnold Rothstein walked out of the Ansonia onto Broadway. It was raining in New York, adding to the unreality of following the ball game in a crowded room. He flagged a taxi and instructed the driver to take him to his offices on West 46th Street, the site of one of gambling clubs. The taxi sped down Broadway to Times Square. Despite the rain, several thousand people were gathered beneath the Times Building watching the re-enactment of the game. Dummy figures were spread out in position on a huge board simulating a ball field. Rothstein got a glimpse of it. He could see the huge green diamond and, on it, the pawns of his own power. Cicotte had given the sign and Rothstein was pleased. He had decided he would plunge another $100,000 on the Reds.

Charles Comiskey sat in a box along the first base line. All day he'd been telling himself that maybe he'd been making a mountain out of this thing. Perhaps all the filthy talk was really much too fantastic for credulity. He'd let himself be terrorized by it. He'd let a bunch of tinhorn gamblers and pack-rat rumormongers shake him up. He'd been in the world of baseball all his life and never so much as dreamt anything like this could possibly happen to him. The whole thing was preposterous. These boys would never let themselves in for such nonsense.

Before the fourth inning began, Cicotte threw five warm-up pitches to Schalk. Simple warm-up tosses, but the Cracker fired the ball back to him faster than the pitcher had. Another Schalk message to look alive. Cicotte tried to ignore it. He didn't want any trouble from Schalk now. He'd thrown only three innings, but suddenly he was tired. Apparently, it was taking more out of him to lose a game than to win one. He had to let them hit the key blow without tipping his hand. He had to fool everybody, including Schalk, a feat as difficult as pitching a no-hitter.

It was a 1–1 ball game. The outfielders were set. Joe Jackson out in left, his hands resting on his knees. Cicotte could ask himself: was Jackson going to help him lose this ball game? And Felsch in center. Would he drop one in the clutch? Cicotte was afraid that they would not. They all wanted to look good. They would leave it up to him to lose this ball game. It figured. *He* got the ten grand.

"Batter up . . . let's go!" Rigler barked.

Cicotte turned and toed the rubber. He looked at Edd Roush, waving his big bat at him. Schalk went into his squat and signaled for a knuckler. Cicotte took his time, wound up, and let it go. He took something off it, not much, just enough to give Roush time to get a decent look at the wobbles as the ball floated to him. The big man took a big cut at the ball and laid a lot of wood on it. Cicotte knew at once it would go a long way.

He watched Happy Felsch take off for it. Deep, deep into center field he raced, glancing artfully over his shoulder as the towering shot soared toward the fence. Cicotte figured Felsch would short leg it, and the ball would drop, roll to the wall. It should be good for a triple. But Hap seemed to gather speed as the ball started sinking. Ten feet from the wall, he reached out on the dead run and pulled it in. The crowd bellowed at the thrill of it, furious at Felsch's robbery. Cicotte turned back to the mound, knowing how right he had been: they would all dump it on him.

He reared back this time and threw his fast ball right at Pat Duncan's head. The batter fell away, just in time. Cicotte's fast ball really had something on it when he got mad. His next pitch, a curve, hung in the air and Duncan slapped at it neatly, into right center for a base hit. The crowd came alive again. A base hit in Cincinnati sounded like a batting rally.

He faced Larry Kopf now. Kopf lashed at the first pitch, a fast ball right down the pipe. But all he could do was bound it back at the mound. Cicotte gloved it, an instantaneous, protective reflex. All his years in baseball governed his move now. He turned to start the simple double play: Cicotte to Risberg to Gandil. But this time he turned slowly. He hesitated. His throw to Risberg was deliberately high. He was in time to get Duncan racing to second, but he didn't give the Swede enough time to complete the play. Kopf beat the throw to first by a full step.

In the press box, Hugh Fullerton saw the play and didn't like it at all. He turned to Matty, and as if on cue, their eyes met. Gravely, Matty nodded. It didn't look right to him either. Fullerton recorded the play on the score card and penciled a heavy circle around it. This was the first one.

Yet it seemed strange to him. What for? If Cicotte had delayed intentionally, wasn't it a stupid move? He had two out now and a runner on first, hardly a threatening position to be in. If he wanted to throw the game, he might better have pitched the ball out of Risberg's reach, into center field.

Fullerton leaned forward, more nervous than he'd been since the opening pitch.

"Greasy" Neale was waiting at the plate. Cicotte glanced over his shoulder at Kopf on first, then pitched. Neale cut hard, sent a hard shot on the ground through the middle. Risberg cut sharply to his left and stopped it, but he couldn't make the play. There were runners on first and second now.

Ivy Wingo, Reds' catcher, stepped in to hit. He took one cut at the ball and lined a single to right, scoring Kopf, sending Neale to third. Wingo took second as Shano Collins threw desperately to the plate, hoping to cut down the front runner. The crowd was bellowing with joy now. There was only one run in, but it sounded like a dozen.

To Fullerton, Cicotte seemed angry. He pawed the mound, busying himself until the dust had cleared. Schalk roared at him from behind the plate. It all seemed exaggerated, for there was little to sweat about. Two out and the pitcher up, Dutch Reuther, no better than a fair hitter.

Cicotte curved him, low and away. Ball one. Then Reuther took a vicious cut and lashed a tremendous drive to left center. Jackson and Felsch took off after it, but they couldn't get near it. The crowd leaped to its feet and watched Reuther pull into third base standing up. Two more runs had crossed the plate.

The noise was deafening.

Fullerton turned back to Matty and saw his smile. The Reds had been his ball club only a year before. He must feel proud of them now.

"When the bottom of the order starts hitting you, it just isn't your day," Matty said.

It seemed clear to the greatest pitcher of them all that it was just a question of Cicotte not having his best stuff today.

In the dugout, Kid Gleason just sat there, unwilling to believe what he saw. A bunch of .250 hitters were teeing off on his ace. It didn't make sense. Surely Cicotte would pitch to Rath now and retire the side. He would settle down for the remainder of the game while the big Chicago hitters started moving. They would open up for a big inning or two, just as they'd done dozens of times during the summer. That's the way it would go.

Out in the field, the infielders had gathered around Cicotte. Gleason knew what they were doing: keeping him company till this screaming mob subsided.

In the bull pen, he had Roy Wilkinson warming up. Gleason debated about pulling Cicotte with the score at 4–1, then decided to stick with his original estimate. They'd win this game with Cicotte.

Gleason moved to the dugout steps. "All right!" he hollered at the conference on the field. "Let's get the inning over!"

The boys jogged back to their positions and Cicotte went to work on Rath. Immediately, Gleason feared he was making a mistake. The pitch was a badly thrown curve ball, down and away. His second one missed by even more. Schalk was raging. Cicotte was tight-lipped and grim. Rath got set for the third pitch and lashed a hard shot that Weaver dove for futilely. Reuther scored while Rath beat the throw into second. Gleason moved to the top step of the dougout; Cicotte threw one bad pitch after another to Jake Daubert, moving the count to three and one. Then bang, another shot through the infield, and Rath scored from second. The score, 6–1.

At this point, Gleason charged out of the dugout. The crowd screamed when they saw him, enjoying his anger and his grief. He stood on the baseline and hollered at Cicotte. It was as if he was afraid to go all the way to the mound, afraid of what he might do.

"That's all, goddammit. That's all!"

He waved to the bull pen for Wilkinson to finish the fourth inning and then turned abruptly back to the dugout.

The city of Cincinnati was loyal to its 45,000 school kids. The 45,000 school kids were extremely loyal to the Cincinnati ball club. The principals of its several hundreds schools were instructed to post the score on convenient bulletin boards. At three o'clock, just before dismissal, the halls were crowded in front of the handmade scoreboards. They read:

CHICAGO	0	1	0	0
CINCINNATI	1	0	0	

The kids wondered why the score to complete the fourth inning was taking so long. They grabbed their books and empty lunch boxes and hurried into the warm October sunshine to find out.

In the press box, Ring Lardner was already writing his syndicated article. ". . . The White Sox only chance at this point was to keep the

Reds hitting until darkness fell and made it an unfinished legal game. But Heinie Groh finally hit a ball that Felsch could not help from catching and gummed up another piece of strategem."

If the ball game was death, the White Sox locker room was the morgue. The game finally ended at 9–1. The ballplayers showered in total silence.

Ray Schalk was boiling with the defeat. There is something unique about the position of a catcher that intensifies the emotion of a ball game. He, alone, sees the entire action in front of him, feels the presence of the umpire behind him, urges his will on every pitch, on every ball-strike decision. He squats behind the hitter, hollering through an iron-leather mask, working a pitcher, harassing the batters, getting meaning out of every pitch. Schalk was relentless. The pitcher was his own special baby; the infielders were his nephews. He barked at them all, hustled them, made them work, made them think, made them play ball. And when they didn't, he raged.

Still, like the others, he kept silent now. Even when Gleason came in, glaring at them all with the look of an injured lion—a look that Schalk had never seen before.

Kid Gleason just stood there, staring out over the locker room. Instinct told him he was going to be a loser. He looked at the players, trying to find the answer in their faces. Where was Cicotte? Someone said he had already left. He had showered early and taken off. Gleason scowled. He had to find out the truth. He had to find out what he did not want to know.

Lefty Williams, Joe Jackson, and Fred McMullin drove back to the Sinton with Sammy Pass, the businessman who, out of his love for these boys, had bet with Attell. At this unhappy moment, he tried to be cheerful: "We'll get them tomorrow, yeah?"

"Yeah," someone said.

Sammy was undaunted. "You'd better win." He grinned. "I got three thousand soldiers marching on you guys!"

Lefty Williams was sitting next to him. "Sammy, I don't think you should risk your dough on us." His voice was pitched low, lower than usual. He was obviously uneasy.

"What do you mean?" Pass asked. "Isn't your arm okay?"

Williams nodded. "My arm's all right."

"Well, aren't you guys gonna win?"

Williams shrugged. "Don't you know, Sammy . . . anything can happen in baseball . . ."

4

Abe Attell's room at the Sinton Hotel was a scene of triumph. The big sample room #708 was crowded with his partners assorting piles of newly won money. Attell was glowing. This was an easier way to make a buck than going twenty bloody rounds with "Harlem Tommy" Murphy! There was $45,000 in front of him, $16,000 of which was his, and he drew a fast arithmetic picture of a five-game parlay, in brilliant multiples of 16,000, give-or-take a loss here and there. What tickled him most was that it had cost him nothing. Not a dime. That there were eight ballplayers out there waiting for him to pay off bothered him not a all. For the first time in his life he felt like a really smart man.

Sleepy Bill Burns had not seen the game. His wife had come north from Texas and they were visiting friends in Norwood, a suburb of Cincinnati. That evening, he drove back to town and stopped at the Sinton, to pick up Billy Maharg. It had been agreed that Maharg would take the first payment of $20,000 from Attell and deliver it to Gandil. Out of that sum, Burns would be apportioned a share equal to that of the players. Together with what he had bet, approximately $3,500, he, too, saw himself pyramiding his stake into a substantial sum.

Maharg was waiting for him in the lobby. They smiled and shook hands. Everything was going fine. They went up to room #708 and confronted Attell.

But the Little Champ, Burns was quick to note, was not happy to see them. Burns simply asked him for the money for the players, and Attell, not so simply, refused him. He had his excuses ready, but he was not an accomplished liar. "The money is all out on bets, Bill," he said. "The players will have to wait!"

Burns got riled. He didn't like Attell, that dapper little Broadway character. His first reaction had been not to trust him. Now his suspicions were being verified.

Burns went after him. The ballplayers were relying on him, he said. They weren't going to throw ball games without getting their money.

Attell avoided him. He had a phone call to make.

Burns turned to Maharg, grunting his contempt. The two conspirators then left and made their way to Gandil's room. Their evening was not going to be a pleasant one.

When Burns bluntly told the players the disappointing news, they looked at each other, unable to think of anything to say. Burns told them they shouldn't worry. In the gambling world things like this happen. The cash goes out on bets: it takes time to rake it in. He felt sure they'd get their money tomorrow.

Gandil didn't like it and said so. He, too, felt a responsibility. Lefty Williams was scheduled to pitch the second game. You couldn't expect him to throw it without getting paid off! Burns allowed that this was true. He said he'd arrange for Gandil and Williams to meet with Attell the next morning, before the game. Williams would be assured that everything was being taken care of. Then Burns left the room as abruptly as he had left Attell's. His one comment to Maharg was that he was glad he wasn't a ballplayer any more.

Kid Gleason left the Sinton Hotel for dinner with his wife around eight o'clock. He had tried several times to see Charles Comiskey. He wanted desperately to talk to him. But Comiskey, as usual, was not available. At dinner, as a result, Gleason had eaten very little. His wife, who knew nothing of his suspicions, thought only that defeat was terribly hard for him. Well, they would win tomorrow. Everything would be all right.

But Gleason's stomach was filling up with the juices of his rage. At the entrance to the Sinton, he told his wife he didn't want to go inside yet. He wanted to take a walk. She smiled sympathetically, and went in by herself. It was a mistake: she should not have left him.

Once he was alone, he became the prey of every sardonic wise guy who felt like getting in his licks:

"Hey, Gleason, that's some job you did out there today!"

"What a ball club! Nine bums and a dope to run 'em!"

"Whattaya wanna bet you lose five straight!"

Gleason ignored them, or tried to. They followed him down the street, taunting him, baiting him. Their voices grew louder and closer. Nothing stopped them. It was as if they were gathering strength from his silence. Eventually he hated them too much to continue, and turned back to the hotel. His walk was over almost before it had begun.

Encouraged by this victory, his tormentors turned back with him. When he moved into the lobby, his blood was boiling. He saw Cicotte and Risberg, sprawled in big overstuffed chairs, laughing with a couple of strangers as if this was all a businessman's convention.

"Cicotte! Whattaya laughing at, eh?" he snapped.

For here suddenly was the real enemy, these two grinning faces, and he ripped into both players with a quick, uncontrollable torrent of words.

"You two think you can kid me? You busher, Risberg! You think I don't know what you're doing out there? Cicotte, you sonovabitch! Anybody who says he can't see what you're doing out there is either blind, stupid, or a goddam liar!"

Then he realized what he'd done. He looked into the blanching faces of his two ballplayers, saw the thunderstruck reaction of maybe a hundred popeyed lobby idlers. A strong supporting hand on his arm drew him away. It was the newspaper writer, Hugh Fullerton.

"Come on, Kid," Fullerton was saying. "Tomorrow's another day."

Gleason, like a schoolboy who had just been caught cheating on a test, walked to the elevator and went up to his room.

Charles Albert Comiskey was a big man. Everything about him was big, especially his nose. In the baseball world, he was known as the "Old Roman" because of that nose. As a personality, he lived up to the grandeur of the title. Late this night, however, he was having his troubles. There were too many reports, not only from shoeshine boys, but from the so-called horse's mouth. For one, the Chicago gambler and sportsman, Monte Tennes, had come to him an hour before. He related as how Joe Pesch, a familiar gambling figure from St. Louis, had told him during the latter part of August that he'd been active in the baseball world and was expanding his influence. Pesch had claimed that he'd sewed up Gandil, Risberg, and Felsch, placing them on a payroll for $200 a week. For this, they supposedly threw one or two ball games a week. Pesch had hoped that Tennes might like to come in on such an arrangement. Tennes told Comiskey that he had not believed the story at the time. Gamblers were famous for handing out false reports as readily as sound ones. It was a world where everyone wanted to play the big shot. But tonight, Tennes was not so sure: he'd heard enough to make him question the honesty of the Series. Enough, he added, to bet a big chunk against Mr. Comiskey's ball club.

By the time the Old Roman was settled in his hotel suite, he'd heard a lot more. Everything was piling up on him. He was confronted with a frightening realization, permanent and irrevocable, like the sudden, blatant knowledge that one had an incurable disease. In all his life, he'd never really known anything like it, and it would be there to cope with tomorrow, and the day after, and the day after that, and on and on.

He tried to shake it off, to shut his mind to it so that it would go away. The evidence, such as it was, was far from conclusive. Perhaps he had allowed his suspicions to sway his judgment; perhaps he had read into that ball game today a meaning that was not valid at all. Perhaps, as the sportswriters were headlining, the White Sox were simply victims of overconfidence!

Comiskey was not in the habit of deluding himself. He was not going to delude himself now. It was well after eleven o'clock, but he went to the phone and called Kid Gleason, asking him to come up.

When the Kid arrived, Comiskey stared at that tormented face and knew what was on his manager's mind. Gleason reached into his pocket and withdrew a batch of telegrams. New York, Philadelphia, New Orleans, Havana. From gamblers, he explained, warning him that the Series was being fixed. "How do you like that!" he cried. "I don't even know these guys!"

Comiskey wasn't interested in Gleason's telegrams: he had several of his own. He asked the Kid what he thought of that afternoon's game. Gleason restrained his anger and simply said that he'd never seen his club play like such a bunch of bushers. That wasn't exactly what Comiskey meant by the question. Point blank, he asked, "Do you think they're throwing the Series?" Gleason said he had no way of knowing. Comiskey flared: "Answer me!" Gleason then admitted he felt there was something wrong, but he knew nothing for certain. In the last analysis, he just couldn't believe that the worst was happening. It was too fantastic. How could anyone do a thing like that?

Comiskey could have told him, but he didn't bother. He ordered him to keep his eyes and ears open. They would talk about it again tomorrow.

The night was going to be a long one for the Old Roman. Sometime around 2:30 A.M., he decided that it was impossible to sleep. He had to face this problem, one way or another. But its gigantic implications tended to paralyze him. Could anyone do anything to stop such a frame-up? How could it be attacked without exposing the mess to the public? What was the smartest thing to do to protect baseball? To protect his own million-dollar investment?

Desperation drove him to action. He would turn this problem over to baseball's National Commission.

This Commission had been ruling baseball for seven years. Its chairman was Garry Herrmann. Herrmann, to complicate matters, was also owner of the Cincinnati Reds. It would be impossible to confront him with this problem.

The proper official, therefore, was the President of the American League. His name was Byron Bancroft Johnson. But here, too, was an impossibility: Comiskey and Johnson were not on speaking terms. Their history—together and apart—had been a long and dramatic one. It had begun, ironically, in this very town, a quarter of a century before. Comiskey was managing the Cincinnati club for owner John T. Brush in 1893. Ban Johnson, a few years out of college, was a young reporter for the *Commercial-Gazette*. They used to meet regularly at a tavern in Cincinnati's somewhat disreputable Vine Street, the Ten Minute Club (so named because every drinker was obliged to summon his waiter for another round every ten minutes). The two serious friends would drink and discuss the world of baseball, and here was spawned the idea for the formation of the American League.

It was Comiskey who was responsible for Johnson's executive career in baseball. In the autumn of 1893, Brush sent his manager on a scouting tour of the Southwest. There Comiskey saw great interest in reviving the recently disbanded Western League; eventually, he induced its members to reorganize, with Ban Johnson as President. Johnson ran the League so well that Comiskey left Cincinnati, bought a franchise in it, and ran a club in St. Paul. Connie Mack followed him at Milwaukee.

The Western League grew rapidly under Johnson's vigorous leadership. His ambition grew with it, spurred by the growing dissatisfaction with the whole National League operation.

The time was ripe for a rival league. Johnson met with millionaire coal magnate, Charles W. Somers, who was willing to put up a fortune to get it going. Johnson was elected president—again, largely through Comiskey's efforts—for a term of twenty years. In 1901, the American League went into operation.

It was inevitable that these two authoritarian figures should clash. Like Comiskey, Ban Johnson was a big man, mentally and physically. He weighed almost 300 pounds, but lived a vigorous, spirited life. He hunted from Canada to Mexico, much in the flamboyant manner of his contemporary, Teddy Roosevelt, whom he resembled. Descended from a long line of educators and ministers, he had a rigorous mind and a forceful, stentorian style of speaking. He was fond of poetry (he would recite "Barbara Frietchie" at the drop of a hat) and American military history (he could describe the strategy and action of all leading battles of the Civil War). He was also fond of conflict . . . so much so, in fact, that he was always at war.

Between Comiskey and his friend, there was reasonable harmony in the first years of the American League. In 1905, however, the rift began. Johnson saw fit to suspend one of Comiskey's ballplayers, James "Ducky" Holmes, for using abusive language to an umpire. Comiskey was furious, not so much for the suspension, but because he was not informed of it until a few minutes before game time.

Johnson snarled at Comiskey's protest. "If Comiskey doesn't like the punishment, he is at liberty to pull out of the American League. I regard the whole matter as closed!"

Comiskey stayed in the League. He merely pulled out of the office he'd been sharing with Johnson in the Fisher Building.

There were other incidents, trivial enough on the surface, yet irritants to such rival personalities. In 1907, in the heat of a tight pennant race, Comiskey's playing-manager, Fielder Jones, was suspended. He had earned the dubious honor (with Clark Griffith, an ex-Comiskey manager) of being ordered off the field more often than anyone in the majors. Coincident with this, Johnson sent Comiskey a dozen bass, the fruits of a successful fishing trip. Comiskey took it badly: "Does Johnson expect me to play fish in my outfield?"

(This fish story was repeated many times, inflated in importance as the key to the Comiskey-Johnson feud. In the course of recounting, it changed in size and flavor, as such stories often will. Many years later, it would turn up again in this form: It was Comiskey who had caught a giant trout, and as a peace offering, packed it in ice and sent it to Johnson. But the package was delayed, the weather inordinately hot, and by the time the trout reached Johnson, the smell was unbearable. Johnson, it was said, took it personally.)

Publicly, these rifts were repeatedly patched up. There were pictures of Comiskey and Johnson shaking hands, words of mutual admiration, American League meetings seemingly without enmity. Then, in 1918, the rivaly exploded into permanent war:

An obscure pitcher named Jack Quinn of the Pacific Coast League was signed by Comiskey to bolster his war-riddled pitching staff. But the New York Yankees insisted they had purchased him first. When Johnson, sitting in judgment, awarded Quinn to New York, Comiskey became livid. The affair marked the end of their compatibility.

Now, on this troubled night, back again in Cincinnati after a turbulent twenty-five years, Comiskey realized that he would be forced to eat crow. If he took his problem to baseball's executives, sooner or later it would have to get to Ban Johnson. Comiskey needed help. He needed a friend, not an enemy. The President of the National League, John Heydler, was perhaps such a friend. The Old Roman put on his robe, went and knocked on Heydler's door.

It was some moments before Heydler responded. When he heard who it was, he immediately got out of bed and admitted him. Comiskey apologized for the lateness of the visit, but said urgency demanded it. Heydler was polite and attentive as Comiskey proceeded to explain.

When he finished, Heydler gasped. "Impossible!" It was all he could say.

Comiskey was adamant in his belief that something terrible was going on. He admitted he had no proof. He knew that there were always wild rumors at World Series time. But this was more than that!

Heydler shook his head and insisted: "You can't fix a World Series, Commy!"

Though Comiskey had nothing more to say, Heydler saw that he was far from satisfied. He started dressing, knowing that Comiskey was not going to confront Ban Johnson with this or anything else. It would be up to Heydler to do it for him.

It was close to 3 A.M. when they got to Johnson's room. He, too, had to be awakened. When Heydler told him what was on Comiskey's mind, Ban Johnson roared his contempt in a classically vindictive exhalation: "That is the whelp of a beaten cur!"

The phrase was well turned. Johnson must have felt pleased with himself as he shut them out of his room. It wasn't often that he got a good crack at Comiskey. Any thought that the humiliated Old Roman might have some better cause than being a bad loser was quickly dismissed. Ban Johnson had a rigorous mind, but his ego filled it with blind spots. His hatred of Comiskey would critically plague the development of the Series scandal and alter its history.

Comiskey nodded his appreciation to John Heydler and swallowed his shattered pride. He was through for the night.

5

When Lefty Williams awoke on the morning of October 2, the rising sun was glistening off the rooftops across the street from the hotel. In the adjacent bed was his roommate, Byrd Lynn, second-string catcher, .220 hitter, excellent sleeper, friend.

Lefty had been rooming with Lynn on road trips since their arrival on this club in 1916. They had come to rely on each other, always ready to exchange confidences on any subject that concerned them. Having long since covered the vital areas of their lives, they had more or less stopped talking, though without any breach in their friendship. This lack of conversation suited them both well. Neither was talkative by nature, though both were reasonably intelligent. For the last few days, Williams had maintained a complete silence. Now he speculated as to whether his roommate suspected anything. Lynn was the quiet type whose thoughts were difficult to fathom.

That morning, Chick Gandil woke to the same thought he had taken to sleep: Where the hell was Sport Sullivan? He had been trying to reach him for days. Big-city characters scurried into holes like rats when they wanted to disappear. They couldn't be beaten out with a stick. Gandil never could get accustomed to that. In the small towns of his youth, he could always find his man; somebody always knew where he was. But here, the message was clear enough. When a man owed money, suddenly he just didn't exist. Besides, Gandil could assume that, by this time, Sullivan must be fully aware of their arrangements with Attell. He could disappear and let Attell finance the scheme. Gandil was tasting the bitter fruits of duplicity.

At 10 A.M., Gandil picked up Williams in the lobby of the Sinton and they ambled out into the sunlight. They turned into a side street a few blocks from the hotel and approached a group of men conversing idly. They included Sleepy Bill Burns, Billy Maharg, Abe Attell, and Bennett. The ballplayers nodded to them. It all seemed very casual as their prearranged meeting began. It was indicative of their contempt of exposure that they had chosen such a place to get together. It never bothered them that such a group might attract attention. Significantly, it didn't, despite the fact that Gandil and Williams, and certainly the diminutive Attell, were recognizable figures to any number of passers-by. They were just a group of sporting figures having a chat.

The chat had to do with $20,000, which Gandil demanded, right then and there. Attell shook his head. He just didn't have that kind of ready money. Cash was still out on bets. Attell insisted he was good for it, and pulled out a telegram to prove it. It had arrived the previous evening and read:

ABE ATTELL, SINTON HOTEL, CINCINNATI. AM WIRING YOU
TWENTY GRAND AND WAIVING IDENTIFICATION. A.R.

Gandil wanted to know when they'd get the money. Attell said
he'd have it on the following morning at the latest. He'd give it to
Burns as soon as he got it. Burns could meet Gandil on the side lines
before the game and pay off.

Such an arrangement staggered even Gandil. What was he to do,
hide $20,000 in his jock strap?

Burns was a smooth mediator. He assured Gandil that he could
take care of the payments to everybody's satisfaction. The important
thing of the moment was today's game. There was too much talk going around. Williams had to be careful. He had to be more subtle
than Cicotte had been in the opener in order to make the act look
good.

Williams assured them that he could handle himself, and added
sardonically that, since this was his first World Series start, it was
important for *him* to look good. The Little Champ, pretending to be
amused at Williams's joke, playfully jabbed him a quick one-two, a
reminder of his own former greatness, and beat a hasty retreat.

Burns was aware of Gandil's uneasiness. He assured him that
everything would be all right, that there was nothing to worry about.
Gandil mumbled something about how the whole damn fix was
beginning to stink. How could he expect the other ballplayers to stay
with it?

Burns, aware of his own sticky position, had to sweat at that one.
He was the little man standing in treacherously deep water, trying to
push the overloaded boat across the river because somebody had
stolen the oars. In a moment of almost incredible weakness, he turned
to the surly Gandil and pulled a rabbit out of his hat. "Look," he
offered, "I've got an oil lease on twelve thousand acres of Texas oil
lands. It's worth maybe a hundred and twenty thousand dollars. Suppose I put this up as collateral, just to show how much faith I've got
in Rothstein's word!"

Gandil studied him for a moment. Where was the lease? Could he
see it? Burns nodded. Sure. He had it back at the hotel. Gandil was
placated. He acknowledged that such an arrangement sounded
pretty good. He would talk it over with the players. And then they

separated. For Gandil and Williams, once again it was time to go to Redland Park.

Billy Maharg shook his head critically. "What'd you say a thing like that for?" He was referring to the oil lease. Why should Burns protect Arnold Rothstein's equity? Or Abe Attell's? And what made him so sure that Attell was telling the truth? How did he know that the telegram was even authentic?

Suddenly it seemed vitally important that they verify it, and they headed for the Western Union office. The clerk was reluctantly co-operative, but turned up *no* record of such a telegram to Attell on the previous night! What did this mean? That there would not be any money forthcoming? That Attell had been lying all the way? That Arnold Rothstein was actually not involved?

Burns hurried back to the Sinton. It was not quite 11 A.M., but he wanted a stiff drink to help him think. He didn't like the feel of things any better than Gandil did.

The failure of the Western Union clerk to turn up a record of the telegram lends a beautiful irony to the story, for the truth was that a telegram had been sent to Attell from New York the day before; not by Rothstein, of course, but by Abe's partner, Curly Bennett, at Abe's request.

In New York, Arnold Rothstein watched the odds build against the White Sox. From 8–5 two days ago, they had shifted to even money at game time yesterday, to 5–7 today. Nevertheless, he decided to get more money down, even though he was loading it on the favorite now. It had, of course, crossed his mind that the whole thing was being handled stupidly. The correct way to play this Series would have been for the Sox to win that first game. Then the odds would be at least 2–1 and he would double his money. But this was too much to ask. When half-baked gamblers run the show, anything can happen.

He got down another $85,000 on Cincinnati to win the Series. He knew better than to bet individual games.

6

There were 800 fewer spectators at Redland Park for the second game, October 2. (It was said that there were 800 Cincinnati celebrants who had been unable to get up on this morning.) But no box-office tickets were available and scalpers were still getting $50 a pair. The law, it was repeatedly announced in the press, required all speculators to register at the Internal Revenue Office and pay a Federal tax on half the amount received in excess of the face value of each ticket. Arrests, however, were few and far between. Speculators continued to flood the town despite their failure to comply with the law.

The crowd was less boisterous than the day before. With one big victory under their belt, Cincinnati fans could assume a more gracious, less frantic manner. It became unnecessary to prove their status in the baseball world by screaming at every pitch. Now they could relax and watch the ball game. It was almost as if they didn't have to win this one.

And once again, the truth was, they didn't expect to.

The Cincinnati ballplayers themselves were a little stunned by their previous day's victory. A bunch of .250 Davids had crushed Goliath. It wasn't supposed to have happened that way. But they were pros, even pennant winners, accustomed to winning. If they had done the impossible the day before, it might even be said they had done it all year. Wasn't Pat Moran the Miracle Man? To a pro, yesterday's game was just another ball game. If the White Sox had played like "bush-leaguers" (the papers were full of that kind of phraseology), the Reds had caused it. There was no valid way of analyzing these games. Some days you have it, some you don't.

As for the rumors of a sellout, who paid any attention to them? Not the fans. Not the Cincinnati ballplayers.

Manager Pat Moran sent the veteran Harry "Slim" Sallee to the mound for the second ball game. Sallee, a former St. Louis Cardinal

and New York Giant, had completed his first year with the Reds. At
thirty-five, like Cicotte, he'd had his best year, 21 wins against only
7 defeats. Sallee had pitched for the Giants in the 1917 World Series
against this same Chicago ball club. He was beaten twice. If he knew
the White Sox batters, it could easily be said that they knew him
better.

Sallee felt strong, having had a good rest all week. The warm sun
and the big World Series crowd fed him a little something extra. If he
lacked his normal confidence, facing this great ball club, he was nevertheless determined to make it tough for them. It was a matter of personal pride; he knew he had only a year or two left.

At exactly one minute after two, he faced Shano Collins, took his
first big windup, and cut loose with a hard one. It sailed high and outside, and the umpire Billy Evans called it a ball. The second pitch was
no better. With the count at 3 and 1, Collins slapped back a feeble
grounder. Sallee took his time throwing him out at first. But his control was still shaky against Eddie Collins who worked him for a walk.
He could sense the nervousness of the crowd now, and he pitched
high to Buck Weaver, who lashed at the second pitch and lined to
Kopf at short. Eddie Collins stopped short, then fell all over himself
trying to scramble back to first. Kopf's throw doubled him off for the
third out.

Sallee had been lucky.

Lefty Williams was in his prime. He could throw a sharp-breaking
curve ball, fast or slow, and sometimes neither. He was smart. He
had that rare ability to pitch to spots with incredible skill. He could
shave the outside corner of the plate at the knees, or break a curve
ball right under a hitter's chin. He'd complete entire ball games without walking a man. Hitters hated to bat against him; Williams would
never give them a fat pitch to swing at.

He was a quiet, steady, almost scholarly type on the mound. His
style was careful, almost delicate. His concentration was perfect, like
that of the conductor of a symphony orchestra. Watching him work,
one might get the feeling that he should be allowed to pitch in complete silence.

But when Rath stepped to the plate, the Cincy fans greeted their lead-off man with a roar of welcome. Williams seemed embarrassed by this and waited for the sound to subside.

When, seven years earlier, at nineteen, Ray Schalk had entered the majors, he had weighed less than 150 pounds. Compared with the big men surrounding him, he had always seemed like a little kid.

The Cleveland bench had spent the day jockeying him. "Hey, sonny, where's your momma?" "Raymond, you got your diapers on?" They never stopped; but, then, neither did he. He made plenty of noise and found comfort in bellowing at the White Sox star pitcher, "Big Ed" Walsh (a veteran 27-game winner). Walsh had helped him by bellowing back. Since that day, Schalk had caught almost 900 official games, always with the gritty determination that nobody would handle it any better than he.

But today Schalk was threatened. There was nothing in his training to cope with the special kind of fear he was aware of. He had heard rumors. Were they true? Cicotte's performance yesterday had baffled him. Maybe he just had a bad day. Schalk squatted now, on the brink of anger. He glared at Williams, waiting for the crowd to subside.

"Watch him!" Gleason had said to Schalk in the clubhouse before the game.

Schalk's impatience was getting the best of him. It was only the first inning and already his nerves were raw. "Dammit, Lefty, let's go!" he barked.

Williams nodded. Schalk wriggled his fingers in his crotch, signaling for a curve ball. They'd been over the hitters carefully. Williams would know exactly where to throw, and Schalk got set to receive the pitch.

Williams had one thing on his mind: How could he lose this ball game without looking bad? In six years on this club, he could not remember having seen Cicotte take such a drubbing as he had yesterday. It had crossed his mind that he ought to talk to him, but one look at Cicotte's face as he had left the field had been enough to deter him. He wondered how the proud Cicotte could have swallowed so much, even for $10,000. Williams had repeated the figure to himself many times. Ten grand would be a lot of money on top of his own $2,600 salary. The arithmetic of the deal made a lot of sense to him.

Williams acknowledged Schalk's sign and began pumping. His arm swung up and around with its usual grace. He let the ball go with a sudden snap of his wrist, sending it spinning to the plate. The curve broke sharply and Rath watched it pass. Umpire Billy Evans shot his black-sleeved left arm up and growled, "Ball one!" Williams's second pitch also missed the corner. The crowd yelled, hungry for a base on balls. Rath worked him to a full count. Williams paused for a moment, knowing he should not walk him. It was vital that he stay on the mound for most of this nine-inning game. He put a little something extra on his fast ball and Rath flied feebly to Felsch in center. One out.

Williams turned, got set to pitch to Daubert. Again, when he threw a curve, it broke off wildly. Schalk shook his fist at Williams and barked something about watching his glove. He had failed to do this. He had let himself fall into a sloppiness he always abhorred. In eight pitches thus far, he had tried to control only one of them. This was not the way he wanted things to go. He had to control the ball game. Every pitch had to mean something. If he was going to lose this game, he had to lose it carefully.

His fast ball cut the inside corner for strike one. Then Daubert fouled back a good curve. Strike two. Williams curved him again, and Daubert rapped feebly to Risberg who threw perfectly to Gandil at first. Two outs.

Heinie Groh faced Williams now, waving that crazy bottle bat of his as if he were a cop directing traffic. Groh swatted the first pitch to right. Shano Collins made a mad dash for it and picked it right off his shoes for the third out.

Chick Gandil moved out of the dugout as Joe Jackson blooped a cheap double to center field. He grabbed his two bats, swung them back and forth a few times to get loose, then knelt in the batter's circle. Hap Felsch was up and would sacrifice, sending Joe to third. It would then be up to Gandil to keep him there, not so easy to do with one out. The infield had moved in on the grass, thinking only of keeping that runner from scoring. This, of course, gave the hitter a big advantage. All he had to do was slap one by them. . . .

Gandil discarded his second bat and walked to the plate. He checked to see if Gleason would signal for a squeeze play. No. Gandil got set, but for the first time in his life he was actually afraid of rapping out a base hit. This sort of thing took skill.

Sallee took a cautious windup and fired for the low, outside corner. Gandil stepped into the pitch and met it squarely, but without power. He rapped it artfully, directly at Kopf, the shortstop. Kopf fielded it cleanly, held Jackson at third, then threw to first in time to get Gandil.

Gandil raced past first, turned back to the dugout. He had played his role skillfully. As an added gesture, he kicked at the earth in simulated anger.

Two out, now and Risberg moved to the plate. Gandil could rely on the Swede. He moved into a corner of the dugout, but didn't have to stay there long: Risberg flied to right field on the second pitch, ending the inning. The threat was over. No score.

Kid Gleason was having another bad day. The previous night's explosion of anger had brought him no relief. Now, he no longer knew what to think or how to act, though at the moment, his boys were looking good out there. They were starting to hit the ball hard. There was that wonderful feeling in the air of the pending big eruption, the kind of big inning that had won so many games for him all season. Williams, though a bit shaky at the start, seemed sharp. He moved through the bottom of the second without any trouble. In the top of the third inning, Schalk blasted a tremendous drive to the left-field roof, just foul, then lined sharply to Roush in left center. Williams singled to left. Shano Collins hit another line smash to left that Duncan was lucky to get a glove on. Eddie Collins ended the inning with a shot to third that Groh caught to protect himself. They were hitting the ball hard. Sooner or later, they'd start to drop safely. That's the way of baseball.

To end the third inning, Williams was brilliant again. He fanned Greasy Neale. Reds catcher, Bill Rariden, skied to Jackson in shallow left field. Sallee popped up to Weaver.

When Weaver and Jackson opened the fourth with singles back to back, Gleason was ready for the turning point. He had Felsch sacrifice again, moving the two runners to scoring position. With one out and the infield in close, surely Gandil could push one through this time! But Gandil grounded to Daubert at first base, and Daubert caught Weaver at the plate. Risberg followed by looking sick again, popping feebly to Daubert. Another inning without score.

Gleason had been through this same pattern of defeat two innings before.

Up in the press box, Hugh Fullerton was enjoying the game. He watched Lefty Williams take the mound at the bottom of the fourth, confident that he was going to have another fine day. Fullerton had seen this great ball club frequently enough to sense the pattern of the game. Like Gleason, he anticipated a big White Sox inning to come.

Williams's first pitch to Rath was low and outside. His second was high, just missing. The Cincinnati crowd started roaring again, impatient to break the 0–0 deadlock. Williams pawed the dirt around the mound with his spikes. It was something to do while he took a breather. Gandil left his position and sauntered to the mound. The big first baseman put his hand on Williams's shoulder and talked earnestly to him.

The ball game waited for the conference to end, but not the crowd. Any sign of Chicago weakness was inspirational. They started to get on Williams with all they had.

Williams got set and threw. Rath took strike one, right down the middle. The count moved cautiously to three and two. Williams missed the plate with a bad pitch. Rath drew the first base on balls, and the crowd screamed approval.

Daubert followed with a sacrifice bunt, moving Rath to second, the first Cincinnati runner in scoring position. Heinie Groh also worked the count to three and two. Williams seemed nervous now. He was taking more time than usual. Schalk was yelling at him, but the crowd drowned him out. Williams called for the ball and threw. The pitch was high, and Groh walked.

This brought big Edd Roush, cleanup hitter, to the plate. The steady, relentless roaring of the crowd was dominating the stadium. Williams breathed deeply, studied Schalk's signals, checked the runners and threw. Low. Ball one. Schalk snapped the ball back to him, unashamed of his anger. Williams toed the rubber again, determined to keep pitching. Again, low. Ball two. The crowd added another layer of sound; it seemed to have unlimited resources.

Schalk pushed his mask to the top of his head and stalked out to the mound, hollering at Williams all the way. What he said to the troubled pitcher, Fullerton, of course, did not know. But it was clear he was saying plenty. He turned back to the plate, still raging, then stopped to holler a few words toward Gleason in the dugout. Williams watched and listened, never put in a word.

As Williams got set for the next pitch, so did the crowd. A shout more penetrating than Fullerton had ever heard seemed to swell with the movement of the pitcher's arm. Roush swung. The bat leveled off at the fat pitch and met the ball squarely. So great was the roar of the crowd that Fullerton could not hear the contact. But what he saw was enough: Roush had singled sharply to center. Rath sped around to score, and Groh slid safely into third.

Fullerton wrote himself a note: "Never heard so much noise!"

There was more to come. Every pitch sounded like a crisis. Williams worked steadily, maintaining his poise. He seemed indifferent to the crowd now, but his control had deserted him. With the count two and two, Roush made a dash for second. But Schalk rifled a perfect throw to Risberg, cutting him down.

To Fullerton the throw was a vindicating one. It flaunted the greatness of the Sox in the face of 30,000 enemies. As Roush trotted almost guiltily off the field, the bedlam seemed to fade with him.

The silence was short-lived. Williams walked Duncan on two more pitches, putting a man back on first. Three walks in one inning. Williams had never been so wild.

Suddenly the alien roar of a plane intruded on the stadium. Everyone looked up, saw the plane circle lower and lower, hovering over the diamond. Then, from the cockpit, the figure of a man dropped out, plummeted weirdly to the playing field, its arms and legs flailing in descent. Men gasped. Women screamed in fright. Then it became apparent that the figure was only a dummy. It landed in the outfield, loose and lifeless, a ludicrous, meaningless joke. A stout policeman ran out to retrieve it, hurried away, dragging the floppy form behind him. He laid it on the ground against the left field barrier and used it for a seat.

The crowd laughed nervously as Williams went back to work on Kopf. On the next pitch, Kopf leaned into a hanging curve ball and smashed it into deep left field. Groh jogged merrily across the plate, followed by Duncan. Kopf pulled into third with a mighty triple.

Fullerton wrote himself another note: "Three walks, three runs." Grimly, he drew a circle around it.

A moment later, Neale grounded to Eddie Collins, ending the inning. But it didn't seem to matter. The White Sox outhit the Reds ten to four, managed to score two runs in the seventh, but lost the game 4–2.

7

"You can 'pat' Moran, but you can't 'kid' Gleason!"

Every school kid in Cincinnati was rattling it off, thirty times a day.

Kid Gleason watched the players file slowly into the locker room, glared at them brazenly, defiantly, murderously. He didn't care. Let them know how he felt.

When he got to his little dressing room, Schalk was waiting for him. He was hot, sweaty, filthy. His face was lined with dirt, marked by the pressure of the catcher's mask. He was standing by the door, holding his catcher's mitt as if he was still ready to play ball.

"The sonovabitch!" His voice was hoarse, compounding the sound of his rage.

Gleason shut the door behind him. "Williams?" he asked.

"Williams," Schalk replied. "He kept crossing me. In that lousy fourth inning, he crossed me three times! He wouldn't throw the curve!"

Schalk's rage forced Gleason to contain his own. As calmly as he could, he commented, "Well, it happens. . . ."

Schalk wouldn't give him that. "Not with Williams!"

"Never? Not all season?" Gleason asked.

Schalk spit it out. "Never!"

Gleason groped for something to say that would placate him.

But Schalk was not in the mood for discussion. He had sweated for two hours behind that plate. He had come to Gleason for action. He exploded: "Goddammit, Kid . . . you gotta *do* something about this!"

Gleason knew this was true. If he was to pull out this Series, he had to do something. Talk to Comiskey again? What for? He had no more proof today than yesterday. All he had was the cuss words of an angry catcher who never could stand to lose. Who would believe him?

It was apparent that there were no facts. Reality was a vague stink that anyone could smell, but no one knew where it came from.

He crossed to the ballplayers locker room. They had started talking again, not too dispirited: normal chatter after a normal defeat. When they saw Gleason, they subsided, like jabbering kids when the teacher comes into the classroom.

Gleason looked for Williams, but his vision never got past Gandil. He saw Gandil smoking a cigar, complacent and unperturbed, and hatred rose to choke him. Gandil was the enemy, a cutthroat character, tough, shrewd, corrupt. Gleason crossed to the bench where Gandil was sitting. When he spoke, his tone was surprisingly sardonic: "Gandil, you sure had a good day today. . . ."

Gandil looked up at him, almost a little amused. "So did you, Kid!" he replied.

Gleason leaped at the big first baseman, actually got his hands on the ballplayer's throat. Immediately he was pulled off by several players, his whole body lifted from the floor and carried a few feet away.

He shook them off and retreated to his little dressing room. Gandil wouldn't say a word, Gleason knew. He wouldn't dare.

Schalk showered and dressed hurriedly. Since they were heading back to Chicago on the sleeper that night, he had to pack his catcher's gear.

When he got outside, he walked slowly down the ramp, under the grandstand, toward the exit. The empty ball field was messy, littered with discarded programs, old newspapers, and candy wrappers. He looked out at home plate and at the spot behind it where he had squatted through the nine tortured innings.

He stood there waiting for Lefty Williams.

When Williams came out, momentarily alone, Schalk called to him. Lefty turned, nodded impassively, and walked toward the catcher. Schalk grabbed him firmly by the arm and drew him away from the ramp, a few yards under the grandstand that slanted above them. Then he spun him around, and slammed into him, both fists flailing in inept fury. Williams cried out in shock and backed away from this wild onslaught, instinctively covering up to protect himself. Others heard the cry and hurried to stop Schalk. They pulled him off, but not in time to prevent the little catcher from getting in a few licks.

Sleepy Bill Burns had watched the second game with considerable respect for Lefty Williams. Burns, ex-pitcher himself, knew a masterful job when he saw one. Williams had lost that ball game in one inning, but had looked brilliant in the process.

Along with Billy Maharg, Burns went to Attell's room at the Sinton to pick up the $40,000 for the players. Out of this, the ballplayers would pay him a commission. Though the exact amount had not been determined, Burns assumed 10 per cent was not unreasonable. Secretly, he was prepared to accept less.

Attell's room was full of money. Money was being laid out in neat piles, stashed in suitcases, packed in bundles, stored under the mattress. Burns had never seen so much money. He had no idea how much there was, but it gave him a warm, glowing feeling.

Until he asked Attell for $40,000 of it.

Again Attell refused. He simply turned away, not even bothering with an excuse. The man named Bennett moved into the breach. "To hell with them," he snapped. "What do we need them for!"

Burns was staggered, so staggered that he couldn't say anything. How could you answer a man like that! He moved past him and grabbed Attell. He insisted that the money be paid. He even spoke of the masterful job Williams had done. The ballplayers had worked for their dough; they deserved to be paid. Attell didn't think he could strain their loyalty any further, did he?

Attell finally summoned Bennett and the Levi brothers, Ben and

Lou, to a private conference. There was a brief discussion out of Burns's earshot, and when it was over, Attell lifted up a mattress and withdrew a pile of bills. He handed them to Burns, who counted $10,000.

"That's not enough!"

Attell shrugged. "That's it. That's all they can have!"

"They won't accept it, Abe. For Chrissakes, there's eight of them!"

"They'll take it," Attell replied.

Burns exchanged glances with Maharg. This time, he sensed, there was going to be trouble. Attell was threatening the whole set up with this kind of greed and stupidity. Burns also gave more than a passing thought to his own finances. He had won a bundle for himself—so far, close to $12,000. From where he was sitting—on the inside—it could be much, much more. Unless Attell rocked the already shaky boat too severely.

Burns looked at the cash in his hand and wondered how he was going to hand it to Gandil. Almost involuntarily, he held it out to Maharg. "Here, you give it to them!"

Maharg recoiled, as if the money was poisonous. Sensibly enough, he didn't want any part of that assignment.

In the end, Sleepy Bill acquiesced. It was $10,000 or nothing. He would do what he could to keep the ballplayers happy. Maybe he could get $500 out of it himself. He started to leave.

"Wait a minute!" Attell snapped. Burns stopped. He could see Attell's mind racing with new manipulations. "Tell the ballplayers that they should win the third game. Much better for the odds, that way. . . ."

Burns had to smile. Attell's gall was incredible.

With the package of bills hidden under his shirt, Burns made his way to Gandil's room, on a different floor. En route, a door opened and a familiar figure stepped out. It was Kid Gleason. He saw Burns and scowled. Burns smiled in return. "Hya, Kid," he said.

Chick Gandil was not surprised. This confirmation of his suspicions, however, did not mitigate his anger. When he saw the paltry $10,000 Burns tossed on the bed, he was ready to blow up.

"Goddam double cross!" he barked. Risberg and McMullin chimed in. They were drowning men grasping at $10,000 straws.

Burns once again assured them that it was only a delay, that they would be paid in full. Immediately Gandil began thinking how he, too, could play this game. It was not without irony that Burns himself supplied him with an idea by casually suggesting that the ballplayers think in terms of winning the third game. It would level the odds again.

Gandil said he'd think about it. He took the $10,000 and put it in the lining of his suitcase. It was time to start packing again. They were all making the 11 P.M. sleeper back to Chicago.

For a thirty-four-year-old, Ringgold Wilmer Lardner was doing fine. He was an established writer whose column appeared in newspapers throughout the country. He could write about pretty much anything he chose; he was not confined to sport. Readers liked his sardonic style, his amused cynicism, and increasingly emerging in his columns, his bitterness. Three years earlier, he had published his first collection of short stories, some of them about baseball.

Lardner was a tall, dark-haired, neat-looking man. His somber face seemed never to smile, though his friends knew this was only a façade. Hugh Fullerton described him as wearing "the look and manner of Rameses II with his wrappings off." If Lardner didn't laugh much himself, he made others roar.

Like Fullerton, he was a great baseball fan. He found in the game the finest expression of competitive athletics. In 1919 ballplayers were heroes. He constantly thought of them as big men and himself as a kid. A major-league star was someone who had used his talent to get to the very top. And when, as a result of his work, Lardner became friendly with them, even then he could not get over his adulation. It was a strange thing to see this bright, cynical, misanthropic writer hanging around the lobbies and pool halls, just to be with a bunch of rather slow-witted ballplayers.

Lardner lived in Chicago, and as a consequence, his great admiration centered on the White Sox. Among them, his favorite was Eddie Cicotte. Lardner believed him to the finest pitcher around. He liked Cicotte's cleverness, his artful use of the knuckle ball, the incredibly deceptive "shine ball." He saw Cicotte as the image of the "little man," once abused and discarded, then rising above the conventional prejudice of small-minded baseball owners against lack of size and power. Besides, Cicotte was a colorful character. A funny guy, capable of rare pranks and wisecracks, adept at the hilarious banter of locker rooms and hotel lobbies. He could almost make Lardner laugh.

For the past few days, however, Ring Lardner had been swallowing all the rumors. He had seen his hero destroyed in the first game, other idols smashed in the second. No matter how much he hated to admit it—especially to himself—it was not in him to resist the logic of his cynicism. The sellout was on. He could smell it. Nothing more; just smell it.

But like all the others with sensitive noses, he could not be certain. The situation rendered him helpless. After that first game, Lardner had asked Cicotte to come up to his room for a drink. Cicotte came, and the writer put the big question to him. It was childish and naïve of him, and Cicotte had to laugh. No, the great pitcher had sighed, he was merely off form, that was all. There was nothing going on out there. Just off form.

Lardner wanted to believe it, but he couldn't.

After the second game, he returned to the Sinton and started drinking. He wrote his daily column with a bottle beside the typewriter: ". . . There's a wild rumor going around that Mr. Gleason wants the fourth inning removed for the rest of the Serious, and I don't care which inning they do cut out or maybe even two, but if they eliminate an inning the Sox maybe will win a game which will merely elongate the Serious so whatever happens we are the losers."

That night, Lardner was aboard the train heading west to Chicago, along with the entire personnel of both clubs. His bottle went with him. He sat there drinking with other newspapermen, letting the pinochle, poker, baseball, smoke-filled, whisky-lined, dirty-joke jabber swirl around him. Others barely noted how untypically silent he was. Then he rose from his seat, slightly unsteady on his pins, and moved through the rattling train to a certain Pullman.

Here, members of the Chicago White Sox were playing a few hands of poker before getting into their berths. Lardner moved conspicuously into the car and started reeling down the aisle. Any of them who had not noticed his arrival, quickly became aware of it. Lardner burst loudly into song:

> "*I'm forever blowing ball games,*
> *Pretty ball games in the air.*
> *I come from Chi*
> *I hardly try*
> *Just go to bat and fade and die;*
> *Fortune's coming my way,*
> *That's why I don't care.*
> *I'm forever blowing ball games,*
> *And the gamblers treat us fair. . . ."*

Nobody even told him to shut up.

8

On Friday, October 3, there was a message from Abe Attell waiting for Bill Burns when he checked into Chicago's Hotel Sherman around 8:40 in the morning. Attell wanted to see him. Burns had his bags placed in his room and called Attell's.

The Little Champ, it seemed, was worried. What did Burns think the players were going to do for the third game? Burns laughed. How in hell did *he* know? Attell acknowledged that he understood why the players might be annoyed, but he asked Burns to bear with him. It would all come out okay, and Burns would be well taken care of. If only they could be sure of the ballplayers. . . .

It all boiled down to one thing: how were they going to keep this deal going and the big dough rolling in? Attell wasn't willing to give the players any more than the paltry $10,000 of the previous night. Burns had to weigh the alternatives. Either he went along with Attell or he pulled out completely. He hated both. But it was glaringly apparent to him that there was no possible money to be gained by pulling out.

Attell was smiling as if he had known this all along. He suggested that Burns go see the ballplayers again. After all, they knew him, trusted him, liked him. Wasn't that his function in this whole setup?

Much revolved around the third game: just what were the ballplayers planning to do with it?

Burns said he would find out. He went to his room and called up Gandil at the Warner Hotel. "What about the game today?" he asked. Gandil replied that the boys had talked it over and that it would go exactly like the first two. Burns thanked him and went back to tell Attell.

But Attell was skeptical. Did Burns believe that? After all, Dickie Kerr was going to pitch, and Kerr was not in on the fix. Burns, of course, knew that. But he also remembered the ballplayers saying that they wouldn't win behind Kerr because he was a "busher." They'd save their victories for Cicotte and Williams. Burns could understand that: these boys were real cliquish.

Burns left hurriedly to join his partner, Billy Maharg. Together, they scraped together every dime they could, anxious to parlay their previous two wins into a huge pot. The Sox were going to lose number three!

Chick Gandil had lied. If he could, he was going to make Burns and Attell sweat. And he was going to force Sport Sullivan out of the woodwork. The ballplayers had not met and talked things over. Nor did they have any intention of letting the third game "go exactly like the first two." Their anger at the failure to receive payment was enough to preclude any further discussion. As for the third game, they would go to Comiskey Park without any clear idea as to what was expected of them or what they expected of each other.

The truth was, *nobody* knew how the third game would go.

Comiskey Park was decorated for the occasion. It was a fine-looking, double-tiered ball park, with a pleasant background of trees, church steeples, and new public buildings—this despite its reputation of being located in the stockyards region of the South Side. To add to the festivities, two brass bands paraded through the aisles, one from Cincinnati, playing the old tunes, and a sharper band from the big city of Chicago, playing the new. Several thousand Cincinnati fans had made the all-night trip, and set up headquarters at Chicago's huge Congress Hotel. They'd spent a blustering morning parading through the streets with giant red pennants. In hoarse voices, they sang of their

victories like a bunch of drunken college kids. Chicagoans saw them
and heard them and found them silly. They took their baseball seriously in Chicago.

Here the women were fast becoming as ardent fans as the men.
It was estimated that more women attended the third game on this
day than any previous ball game. In addition to the flashing colors of
their hats and gowns, they were capable of greeting key players with
plenty of vocal power. Shyness was passée. Women shouted at the
ballplayers as freely as the men did. They also felt free to use horns,
klaxons, and bells. It was, perhaps, significant that Charles Comiskey was the club owner who originated Ladies Day on which women
were admitted free.

In the all-night bleacher line, there were some 2,000 men and
boys, sustaining themselves with crap games and flasks and giant
sandwiches. By 9 A.M., the line had swelled to 5,000. Shortly before
the gates opened, two travelers, all the way from Denver, Colorado,
approached the front of the line. They had come to see the Series,
but there were no tickets available. Could they buy a place at the
front of this line? Two youngsters obliged them, and walked away
with $20 for their night's vigil.

Abe Attell didn't like the feel of things. Burns's report made
everything seem too simple. "The third game will go like the first
two!" Just because Gandil said so? That didn't sit right. To Attell,
who had broken all his own promises, it figured that the players would
never keep theirs to him. He had to go on his instinct. That was the
way he operated.

It was almost noon. He didn't have much time. He got on the
telephone and started working fast. To play this one safe, he would
hedge his bets on Cincinnati. He would take whatever he could get
on Chicago. . . .

Damon Runyon wrote of the White Sox third-game pitcher:
"Take Dickie Kerr, now, a wee hop o' my thumb. Not much taller
than a walking stick . . . the tiniest of the baseball brood. Won't
weigh 90 lbs soaking wet, an astute scout once reported after a look
at Kerr. Too small for a pitcher, especially a left-handed pitcher. Too
small for too much of anything, except, perhaps, a watch charm. . . ."

Little Dickie Kerr had been born in St. Louis, twenty-six years before. He was late getting to the major leagues because of his size. Kid Gleason liked him and used him in 39 games. He amassed an impressive rookie year, winning 13 and losing 8. He had a sneaky fast ball and good control. He relied on both. What he did with his curve ball was icing on the cake.

On this Friday afternoon, in front of the somewhat amazed and thoroughly delighted eyes of 29,000 Chicago fans, little Dickie Kerr was sharper than ever. His fast ball had a real hop on it, causing the Reds to pop up. His curve ball dropped with startling suddenness, and they hit feeble grounders to the infielders. All his pitches had eyes. Perfectly placed, perfectly timed. He was so good, there was probably nothing Gandil and company could have done to alter his victory, even if they'd tried.

It took less than ninety minutes for him to go the route. The White Sox walked off the field, 3–0 victors, while the entire grandstand stood up and wildly cheered Kerr for the finest pitching performance they had ever seen.

The game was won in the second inning. Joe Jackson opened with a single to left. Felsch, as it happened so often in the Series, had bunted for the sacrifice. But Ray Fischer, the Reds' pitcher, had rushed his throw to force Jackson at second, and heaved the ball into the outfield. It ended up with Jackson on third and Felsch on second. Gandil stepped up to the plate with the infield drawn in, hoping to cut the run off at the plate. This time, the big first baseman rapped one through the middle, into center field, scoring Jackson and Felsch, and ran to first base listening to the bedlam of the crowd. The entire White Sox bench stood up to cheer him, some throwing hats in the air. Suddenly, Gandil had become a hero.

Sleepy Bill Burns was a very unhappy man, for the surprising Chicago victory left him broke. He had worked on the project for weeks, only to blow the potential gains all in one day. In his pre-Series discussions with Maharg, they had both recognized the dangers of game-by-game betting. The safest procedure was to bet on the Series itself. But this would have limited his take considerably. He was hungry for a real killing, and one bet seemed painfully inadequate. So at the end of two games, he had parlayed his $4,500 stake to over $12,000. At the end of three, however, he had nothing.

Up in Attell's room, he found excitement and joy, but he heard a tale of woe. Attell and Bennett claimed they had lost. In fact, the Little Champ was blaming *him* for it. Hadn't Burns told him that the Sox were going to throw this one too? Burns was ready to spit at him. Attell became compliant and philosophical. Well, maybe they had to expect days like this. It happens. The thing to do was to forget it and recoup tomorrow. They would set up something new.

Like what? Burns asked. Attell said he was in position to make a solid offer. "I'll put up twenty thousand of my own money. And they'll get it, too. *If* they lose the next game!"

Burns was about to ask where such a heavy loser was going to get $20,000 so quickly. But then, there was Bennett; and in New York, there was Arnold Rothstein. Or maybe Attell was lying again, lying about losing, lying about paying off. Maybe anything. Burns shrugged and said he would pass this on to the players. He'd go over to the Warner Hotel right away, but he doubted they would go for any more promises. He faced the Little Champ and tried to smile: Why didn't Attell put up the twenty grand right now, *before* the game. That would go a long way toward insuring the defeat.

Attell shook his head, then spoke the words of a true deceiver: "I don't trust them ballplayers any more!"

Attell was so preposterous, Burns had to laugh. How could anyone talk to a man like that?

About 9:30, Burns walked into the Warner Hotel, fully aware of how the odds were stacked against him. This would be like pitching against Cobb. But maybe he could make them feel guilty. He had lost a fortune today. All because of them.

But as soon as he entered Gandil's room, he knew he was in for trouble. There was no sympathy in their sparse greeting. Whatever they had done to him was not their affair. These guys were not his friends today . . . if they had ever been.

"Just left Attell . . ." he began, bringing out that promising, hopeful, prosperous ring in his Texas drawl. "The little guy ain't too sore at you guys—yet. He went down in the crash today. You hurt him bad, I guess."

There was an amused chortle from someplace in the room. Burns looked over toward the sound, wondering who it was. Williams? No. Weaver, probably.

"Anyway, he's got twenty grand for you. . . ."

Pause.

Gandil asked to see it.

Burns shook his head. "Not so fast, Chick. He's got the dough . . . but he wants to see the score first before he gives it to you." Then he added, somewhat furtively, "After today, can't say you could blame him."

Again, the chortle.

"Same old crap," Williams said.

Burns tried to convince them that this was different. But they told him they were no longer interested. Everything about them was hostile. Burns saw it: they were through. The whole deal was finished.

"All right," Burns conceded. "We'll drop the whole business. But I want my share of the ten thousand I got you."

Gandil thought for a moment, then grinned. "Sorry, Bill," he said softly. "It's all out on bets."

This time, there were several laughs. In fact, they all laughed; except Burns. He was in no mood for jokes. He was dead broke. He had done his best for them all. Now he wanted what he thought he deserved: a commission, not wisecracks. "I tell you, I want my share! You give me a grand," he roared. "Or I'll tell everything!"

Gandil just turned away. Nobody said anything.

Burns left, returned to the Sherman Hotel, and told Attell that it was all off. Then he went out and got drunk. For Sleepy Bill Burns and his partner, Billy Maharg, the fixing of the World Series had ended.

9

On October 4, sometime around 1 A.M., Joseph "Sport" Sullivan entered the lobby of the Ansonia Hotel in New York, en route to his room. He had just left Arnold Rothstein at his office on West 46th

Street, after giving a cautious accounting of his mission to Chicago and Cincinnati. (He had, of course, omitted the fact that he'd paid the ballplayers only a part of the $40,000 that was given him.) The victory in the third game did not bother either of them. Their principal money was bet on the Series, as Rothstein had advised. Sullivan left the meeting feeling elated. He had carried it all off well and Rothstein had seemed pleased. Sullivan was not only going to make himself a bundle of money, he was also making himself solid with the great A.R.

His elation, however, did not survive his trip to the front desk where he would pick up his key. It was, at least, threatened. He was approached by a gambler named Pete Manlis, who startled him by indicating he had a good sum of money he'd like to get down—on the White Sox! He wanted to know what odds Sullivan was giving. It was an ominous, eerie moment, for Sullivan knew this man to be a friend of Rothstein's. Why should Manlis suddenly want to bet on Chicago?

Sullivan told him that he had all his money down, and therefore was not interested in any further wagering. Having thus cleared the decks, he tried to learn what Manlis had heard—if anything. Sullivan learned only enough to make him wary.

Upstairs in his room, he brooded about it. Had something happened with the ballplayers since he'd left Cincinnati? Had they gone sour on the deal? On him? He could readily see where they might. Had he acted foolishly by disappearing?

It worried him. If something new was up, what if Rothstein should hear of it? And what chance was there that he would not?

Perhaps the thing to do was to call Gandil. . . . No. It was late, too late to call. He must not let on that there was any room for doubt, any fear of trouble. He would call at a reasonable hour just to say hello, and in the process, he would find out which way the wind was blowing.

At a few mintues before nine the next morning, Sullivan learned the validity of his fears. Gandil was crystal clear about it. Nobody trusted anybody any more. Gandil could no longer get the ballplayers to do anything on faith. They'd decided to drop the whole business.

Sullivan let his mind race over the possibilities if this decision were allowed to stand. It was two games to one against the White Sox, still a wide-open Series. He could see himself in all kinds of trouble if the Sox should go ahead and win it. There was no doubt in his mind that he had to stop this, and since it was just a question of money . . .

He told Gandil how well he understood the matter. Just to prove his own good faith, he would wire $20,000 immediately. They were to continue with the original plan. He reminded Gandil of the money waiting for them in the Congress Hotel safe: another $40,000.

Gandil allowed that $20,000 would be a healthy argument. He believed that if it was received the players would go on with the fix. But that also meant another $20,000 before the fifth game, too. Sullivan quickly agreed. Of course, of course. He added reassuringly that he would meet them back in Cincinnati on Monday for the sixth and seventh games.

Sullivan hung up, aware of the big problem he faced: the raising of $20,000. He could assume that one such payment would suffice, and though he had agreed to pay that amount again before the following game, he had no such intention. The assumption was one he would later regret.

He got back on the phone and began calling colleagues in Boston. Using all his bargaining power, pleading desperation and potential personal disaster, he managed to raise the twenty grand before the morning was over.

Dickie Kerr's victory on the day before had had great impact. In the locker room, the mood of the White Sox was triumphant. When the players stepped out on the field, the early crowd greeted them all like heroes again. Nobody really believed they could lose; these White Sox had to be winners. There was no other way to think of them.

Gleason asked Cicotte how he felt, and Cicotte smiled reassuringly: Gleason didn't believe all those wild rumors about how his arm was through, did he?

The weather was fine, again. Temperature around 70°. There were almost 34,000 in the stands as Cicotte walked to the mound, and they gave him an appreciative and glowing reception. It was going to be another tough day for him. He hated to lose in his home ball park.

He threw the first pitch past Maurice Rath for a called strike, and the huge crowd roared in approval.

He set the Reds down easily in the first two innings. In the bottom of the second, the Sox fell back into a familiar pattern: Jackson doubled and Felsch once again sacrificed him to third. Gleason was still playing for one run at a time. Gandil faced the pitcher, Jimmy Ring, and once again failed to drive in the run: he popped feebly to Groh, a few feet in front of the plate. Risberg walked. Schalk was intentionally walked after Risberg took second on a passed ball. The crowd roared as Cicotte himself stepped to the plate with the bases loaded. He was a fair hitter for a pitcher. He grounded sharply to Kopf at short, ending the inning.

Cicotte set the Reds down in order in the third and fourth. There was no score in the game as Big Edd Roush came to bat in the fifth. He tapped a slow roller in front of the plate, and Schalk pounced on it like a cat, threw him out at first. Duncan then lashed a bounder back to the mound. Immediately Cicotte reacted, knowing that he had to make his move. He knocked it down, then threw hurriedly and wildly to first. Gandil let the throw get away from him, and Duncan made second, despite a desperate throw by Schalk, who was backing up the play. Then with 2 and 2 on him Kopf lined a single to Jackson in left. Jackson rifled a perfect throw to the plate to cut off the run. But Cicotte interceded. He stepped in front of the ball to cut it off. Artfully, as if to hurry his throw to second base, he allowed the ball to deflect off his glove. It rolled to the stands behind home plate. Duncan scored easily and Kopf went to second. Jackson was playing Neale shallow, and the hitter cracked one over his head for a double, scoring Kopf. When the inning ended, the Reds had two runs on two hits—and two Cicotte errors.

In the press box, Hugh Fullerton had drawn a large circle around the two Cicotte fielding plays. When the game ended less than an hour later, the score was still 2-0.

Except for that disastrous fifth inning, Cicotte had been masterful. He had given up only five hits. Cincinnati pitcher Jimmy Ring walked off the field a little staggered by his own performance: a three-hit shutout. He had never been so effective.

It was a drab, cloudy Saturday night in Chicago. The celebrating was done by 1,000 Cincinnati fans. They had brought their band with them, and they took over the Loop, singing loud, drunken songs.

Kid Gleason was telling a reporter: "Once more, luck favored the Reds. They would never have scored on Cicotte if it hadn't been for his own two errors. Cincy didn't hit him half as hard as Ring was hit. Cicotte threw his own game away . . . it was nothing but hard luck that beat the White Sox. I don't believe that all the luck of the Series can be on one side. . . ."

Ring Lardner was writing in a different vein: "As for today's game, they was a scribe downtown this AM saying that 2 men asked who was going to pitch today and the scribe said Cicotte and 1 of the men said you are crazy as Cicotte has such a sore arm that he can't wash the back of his neck. So when we come out to the park this scribe told me about it and I said they wasn't nothing in the rules of today's game that required Cicotte to wash the back of his neck. 'Well,' said the other expert, 'the man was just speaking figurative and meant that Eddie had a sore arm.' 'Well,' I said, 'if he has only one sore arm he can still wash the back of his neck as I only use 1 even when I am going to a party.'

'The back of your neck looks like it,' said the other expert. 'Yes,' I said. 'But what is the differents or not about Cicotte only having 1 sore arm as he only pitches with 1 arm.' 'Yes, you bum, but that is the arm that the man said was sore.'

That is the kind of clever repartee that goes on between the experts and no hard feelings on neither side."

Chick Gandil counted out the twenty crisp one-thousand-dollar bills he received from Sport Sullivan. The cash had been delivered to him by a nameless man, and it relieved him to get it. He had never handled so much money at one time. In a few days, he'd be handling a whole lot more. Temporarily content with the $10,000 Burns had delivered a few days before, Gandil was willing to dispose of this fresh bundle to his money-hungry colleagues. He had promised $5,000 to Risberg. The Swede had been dogging him for the money and would probably cost him a lot more before they were through. He would give $5,000 to Hap Felsch, five thousand each to Williams and Jackson. Cicotte already had his ten. McMullin, the substitute, would have to wait. Weaver would get nothing. Gandil knew by now that Weaver had excluded himself.

For all the confusion, the fix was still on.

10

It was raining hard on Sunday morning, October 5, the first bad day of the Series. The White Sox gathered in the locker room before noon, though it was obvious there would not be a game. They just sat around and talked, neither discouraged nor depressed. To visiting reporters, they did not seem angry except, perhaps, at themselves, at their failure to live up to expectations. When they spoke, they were critical of each other and the various plays they had handled badly. Most of them acted as though they were still going to win, despite being behind three games to one. When one of the reporters lightly commented: "Well, the loser's share might come to maybe four thousand dollars" he was told, bluntly enough, to go to hell.

Gleason sat there and listened. He was nervous and restless. Reporters hovered over him, prodding him to talk. "I don't know what's the matter. . . . It's the best team that ever went into a World Series, but it ain't playing baseball . . . we'll take 'em tomorrow. You'll see, we'll take 'em!"

But when an out-of-town newspaperman asked the obvious question: "Will it be Williams tomorrow, Kid?" Gleason scowled and replied, "No. I think I'll go in myself."

By Monday afternoon, October 6, the sun had broken through and there was a clean, fresh feeling to the day. The crowd responded to it after the wasted rainy Sunday. It was a big crowd, the biggest crowd of the Series so far. They had come to see Chicago win. They felt they had a right to expect it. Williams would not fail them again.

Williams, unfortunately, had other commitments. On the previous night he had been called into Gandil's room where he was given two dirty envelopes, each containing $5,000 cash. Gandil had told him to keep one, to give the other to Jackson. Williams had taken them without saying anything. He gave Jackson his envelope and still said nothing. Nor did Jackson, who merely nodded and took the money.

Nobody talked about it. To Williams, $5,000 was more than he had expected after those first few days. He would go to work on the mound this afternoon with expectations of getting maybe $10,000 more.

He took his final warm-up pitches and watched Schalk snap a clothesline throw to second. There was anger in Schalk already. Williams knew the catcher was going to try to keep him honest this time if he had to kill him in the process. He knew he would have to be extra careful. He would have to look brilliant in defeat.

If Gleason had any doubts about using Williams, they were soon dispelled. Williams was red-hot. Schalk was working him in that steady, controlled, brilliant pattern of pitches that had won 23 games for the left-hander this season. The Cincinnati Reds couldn't get any wood on him. Four innings went by, and Williams held them hitless.

Only one man had reached first, on an error by Eddie Collins. The left-hander seemed invincible.

But Hod Eller, pitching for the Reds, was even more remarkable. He had allowed the Sox only two feeble hits, had fanned six in a row through the second and third innings. The crowd was on edge, waiting for the explosion. Something had to happen soon.

With two out in the fifth, Williams finally gave up a hit to Kopf, who singled to left. But he died on first a moment later. The shutout continued.

Then in the sixth, Eller led off with a fly ball to left center. Jackson and Felsch took off after it. For a moment it seemed as if either one could get to it. A moment later, it was apparent that neither would. The ball fell between them, and Eller raced around first. Felsch picked the ball up and threw badly to Risberg at second. The Swede played the ball listlessly, allowing it to roll away from him. Eller, standing at second, dashed for third. Risberg's throw to Weaver was late, and Eller was suddenly a terrible threat!

The White Sox infield moved in on the grass, hoping to cut off the run at the plate. It made things easier for Rath, who slapped a hit by Eddie Collins, a drive that would easily have been caught if the infielder had been in normal position. In less than a minute, Williams's shutout ended.

Daubert then sacrificed Rath to second, bringing Heinie Groh to the plate. Williams worked him carefully. Schalk, sensing the crisis, drove him hard. If Williams got out of the inning, it was still an open ball game. Williams responded, curving Groh beautifully on the outside. But umpire Rigler didn't like the pitch. Schalk, eager and tense, protested. Rigler ignored him. Aggravated, Schalk barked at him, angrily this time. And when, with a full count, Rigler called a doubtful pitch another ball, Schalk wheeled on him with greater fury than before. Rigler snarled, but said nothing.

Then Big Edd Roush sent a towering shot to deep center field. Felsch turned at the crack of the bat and tore after it. To the 34,000 Chicago fans who watched it, there was no doubt but that old Hap would pull it in. He had easily bagged dozens of such drives all season. It was just a question of watching how neatly he would handle it.

But not this time. Felsch turned too soon, slowing down, then started again, turning again. He didn't seem to know where the ball was. Then he saw it again, and with a great burst of speed, caught up with it. As it ended its long descent, Happy reached out with two hands and grabbed it . . . only to drop it as he completed his stride. The ball rolled away from him. He went after it, slipped, fell, got up and went after it again. He grabbed it, dropped it, grabbed it again. Finally, he cut loose with his great arm, beginning the long relay to the plate. Eddie Collins, waiting for the throw, pivoted, and threw rapidly to the plate as Heinie Groh raced in. Schalk caught it and dived at the sliding runner. Rigler spread his arms wide. "Safe!" Schalk was on his feet immediately, roaring at Rigler over the bedlam. He was livid this time, pushing into the big umpire, bumping him, pushing him again, spitting out a wave of unheard abuse.

By the time the turbulent moment ended, the crowd had absorbed what had happened. The Reds had scored a total of three runs and Schalk was thrown out of the game. Roush scored on a sacrifice fly before the Reds were retired. Four runs were more than enough: the White Sox were helpless before Hod Eller's shine ball.

In the press box, Hugh Fullerton was disgusted. Whatever he knew about baseball now seemed meaningless. It didn't make sense anymore. There was no "dope" worth writing about. "When Felsch misses a fly ball like Roush's, and like the one before from Eller— then, well, what's the use?"

The statistics pointed even more directly at the Sox's failure:

the great hitting team had produced no more than six runs in five games! They hadn't scored in the last 22 innings! Kid Gleason could do a lot of crying over that. He couldn't understand it. "Something is wrong," he told the press. "I don't know what it is. The team that won the pennant for me this summer would have made about fifteen hits off Eller in August. It wasn't the same team that faced him today. The Sox are in a terrible batting slump. It is the worst slump a team ever had. Sometimes I feel like going up and hitting myself. . . ."

If Gleason was down, he was not yet out. He made sure everyone knew that. There had to be a chance for them. The whole history of his ball club backed him up. It was not in him to give up. Even if everything pointed to the sellout, he would not give up. "I'm going to send Dickie Kerr to the slab tomorrow. Maybe, if he wins, I'll send him back the next day, and if he wins that one, I'll send him back again!"

The evening papers carried the attendance records and gate receipts. The figures had a special importance to the ballplayers, since they shared in the take of the first five games only. The winning share would come to over $5,000 per player. To the loser, $3,254. The receipts of the remaining games would be divided between the two club owners and the National Commission.

11

The city of Cincinnati was nearly paralyzed at the return of their ball club on October 7. One more game would clinch it for them, no small matter to a city with an inferiority complex over its secondary status among American metropoli.

There was jubilation to the day, much more joyous than before the opener. Here there was inevitable victory; a week ago there had been probable defeat. The people of the city poured into the streets, strolling in the early autumn sunshine. Bands paraded through town en route to the ball park playing "Hail, Hail, the Gang's All Here!"

A rumor spread through the crowds that there were several thousand seats still available for the game. As a result, a jam-up began before noon. All traffic leading out of the city was blocked. It was the biggest turnout in Cincinnati's history. Ten thousand were turned away, while over 32,000 squeezed into Redland Park, paying a record $101,768. They did not come to see a ball game; they came to dance on the White Sox's grave.

The cost of the burial, as it had been agreed, was another $20,000 payment. The Chicago ballplayers arrived by Pullman sleeper in Cincinnati at seven in the morning and immediately checked into the Sinton Hotel. Gandil and Company expected a visit from Sullivan, as he had promised on the phone. But the gravedigger from Boston failed to show up.

Gandil stewed in his hotel room waiting for the phone to ring. Around 9:30 there was a a knock on his door. He leaped to it expectantly, but it was only Swede Risberg, who had come to share the vigil. They waited together, until finally it was time to go to the ball park.

In the locker room, the other ballplayers in the fix took one look at their leader and knew at once what the score was. Nothing was said. It had all been thrashed out too many times before. The fix had become a tired nightmare to them. They were sick of it.

If there was no cash, there would be no corpse.

The ball game began as a beautiful Cincinnati dream. It was a large party for the local fans. They roared with laughter as the White Sox committed three errors, permitting four Cincinnati runs to score. Dutch Reuther, greatest local hero of them, meanwhile, mowed them down. For five glorious innings, the taste of victory grew more and more delicious.

Then suddenly, for the first time in the Series, the White Sox burst explosively into the ball game. Buck Weaver opened the sixth by popping a short fly ball into left that Kopf and Duncan allowed to fall between them. Jackson slashed a vicious single to center, scoring Weaver. Happy Felsch followed with a longer shot that scored Jackson all the way from first. After Gandil and Risberg failed to hit, Ray Schalk drove a single to left, scoring Felsch. When the dust had cleared, Cincinnati fans knew that the party was over.

Reuther was replaced by Jimmy Ring, and the score was tied at 4 all.

From the seventh inning on, it was a tight ball game. The Reds kept pecking away at Kerr, always threatening. But the fans saw the plucky little man pitch his way out, time after time. There was no change of scoring going into the tenth.

Then Buck Weaver opened up again, lashing another double to left. Jackson pushed him around to third with an infield single. Hap Felsch struck out, but Chick Gandil dropped a single to center and Weaver jogged across the plate, making it 5–4. Then Dickie Kerr retired the Reds in order, ending the ball game.

The good people of Cincinnati would have to wait.

On the following morning, October 8, there was a new mood in the White Sox locker room. They were losing the Series 4 games to 2. In order to win, they had to take three games in a row. Hugh Fullerton stood among them and responded to their spirit; by God, anyone would think *this* is the winning ball club! He had been around ballplayers long enough to know when it was real and meaningful. These boys were genuinely charged with a fresh sense of their own power. The sight of it delighted him. This was more than just a comeback: it dispelled the ugly rumors of the sellout; it re-established his faith in their honesty. More than anything else, Fullerton rejoiced in that. He *had* to believe in that.

"Cicotte is going to win today!" Gleason was saying. "He came to me this morning and he told me that he wanted to pitch. He said he would beat those guys and I believe him." The Kid was eager to talk, to show how he felt. It was a big, honest feeling, with no propaganda working. He believed. Kid Gleason had to believe, and Hugh Fullerton loved him for it.

Fullerton could go back to his job with his old buoyancy. He greeted Christy Mathewson in the press box with a resounding slap on the back.

All week, Joe Jackson had been a disappointment to himself, playing ball with only a part of himself working. He tried to hit, he didn't try to hit. Half the time, he didn't know whether he was trying or

not. He had taken only one real vicious cut at the ball with his famous
black bat and conveniently failed to make contact.

The $5,000 Lefty Williams had handed him in that old envelope
was part payment for his lethargy. But now, like the others in the
jubilant locker room that afternoon, Jackson wanted to win. Winning
was in the air. It was as if the White Sox had had enough of defeat.
The mood had started in the fifth inning of the previous game when
they finally pushed across a run. It had mushroomed in the sixth
when they had smashed out four hits and finally tied the score. They
had known they would win. Everybody in that earsplitting crowd
had known it.

It was the same today.

Once again, the weather was beautiful. Garry Herrmann, owner
of the Reds, could bask in it. He had been primarily responsible for
lengthening the Series to the best 5 out of 9 games. The Series that
would have been over in Chicago, two days ago, was already stretched
two games. Yesterday, they had taken in over $100,000. He had
reason to expect it again today. In the face of the probable tripling of
receipts (the Series would surely break all attendance records), his
club's victory under the old 7-game schedule seemed unimportant.

But today, the fans of Cincinnati deserted him. Despite the sunshine, despite the glorious possibility of clinching the world's championship, despite everything, they did not show. The previous day's
incredibly mismanaged traffic problem was enough to keep thousands
away. If they were told today that there were many choice seats
available, they had been told the same on the day before. Who would
battle that jam-up two days in a row, only to be turned back after
storming the bastion for two impossible hours? Besides, Cincy fans
had a sinking, undeniable, uncontrollable premonition of another defeat. They weren't going to suffer through that. There were even
vicious rumors floating around town that Herrmann had seen to it that
the Series would go this far, that he had bribed his own ballplayers
to throw yesterday's game! Fans recalled that crucial play at the start
of the fateful three-run sixth inning when Kopf and Duncan played
Alphonse and Gaston with Buck Weaver's fly ball. A sure out dropped
for a double, starting the White Sox rally. And what about reports
that Dutch Reuther had been out on the town the night before?

If the more sensible fans repudiated this kind of talk, it was nevertheless persuasive. It was the kind of corrupt manipulation in which many people had come to believe. So only 13,923 fans paid to see the seventh game, considerably less than half of capacity. If Garry Herrmann suffered most, ticket scalpers, too, finally took a real beating. As late as 11 A.M. they were holding out for $30 a pair. Two hours later, they were unloading choice seats at face value, happy to get rid of them. The abused fans who remained at home could at least take some satisfaction from that.

To the Cincinnati ball club, Redland Park seemed like a morgue. They could smirk at the low attendance (it didn't affect their pocketbooks), but they didn't like the feeling it gave them. This was their home park. They had been playing their hearts out—and winning. They had a right to feel supported, not deserted. But what bothered them most was their own sense of foreboding. The smell of defeat was everywhere, and it choked them up. To resist this, the Reds moved to the top of the dugout early in the afternoon. They began riding the key White Sox ballplayers, even before game time. They jumped on Felsch unmercifully. "Hey, Hap . . . drop one of mine, will you? I want a triple, too!" Or on Jackson: "Hey, professor, read any good books lately?" Or on Schalk: "Cracker, you gonna play the *whole* game today?" And when they got to Cicotte, they hooted him for being a loser, for throwing his game away, for every bad pitch he made. They teamed up on each of them, on and on, over and over, louder and funnier, never stopping.

Warming up, Eddie Cicotte ignored the cries. He was indifferent to everyone, to the bench, to the fans, to his own teammates. His throws were as powerful and perfect as any he had ever pitched. They would be that way in the game. Humiliated by the previous losses and by Kerr's victories, Cicotte was a man who could no longer tolerate defeat.

The ball game had Chicago's name on it. From the first inning, the outcome was apparent. They jumped on Sallee for a run in the first, then another in the third. The clean, tight, defensive work of the Reds started to crumble. Bad throw. Booted ground ball. Misjudged fly ball. Error. Error. In the fifth inning, in the face of tremendous abuse from the Cincinnati bench, Jackson crashed a vicious double to left, scoring two more. Sallee was finished. So were the Reds.

Cicotte, meanwhile, was brilliant. He dominated the hitters as if he owned them. Only in the sixth could they push across a run and threaten further trouble, but the rally was quickly snuffed out. It took less than 100 minutes for the Sox to win again, 4–1.

Hugh Fullerton was smiling. "I am beginning to believe the 'dope' again. The White Sox played their American League brand of baseball today. They attacked with vigor and determination. They fielded perfectly. At last, they were fighting. Cicotte got his revenge."

On the night train back to Chicago, Kid Gleason was his old buoyant self as he made his daily statement to the press: "For the second day in a row, my gang played the kind of baseball it has been playing all season. Even though we are still one game behind, we will win for sure. All I wanted to see was my gang get back in form. All it has to do now is to keep that form and the Reds can't possibly win a game."

Pat Moran, Cincinnati manager, was worried. He had pitcher Hod Eller ready to pitch tomorrow's game. Eller had been masterful in the fifth game, but Moran guessed that the Sox would jump all over him this time. It was not a pleasant prospect. He could sense his entire ball club in a sweat. After being so far in front, they were now afraid of losing. Playing in Comiskey Park, in a hostile atmosphere, wasn't going to help. The giant city would line up against them. Ask any old ballplayer and he'd tell you: when an angry club gets rolling, it's almost impossible to stop it.

In New York, Arnold Rothstein was also worried. He did not have to remind himself how little he had liked this whole scheme from the beginning. His qualms had persisted. Too many people involved. Too many fly-by-night amateurs sticking their grubby, inept fingers in the pie. Too many unstable characters. He repeatedly referred to the ballplayers as "a bunch of dumb rubes." And to him the ultimate definition of a rube was "a talented guy who consented to work for peanuts." He hated to do business with rubes.

He had no intention of being taken by them.

Joseph "Sport" Sullivan was more than worried: he was running scared. When the report of the seventh game came through, everything suddenly changed. It was more than his money at stake now. More than his reputation. He had the terrible feeling that it was his neck. When he returned to his hotel that evening, the sight of a message in his mailbox was no surprise. He did not have to read it to know its content: Arnold Rothstein wished to see him.

The meeting took place in the foyer of Rothstein's Riverside Drive apartment. It was simple enough. Rothstein was polite. There was no show of anger. Certainly none of fear. His coolness lent a businesslike tone to his message. He merely suggested that Sullivan see to it that the Series end tomorrow. He did not think it wise that it be allowed to go to the ninth game. He did not even think it wise that the outcome of the eighth game be held in suspense, for the purpose of public show, for the ballplayer's pride, or for any other reason. In short, he hoped to see the Series end quickly, in the first inning, if such a thing were possible.

Then he excused himself with a near-smile. He thanked Sullivan for dropping by. He was extremely busy. There were people waiting for him inside.

Sullivan walked back to the Ansonia. For a moment, he felt relief: A.R. seemed anything but menacing. Then, however, the impact of the message cut through to him and he became fully aware of the nature of this assignment. His fear came back to him. How in hell was he going to pull this off?

He saw now how badly he'd handled the whole thing. He had lost control of the ballplayers, having taken too much for granted. Gandil's collusion, for example. Or, at least, what he thought was Gandil's power. He knew Gandil's hunger for money as well as he knew his own. But Gandil was clearly out of control. There had to be a surer way.

Lefty Williams would pitch tomorrow. Sullivan, sitting here in New York, had to get to him before game time. He had to be sure that Williams was in the bag.

The only way was a frightening one. Desperate situations demanded desperate solutions. The big Boston gambler got on the phone and called a man in Chicago, who could handle such things. Known as Harry F., he was a man schooled in the finer arts of persuasion. Sullivan knew he need only present the problem to have the other apply his craft in a professional manner. So Harry F. was asked to make contact with Lefty Williams and persuade him to see to it that Cincinnati be assured of victory before the end of the first inning. As supplementary information, Sullivan told him that Williams had a wife, but no children. The other replied that children were desirable in these circumstances, but generally not necessary: a wife would be more than adequate.

It took less than five minutes to set this project in motion. In a bored rasping voice, Harry F. assured Sullivan of his skill and discretion—and his impeccable record. He also assumed that $500 would be wired to him immediately, *before* he made his contact. Sullivan, of course, eagerly complied. He hung up with a knowledge of his deep and lasting respect for the invention of the telephone.

Then, he started to sweat. He did not like to think of himself as a man of violence. The fact that nobody was going to get hurt (or so he had to believe) gave him but little peace. The very concept of a raw threat unnerved him. It was some relief that he would probably never know exactly what took place.

12

On October 9, there were no brass bands parading down Chicago's Michigan Avenue. There were no pennants, streamers, or banners adorning the Loop. No firecrackers went off. No pranks were played. It wasn't a party day for the citizens of Chicago.

But everyone was talking baseball. The tension was there. It was all over town. But unlike Cincinnati, the attitude toward the day was professional. They would take their victory—or defeat—in stride.

They jammed Comiskey Park again, a capacity 33,000. They came wearing their loyalty on their sleeves. If there was little fancy fanfare, there was tremendous enthusiasm. They came to see a great ball club play ball. They were not johnny-come-lately World Series fans, these White Sox rooters. They were 33,000 repeats from 89 home games a season. Their love for the White Sox during the decade since the completion of Comiskey Park had become as much a part of their lives as their feeling for their churches and schools. They knew the fine points of the game; they could discuss its science; their judgments of players was based on their respect for high standards of play. They would not tolerate showboating or stupidity. They demanded talent and spirit for their 90 cents. There were no better baseball fans anywhere in the major leagues than these Southside Chicagoans.

Kid Gleason was wary. Since he had been badly burned, he could not free himself from his fear of fire. He toyed with the idea of not pitching Lefty Williams. Then who? Could Kerr go again after only one day's rest? He doubted it. Wilkinson? Lowdermilk? James? No, he couldn't trust them. If only Red Faber were in shape. Faber would have made the difference. But it had to be Williams. If percentages meant anything, Williams would be a winner today—if he wanted to be.

He shouted his instructions to them in the locker room that morning. They had to go all out today. "The minute I think any one of you ain't playing ball to win—if I think you're laying down—I'm gonna pull you out even if I have to make an infielder out of a bullpen catcher! I'm gonna tell you this, too: I would use an iron on any sonovabitch who would sell out this ball club!"

When Gleason said "iron" he meant "gun."

Hughie Fullerton fought his way through the crowded ramps to the press box. He was looking forward to the game more than any that preceded it. This was the big comeback game, the most difficult one of them all. It was always easier to win one when you were far behind than when you were snapping right at the top. And, like any real baseball fan, he was full of nervous excitement.

As he approached the press box, he heard his name called and felt a restraining hand on his arm. It was a Chicago gambler whom he knew. (Fullerton never revealed his name.)

"Hello, Fullerton . . . you got your money down today?"

"I don't bet on baseball," Fullerton replied.

"Neither do I," the gambler grinned. "Except today."

Fullerton perked up. "What's that supposed to mean?"

"Cincinnati, friend. Cincinnati to win!"

Fullerton probed. "What makes that such a sure thing?"

The gambler grinned again. "You could've made a real bundle, Hughie . . . tipping one team and betting on the other. . . ."

"Just what do you know?" Fullerton persisted.

The gambler finally replied, "It'll be the biggest first inning you ever saw!"

Claude "Lefty" Williams walked out to the mound to a sustained ovation. It was a statement of their respect for him as much as a rousing plea for another victory. With his usual solemn mien, he did not seem to hear. He neither tipped his cap nor stopped to respond. With typical deliberateness, he toed the rubber and took his warm-up pitches as if every one of them had to be perfect.

The last practice pitch he threw was a curve ball. He snapped it off like the whole World Series was riding on it. It broke sharply, down and away, thrown so viciously that Schalk had trouble hanging on to it. It cut the outside corner just a bit over the knees of the unseen hitter. It was a beautiful, perfect pitch.

It was the last perfect pitch Lefty Williams threw that day.

Behind him, Weaver, Risberg, Collins, and Gandil were tossing the ball around the horn, a final circuit of throws before the game began. Williams turned to watch them. Behind them, Jackson, Nemo Liebold, and Felsch were fanning out over the vast outfield grass. And all around him, the fans of Chicago. This had been his home for four exciting years. He had pitched for this ball club in 144 games. He was twenty-six years old and he thought of himself as a decent man, very good at his job, well liked by those who knew him and worked with him. But Lefty Williams was in trouble. In all his life, he never dreamed that anything like this could happen to him. It seemed so fantastic that even the fact that it was all very logical meant little to him. It would, however, be indelibly recorded in his brain for all time:

Around 7:30 last evening, Williams and his wife were returning from dinner. He had eaten carefully, knowing he was going to pitch the next day. He had seen him then—a man in a bowler hat, standing at the entrance to his building, smoking a cigar. The man recognized him and immediately got ready to greet him. The man was stiff but polite. He wanted to have a word with him, in private, and a nod indicated to Lefty's wife that she should excuse herself.

The man went right to the point. He bluntly told Williams he was to lose the next game. Lefty had shaken his head violently and started to turn away. But the man stopped him, restraining him with a vice-like grip on his arm. No, it wasn't a question of money any more. Williams was not going to get paid another dime! He was going to lose that ball game or something was going to happen to him. Maybe something might happen to his wife, too.

Williams had choked up at the thought of it. His fists had clenched with a sudden desire to tear into the man. But fear had stopped him. He merely stood there, unable to speak or act.

There was more to the threat. It all had to be done in the first inning. The man eyed him, seeking confirmation of this in Williams's eyes. That's right, the man repeated: Williams was not to last even one inning!

"Play ball!" The umpire was yelling it a third time, louder this time, and more demandingly.

Williams stalled a moment more, toeing the dirt in front of the mound. He had, of course, said nothing to his wife, who, as usual, was sitting in a box behind third base. Schalk was barking at him and he turned to go to work.

Maurice Rath stepped up to the plate to lead off for the Reds. The crowd roared approval as Williams threw the first pitch over for a strike. They roared again as Rath cut at the second and fouled it off. Then he popped feebly to Risberg at short and the first man was out. It took less than a minute.

Jake Daubert moved in and took the first pitch for strike one. On the second, he hit a soft liner to short center field. Nemo Liebold raced in for it, desperately trying for a catch off his shoetops. He never made it and it fell for a base hit. (Gleason had shifted Felsch to right after his feeble playing in previous games.) Williams got two strikes over on Heinie Groh, then Groh singled sharply to right. The crowd roared a steady stream of encouragement to Williams. The game was less than three minutes old, but the tension made every pitch a crisis. Schalk walked out to the mound and talked with Williams. In the press box, Christy Mathewson commented to Fullerton that Williams had been throwing only fast balls. He guessed that Schalk was trying to straighten him out. As Schalk walked back to his position, he stared fiercely at the bench, seeking out Gleason. Gleason nodded, signaled the bull pen for Bill James and Roy Wilkinson to get warm.

Big Edd Roush stood in the batter's box, calmly waiting to hit. The infield lay deep, hoping for the ground ball they could convert into a double play. Roush measured the first pitch—another fast ball —and smashed it savagely to right. Daubert scored easily from second, Groh settled on third, and Roush pulled into second standing up. Lefty Williams seemed in a hurry to pitch. Schalk was bellowing at him, shaking his fist. Williams stood tight-lipped on the mound. Behind him, the infield was drawn in, ready to hold Groh on third. Pat Duncan stepped in to hit, laid into the first pitch and sent a screaming liner into the left field seats, foul. Williams seemed flustered. He reared back and threw again. It went high and wide of the plate. Schalk had to leap for it, preventing a wild pitch with a desperate effort. He called for time-out, hollered at Williams again. Williams nodded, demanded the ball. Then Duncan lashed a single to left, right through the drawn-in infielders. Groh and Duncan scored easily. It was already 3–0.

Gleason moved up the dugout steps, scowling murderously. He stared at his bull pen where James was throwing hurriedly, trying to get warmed up. He shouted at Williams. Williams seemed to ignore him, and got set to pitch to Larry Kopf. He threw hard, and Kopf took it for strike one. In the press box, Matty shook his head. Another fast ball. Nothing but fast balls. No wonder Gleason was sore. Gleason was roaring at Williams again as he moved out of the dugout this time. He called to his bull pen for Bill James. That was going to be all for Williams. Fifteen pitches. Four hits. Three runs. Only one out.

Fullerton sat in a nervous sweat, remembering the last words of the Chicago gambler: "It'll be the biggest first inning you ever saw!"

The crowd was stunned. They watched Williams leave the field unable to believe what they saw. They despaired as Bill James gave up another run before the inning ended. In the second, the Reds scored again, making it 5–0.

But to Chicago baseball fans, baseball was a nine-inning game, and this was still their ball club battling to stay alive. They would

battle along with them. When, in the third, Joe Jackson sent a tremendous blast into the right field stands for the first home run of
the Series, they stood up and cheered him as if it was the crucial run
of the game. And though the Reds proceeded to hammer James, then
Wilkinson, for 5 more runs, these 33,000 stalwarts never lost heart.
They stuck with them, inning after inning, roaring with every Chicago
base hit like it was the opening gun for that one big rally that would
win even this one for them. Then, in the eighth, with the score 10–1
against them, they rose to one final, magnificent splash of power.

Liebold opened with a fly to Neale in right. One out. Eddie Collins singled to center on the first pitch. Buck Weaver followed with a
double over first base. Jackson stepped in, waving his big black bat,
and crashed a roaring double to right center, scoring Collins and
Weaver. The crowd was on its feet, yelling for more. This was the
real White Sox club!

In Times Square, New York, there were 5,000 people watching
the game on the simulated diamond. Most of them were losing interest, but suddenly they, too, came alive, sensing the possibility of a
last ditch Chicago rampage. Others paused to watch. Suddenly, the
word was out, passing through the area like a gust of wind. As the
little dummy figure labeled FELSCH stepped to the plate, the 5,000
watchers had almost doubled!

At Comiskey Park, Felsch took a terrific cut at the first pitch,
but popped it up to Daubert. Gandil followed with a long fly to right,
but Neale lost it in the sun and it fell for a triple, scoring Jackson.
Risberg followed with a short fly to center, just eluding Roush's
glove. Gandil scored the fourth run of the inning. The crowd roared
at Schalk to keep it going. But Schalk grounded to Rath, ending the
inning.

It was over. All over. They were beaten. Twenty four White Sox
players and 33,000 White Sox fans.

In the locker room, Gleason was shouting at the reporters: "I
tell you those Reds haven't any business beating us! We played worse
baseball in all but a couple of games than we played all year. I don't
know yet what was the matter. Something was wrong. I didn't like
the betting odds. I wish no one had ever bet a dollar on the team!"

III   THE EXPOSURE

As Jackson departed from the Grand Jury room, a small boy clutched at his sleeve and tagged along after him.

"Say it ain't so, Joe," he pleaded. "Say it ain't so."

"Yes, kid, I'm afraid it is," Jackson replied.

"Well, I never would've thought it," the boy said.

Chicago *Herald and Examiner*
September 30, 1920

1

Hugh Fullerton thought of himself as a good friend of Charles Comiskey. He had considerable admiration for this knowledgeable baseball owner with his great baseball background and his true devotion to the sport. Some years before, Comiskey had given Fullerton his first job and he felt a great loyalty to him. So it was not just to get a story that he went to the Old Roman's office after the final game: he wanted to share Comiskey's grief.

Comiskey, at the moment, was less grieved than angry. He seemed torn apart by his confusions over the reasons for what had happened. Though he could not begin to explain it all, to Fullerton it seemed that he had a desperate need to try.

Kid Gleason was there with him, raging around the office like a wounded little bull. To Gleason, there was no longer any doubt; they had sold him out. Williams had given them the Series on a silver platter. He swore to it. He would bet his life on it. His fury was too much for Comiskey to dispute. The Old Roman nodded at Fullerton and choked on his words: "There are seven boys who will never play ball on this team again!" Apparently, in counting seven rather than eight players, Comiskey had—and with reason—left out Buck Weaver.

Fullerton left the office bewildered. Like his friend, Comiskey, he did not want to believe the worst. He went back to his own office and wrote a tortured column:

"There will be a great deal written about this World Series. There will be a lot of inside stuff that never will be printed. The truth will remain that the team which was the hardest working . . . won. The team . . . which had the individual ability was beaten. They spilled the dope terribly. Almost everything went backward. So much so that an evil-minded person might believe the stories that have been circulated during the Series. The fact is, this Series was lost in the first game, and lost through overconfidence. Forget the suspicious and evil-minded yarns that may be circulated.

"The Reds are not the better ball club, but they played together. Remember that a flivver that keeps running beats a Rolls Royce that is missing on several cylinders. . . ."

His concluding statement, however, was ominous: "Yesterday's, in all probability, is the last game that will be played in any World Series. If the club owners, and those who have the interest of the game at heart, have listened during the Series, they will call off the the annual interleague contest. . . . Yesterday's game also means the disruption of the Chicago White Sox ballclub. There are seven men on the team who will not be there when the gong sounds next Spring. . . ."

On the following day, the ballplayers drifted into the locker room at Comiskey Park to pick up their belongings. For most of them, there was a need to stay together, for one final round of commiseration perhaps. Their final salary checks, pro rata of their annual salary, for nine days' World Series work, was waiting for them. The loser's share would be mailed to them later. They drank coffee as they cleaned out their lockers and discussed plans for the winter back home with their families. Cicotte came in quietly, crossed to his locker, and packed his bag. There was a message for him that Comiskey wanted to see him in the office. He could pick up his check there. But the pitcher was in a hurry to leave. He had no desire to talk with anyone. Comiskey could mail him the check.

Chick Gandil was not so casual about money. According to his calculations, there was supposed to be $40,000 waiting for him in the Congress Hotel safe. (Sullivan had given him $10,000 before the Series, $20,000 more was delivered to him.) The big first baseman was hungry to get his hands on it. But Gandil had not heard from Sullivan since that phone call from New York. Nor had he seen the man named Brown, the money man from New York.

Sport Sullivan, meanwhile, took the night train from New York to Chicago the night the Series ended. He had collected his New York bets. He would take care of his Chicago business in the morning. . . .

He met with Brown (Nat Evans) in the lobby of the Congress

Hotel. Together, they removed the $40,000 Evans had placed in the safe before the Series. Sullivan, as planned, would deliver the sum to Gandil at the Warner Hotel.

When Sullivan arrived at Gandil's room, Risberg and McMullin were waiting with him. Gandil had been right to suspect that the Swede was not going to settle for that earlier payment of $5,000. It could be said that Risberg had good reason: he had made a major contribution to the White Sox defeat. He had barely hit his weight (170) and was no great shakes in the field. He smiled as he saw the forty fresh $1,000 bills that Sullivan withdrew from his coat pocket. The Swede walked away with $15,000: $10,000 for himself, and $5,000 for his friend, utility infielder Fred McMullin, who had not yet received a dime. For McMullin it was easy money: during the Series he had pinch hit twice.

There was no reason to pay Weaver. Though he had attended the pre-Series meetings, he had played baseball only to win. Of this neither Gandil nor anyone else could have had the slightest doubt.

Gandil watched them all go and sat alone with the balance of the cash. He had collected $70,000 from Sullivan, and $10,000 from Attell. Of this, he had distributed $45,000, leaving a tidy $35,000 for himself.

Thirty-five thousand dollars! Since he was a kid, he'd been on the outside looking in the windows of the rich on the other side of the tracks. Now as a man he had learned how it all worked. There were essentially two kinds of people: those who worked for money, and those who simply took it. There was something about the system that allowed smarter men to make a real bundle by being in the know, by bribery, by special favor. This was all right with Gandil. It was merely a problem of finding a way to be one of them. All he had wanted was a piece of the action. He was not going to spend his life slogging it out in the copper mines, or the dingy club fight rings, or even in the world of baseball.

Having come out on top, he was now anxious to leave, to go home to his wife and daughter in California.

Joe Jackson wasn't in any hurry. There was too much on his mind. He went to Comiskey's office and asked to see him. He had come there to talk, but he was told that Comiskey was busy. Jackson said he'd wait. He waited for several hours, during which the secretary asked him what it was he wished to see the boss about. Jackson replied that it was personal and very important. Comiskey, however, did not appear to think so, and Jackson was not admitted into the Old Roman's presence.

Jackson left Chicago that night, with his friend Lefty Williams. They would drive to Savannah, Georgia, where they would spend the winter.

The statistics of the Series were officially announced. Paid attendance, 236,838. The record gross came to $722,354, affording a higher share per player than in any previous Series. The club owners split $281,670, four times the income of the previous (war) year, and twice that of 1917.

Joseph "Sport" Sullivan had won over $50,000. He took his fresh bank roll and skipped off to the horses at Havre de Grace, Maryland, where, it was reported, he was a heavy loser.

Hugh Fullerton finished writing about the Series and took off for Northern Michigan with his fishing gear. The baseball season of 1919 was over and he wanted to forget about it.

2

"Comiskey, Old Comiskey
Who knew every sleeper in every contract
And spent ten g's on Pinkertons
But didn't like paying any player over five.
Who offered an extra ten for evidence that
    any man of his had thrown a ball game
And never paid off when it was given at last.
Who played the hero for the newspapermen
    and Maclay Hoyne
And saved his purse
And had his heart broken all the same . . ."

Nelson Algren

The demise of Charles Comiskey began the day the World Series ended. Out of his intelligence and sensitivity, he realized that there was no direction he could pursue that did not lead to disaster. If he proceeded as if the fix were a reality, he would certainly destroy his ball club and his million-dollar equity. If he hid it, it was a submission to corruption that would surely prove unpalatable to his pride, and might well boomerang to destroy him as well. He immediately turned to his friend and attorney, Alfred Austrian.

Austrian, in his late forties, had become a leading corporation lawyer in Chicago. Born in that city, he spent most of his life there, having left only to go to Harvard Law School, where he graduated with honors in 1891. On his return to Chicago, he started as a clerk for the famous attorney, Levy Mayer, and later became a member of the firm. Austrian was an intelligent, well-rounded, well-liked man. His hobbies, which were imporant to him, included a collection of rare prints, manuscripts, and art treasures. He was the proud possessor of a page from the original Gutenberg Bible. As a sportsman, he was a fine golfer, frequently shooting in the mid-70's. He was also attorney for the National League Chicago Cubs Baseball Club.

Austrian thought Comiskey's White Sox had to be treated as a business. His respect for his client's property, now worth a fortune, was paramount. Whatever he felt about the game of baseball itself, or his client's apparent love for it, was irrelevant to the protection of his equity. He was always quick to make that clear. As a result, he could understand Comiskey's rather highhanded tactics with players' salaries. They were legitimate and legal, as he interpreted them, and kept the club's expenses down, an elementary business tactic. Austrian believed the primary function of a corporation lawyer was to save his client's money. The secondary function was to keep him out of trouble.

Now he was involved in a problem that would require guidance through both functions.

To Austrian, there seemed to be little danger to his client's interests. At least, at this time. If there had been a sellout, as Comiskey so strongly indicated (Austrian was not going to argue the point!), it would take the whole structure of baseball to bring it to prosecution. This, in itself, was highly unlikely. The National Commission was not about to commit such suicide. Baseball, though intent on keeping its skirts clean, was more intent on hiding its dirty underwear.

There was a strong logic to this attitude that could not be denied. The law was in part responsible. Did Comiskey realize how hard it was to prosecute a bribery charge? If the gamblers had passed money to the players, and the players, in collusion with them, had deliberately thrown ball games, how could that be proved? Without firsthand confessions, how could they amass any evidence at all? Hearsay, of course, was inadmissible. And all they had to go on was hearsay. For who was about to talk? Certainly not the gamblers with their closed-mouth traditions. Why would anyone want to incriminate himself?

The long and short of it, therefore, was simply that Comiskey's troubles would be dissipated in time. Rumors would fade away and the public, whatever they believed to be true, would forget by next baseball season. Of this, Austrian was convinced.

Though he was accurate enough, he had omitted something of vital concern to Comiskey: his pride. The Old Roman simply was not ready to give in so quickly to such a betrayal of his achievements in baseball without striking back. He was a baseball man. All his life, he'd been a baseball man. He was getting old now. Was this to be the fruit of his life's work—a ball club of unpunished, unchallenged sellouts?

Austrian was sympathetic, but quickly exposed the alternatives. Surely Comiskey was not prepared to delve into an exposure; to open the door to a difficult, knockdown, drag-out legal fight during which all sorts of matters would reach the public eye. Did Comiskey realize the nature of libel suits to which he might be subjected if he publicly declared that his ballplayers had thrown the Series? Sure, he could fire the suspected players; then they could go out and make a deal for themselves with any club they chose. Thus Comiskey would be sacrificing several hundred thousand dollars' worth of talent! Under the present National Commission, Comiskey would have trouble getting them barred from the game. Austrian was quick to refer to the Hal Chase matter, only a year ago. Hadn't Chase been dumped by Cincinnati for exactly this reason, only to end up on the Giants, in the same league! Did Comiskey enjoy the prospect of seeing Joe

Jackson, for whom he paid $65,000, suddenly playing ball against him?

There was, perhaps, a compromise approach that gradually occurred to them both. It was possible to play it both ways. Comiskey could pursue an "investigation" into the rumors. The public knowledge of the rumors required that. It was a way of protecting himself, especially since there was no likelihood of any "evidence" resulting from it. In fact, Ban Johnson and the National Commission could be relied on to do absolutely nothing. Comiskey would appear as a self-sacrificial knight in armor, dedicated only to the truth at whatever cost to his own selfish interests.

The Old Roman was taken by such a proposal. To be told it was impossible to make a self-sacrificial move; to be forced instead to do only what was profitable was not a difficult pill to swallow, especially since he could look noble in the process. Comiskey could have his cake and eat it too.

On the following day, the Great Whitewash began. Charles Comiskey, owner of the Chicago American League Baseball Club, was quoted in the public press as follows: "There is always a scandal of some kind following a big sporting event like the World Series. These yarns are manufactured out of whole cloth and grow out of bitterness due to losing wagers. I believe my boys fought the battles of the recent World Series on the level, as they have always done. And I would be the first to want information to the contrary—if there be any. I would give $20,000 to anyone unearthing any information to that effect. . . ."

This statement, released by the wire services, appeared in newspapers throughout the country. In Philadelphia, it was read by Billy Maharg. In Dallas, Texas, by Sleepy Bill Burns. Both considered it carefully. Burns, who was still smoldering at the ballplayers, was more than tempted. Twenty grand seemed like a decent return on his anger. He might even enjoy getting even with them. But his instinct led him to mistrust such an involvement. For one thing, he didn't like the thought of what might happen to him if he talked. Arnold Rothstein, for example, might not take it kindly. But beyond that, he could not see himself playing on the same team with Charles Comiskey. Nor could he see Comiskey wanting him on the team. Why should the Old

Roman pay him twenty grand for information that would serve to destroy his ball club? The question was enough to keep him quietly in Texas. . . .

There were others who were not so perceptive. One was Joe Gedeon, second baseman for the St. Louis Browns, who came to Chicago and offered his knowledge of the fix. In front of Harry Grabiner, Alfred Austrian, and Comiskey himself, he revealed the nature of his contacts with it. He named his friend Swede Risberg, exposed his contacts with several St. Louis gamblers including Ben Franklin, the Levi brothers, and Joe Pesch. Gedeon told how he had won $600 through bets they had placed through him.

Comiskey heard him out. Austrian shook his head: it was sparse, useless information. Comiskey told Gedeon he was disappointed with it. Gedeon's disappointment was, perhaps, even greater: he had hopes of getting that $20,000.

Another visitor was the St. Louis theater operator, Harry Redmon. Redmon told them of his contacts with Abe Attell, including a rundown of the actions that took place in Room #708 of the Hotel Sinton. His story, like Gedeon's, was too brittle for this audience. And once again, no money changed hands.

Comiskey would never put the jigsaw puzzle together if he kept throwing away the pieces. If he really wanted the whole story, he could have had it from the horse's mouth. Had not Jackson indicated willingness to talk? What else was necessary to start the snowball rolling? Less than two weeks after the Series, Comiskey had received a letter from Joseph Jefferson Jackson, written by his wife, and postmarked Savannah, Georgia. The letter simply stated he had information that the Series had not been played on the square and offered to reveal what he knew. Comiskey quietly filed the letter, and did not bother to reply.

He played a cautious game. He went to see his friend, Maclay Hoyne, Illinois State's Attorney. Comiskey explained: he had a terrible problem here. His suspicions were overpowering. If this scandal hit the public, Comiskey's ball club would be ruined, and baseball might well go down with him. He wanted Hoyne to see to it that this didn't happen. Comiskey was rigid in his belief that baseball must keep this mess in its own backyard and clean it up in private. He didn't want the legal machinery of the state to touch it. Hoyne was obliging. Despite his official position, he could see it Comiskey's way. For one thing, on the basis of Comiskey's reports, there was little the law could do anyway. No matter how certain the Old Roman was of the fix, without confessions, the evidence was insufficient for indictments.

Comiskey was reassured. He promised to keep in close contact with the State's Attorney.

Of necessity, his next move was a secret one: he hired a Chicago private detective named John Hunter. Hunter was given a list of seven ballplayers whom he was to investigate, the purpose being to discover if any had come into a substantial sum of money. The seven men were accurately listed: Cicotte, Gandil, Jackson, Risberg, Felsch, Williams, and McMullin.

By this time, the World Series accounts had been processed. Twenty-one checks of $3,154.27 each, the losers' shares, were ready to be mailed. But Comiskey withheld eight of them pending "further investigations." This, he felt, would later be considered an effective maneuver, showing how diligently he was pursuing the matter. It could also serve as a tactic to frighten the ballplayers, a show of his own defiance, as it were. Perhaps it would work to inhibit their 1920 salary demands. . . .

Several weeks later, the detective reported his findings: Only Gandil's finances indicated a change in status. He had purchased a new car, a new house, and a sizable quantity of diamonds. Comiskey locked the report in his files. Meanwhile, Cicotte and Weaver began complaining about not receiving their World Series checks. By this time (it was already mid-November) the fix talk had dwindled. It was clear that the matter would soon be forgotten. Comiskey, after discussing it with Austrian, concluded that the danger period had passed. He could proceed with his management of White Sox affairs as if nothing unseemly had occurred. The checks were mailed to the eight ballplayers with a brief apology for their tardiness.

Meanwhile, there was a strange pile-up of civil cases in the South-side courts of Chicago: failure to pay alimony, failure to pay bills, inability to meet mortgages, etc. The magistrates were baffled by it. Then, gradually, a similarity of excuses made this phenomenon understandable: all the defendants claimed they had lost their shirts betting on the White Sox.

3

Whatever lingering concern there was over Comiskey's pursuit of the troublesome 1919 World Series, the American League found itself forgetting it as a result of another typical Ban Johnson-type battle. The trigger for this round was the case of pitcher Carl Mays, a neurotic young star, whom the Boston Red Sox had sold to the New York Yankees. Ban Johnson had issued a dictum invalidating the sale, later declaring that all games Mays appeared in were forfeit.

The case was battled in the courts throughout the fall of 1919. At the annual business meeting of the League in December, this controversy so dominated all discussion that the only action taken was a vote to cut back to the old 154-game schedule.

As a result, no attention was paid to the troublesome questions surrounding the 1919 World Series. When Hugh Fullerton returned from his fishing trip in late fall to discover that no action had been taken on this really vital matter, immediately his anger was stirred. He watched the owners snarling across cities at each other, and foresaw the doom of major-league baseball. If he was being melodramatic, it was righteously so. His love for the game permitted no whitewashing. He insisted on a cleanup. With a sense of outrage, he began a series of articles to jolt the executive world of baseball into action. He would expose, finally, what every decent baseball writer knew, but never had the courage to write. He would break down the hypocritical wall of silence behind which baseball pretended to be holy. He would quote gamblers he had spoken with, recount experiences that indicated dirty work, and above all, name names, lots of names.

When he had finished, he took the material to his editor in Chicago. To his dismay, he was told it was too hot to publish. No newspaper was prepared to tackle anything like this, out of fear of the libel laws. Fullerton, undaunted, took the articles to New York where the New York *Evening World* agreed to print them, providing he watered them down considerably. Fullerton fought them, eventually arrived at a compromise. The articles were hot enough even without his direct accusations and the omission of a number of names.

On December 15, in the midst of the National Baseball Commission meetings, the New York *World* exploded Fullerton's bomb: "Is Big League Baseball Being Run for Gamblers, with Ballplayers in the Deal?" The World Series, he suggested, was tampered with to enrich the gambling clique in many American cities. Actually, he did not state that the Series had been fixed. To avoid libel, his articles merely challenged the evasiveness of the National Commission in the face of some glaring suspicions: "Professional baseball has reached a crisis. The Major Leagues, both owners and players, are on trial. Charges of crookedness amongst owners, accusations of cheating, of tampering with each other's teams, of attempting to syndicate and control ballplayers are bandied about openly. Charges that ballplayers are bribed and games are sold out are made without attempts at refutations by men who have made their fortunes in baseball.

"The National League met and adjourned without even mentioning the subject. The American League, besmirched with scandal, wrangled, fought, and blackguarded each other, then separated without an effort to clear the good name of the sport. They keep silent hoping it will all blow over.

"The time has come for open talk!"

The owners, as usual, thought otherwise. Fullerton's blast, prominently exposed on page one, was nothing more than an irritant. If it finally forced them into making a few statements, it did not lead to action. Harry Frazee of Boston told the press that he agreed with Fullerton: Sure, gamblers were a menace. Something should be done. Another club owner seriously suggested that an appeal be made to the gamblers' patriotism. After all, they were Americans, too. And since this was the national pastime, could they not be asked to respect it? Comiskey, annoyed by the stir Fullerton had created, came through with another denial: "Concerning numerous rumors of dishonesty amongst Chicago players, I am very happy to state that we have discovered nothing to indicate any member of my team double-crossing me or the public last Fall. . . ."

Meanwhile, Manager Pat Moran of the Championship Cincinnati Reds was interviewed at the National League meeting. "I don't take any stock in all this talk about gamblers getting to ballplayers. I watched the White Sox as closely as anyone in the orchard, and if any of them was pulling, they can have the credit for fooling me. Whoever it was, he showed himself a great actor!" Despite his denials, he let another cat out of the bag: "Some piker-gambler tried to get one of my pitchers oiled up with hooch a couple of days before the Series, but I found it out and stopped it."

This last irked Fullerton. He wanted to know exactly who tried to get Moran's pitcher drunk. Why didn't Moran pursue it? Why wasn't there an investigation?

Fullerton's anger ran in direct proportion to the National Commission's indifference. He demanded action. He went further and specified what kind of action. Kenesaw Mountain Landis, a Federal judge in the District of Illinois, should be made arbiter of a special investigation. All suspected ballplayers should be forced to reveal what they knew. If Fullerton was not permitted to name players, he did not hesitate to mention a number of gamblers. He started with Sleepy Bill Burns and Abe Attell, then went down a list that included Monte Tennes, Joe Pesch, Carl Zork, Ben and Lou Levi of St. Louis. Nor did he leave out the illustrious Arnold Rothstein of New York.

The owners winced at such a challenge. Though baseball fans all over the country got stirred up, the National Commission remained dormant. Comiskey responded with another statement, again claiming that the rumors were hogwash, inspired by gamblers who were bitter about losing. Angrily he defied anyone to prove corruption, repeating his $10,000 (sic) offer for any direct evidence. (The $20,000 offer of October 15 had suddenly, inexplicably, been cut in half.) And again, Fullerton blasted back. "I have no proof that any players are guilty. But one thing is certain: gamblers have stated they have put over this thing, and that they have solicited capital from others on the ground that they could control players. This took place during the season and the Chicago White Sox are not the only team involved. This alone calls for investigation!" Fullerton ridiculed Comiskey's naïveté: "The stories that these rumors are all from disgruntled gamblers who had lost on the Series are not true, because I heard them *before* a single game was played!"

About this time, an interview with catcher Ray Schalk appeared in a small Chicago newspaper. Schalk purportedly had spoken with guarded anger, claiming he knew for a fact that seven White Sox players would not be around for the coming season. He did not elaborate. Apparently he had refused to discuss the matter further.

But the statement, such as it was, seemed pregnant with significance. It was picked up by the wire services and reported all over the country. If the members of the National Commission read it, they gave no indication of concern. The Commission's meetings broke up for the Christmas holidays without any discussion of the gambling-corruption problems. In answer to queries, Garry Herrmann stated his position: "The matter rests with Comiskey, who is responsible for the conduct of his players. All investigations into this matter have failed. Why start another investigation of moth-eaten rumors?"

Hugh Fullerton's articles did not result in any action, but they at least kicked up plenty of comment. The *Baseball Magazine,* a national monthly dedicated to bringing news and stories of baseball personalities to its millions of fans, became Fullerton's fierce attacker. The concept that baseball could be corrupt was absolutely alien to the magazine. To fix the World Series was so preposterous as to be almost laughable. Fullerton, therefore, became the enemy. Throughout the winter of 1919–1920, as the rumors persisted, this widely read and respected magazine poured constant abuse on Fullerton's reputation, charged him with devious, dishonest motives, impugned his patriotism, distorted his emphasis, and ridiculed:

> *A dopester whose first name was Hugh*
> *Said the White Sox would win five to two.*
> *But the Reds with a rush*
> *Put the dope on the crush*
> *Now the dopester still bellows "bugh-hugh!"*

Baseball's famous weekly organ, *The Sporting News,* published in St. Louis by Taylor Spink, also rejected the rumors of corruption. In December, their targets were more general than a certain solitary newspaperman: "Because a lot of dirty, long-nosed, thick-lipped, and strong-smelling gamblers butted into the World Series—an American event, by the way—and some of said gentlemen got crossed, stories were peddled that there was something wrong with the way the games were played. Some of the Chicago players laid down for a price, said the scandal mongers. . . . Comiskey has met that by offering $10,000 for any sort of clue that will bear out such a charge. He might as well have offered a million. . . ."

Gradually, *The Sporting News* modified that scurrilous opinion. One of its oldest writers, John B. Sheriden, could indicate his fears, for he had heard more gambling talk at the 1919 Series than he'd heard in over thirty years. He was told by "a conservative and honest gambler" (as distinct from a "dirty, long-nosed, thick-lipped" type): "A man whose betting limit is $100 suddenly bets me $5,000 against $4,000 on Cincinnati! He didn't even ask me for odds. He merely said, 'How much money will you take?'"

Another writer, Joe Vila, had this to say in *The Sporting News:* "Almost anytime you can run into a wise fish on Broadway who will tell you things that make you wonder why there has been no action."

The Sporting News also reported on a novel remedy: perhaps the best way to clean up baseball was to get the ballplayers themselves to do it. They should inform on each other. The National Commission should give medals to those heroic players who exposed the betrayers. After all, it was argued, a player should be the first to root out this evil. "You wouldn't sit down to a poker game with a card player who cheated, would you?"

In New York City, Arnold Rothstein noted the lack of action with a sense of relief. It reaffirmed his sense of order, all these big millionaires running the baseball world like a squawling bunch of idiot kids. He felt he could walk all over them. They were just like politicians; they would end up working for him. He could rob them all blind, then they spent their time and money making sure it was kept a secret. There was no limit to the riches that could be won in a world run in this manner.

Rothstein soon forgot about the World Series. He had important business to get ahead with. Prohibition was taking over, and millions of Americans would want whisky. . . .

4

The year 1920 opened with a blockbuster: on January 5, the New York Yankees announced the purchase of George Herman "Babe" Ruth from Boston for the staggering sum of $125,000. Ruth, not yet twenty-five years old, was an outstanding American League pitcher (90 wins, 39 defeats) plus a record World Series shutout string of 29 consecutive innings. But Colonel Jacob Ruppert was not buying a pitcher. In 1919, Ruth had hit 29 home runs, breaking all records.

From California, where he was wintering, the Babe further shattered precedent by demanding a piece of the sale price. His rebellious attitude, formerly a thorn in Boston owner Harry Frazee's side, forced Ruppert to protect his investment. He kept Ruth happy with a raise to $20,000 a year.

On January 9, Charles Comiskey read the following dispatch in the New York *Times:* SAN FRANCISCO.—Charles Swede Risberg, Chicago White Sox shortstop, announced that he was retiring from baseball and would open a restaurant. He expressed dissatisfaction with his major league salary."

Comiskey was not in good health. He returned to Chicago after the baseball mettings with a bad cold. He was feeling the pressure severely. At sixty, his doctor advised him, a successful man should be able to enjoy certain prerogatives; in his case, essential for his health. He needed a three-week vacation in Florida. The Old Roman, however, felt he had too much important business to handle: he had to put his 1920 baseball team together. If his luck held out, it would be the same club that won the 1919 American League pennant.

He discussed salaries with his secretary, Harry Grabiner. One by one, as the individual contracts were placed before him, he determined maximum figures and set minimums for Grabiner to shoot for. It was a job that Grabiner was well trained to do.

Then he had to do something about Ray Schalk's provocative outburst. He put in a call to Schalk who lived in Chicago—there must not be any further rumors.

On January 16, in newspapers throughout the country, Ray Schalk was quoted as denying his previous statement implying corruption of the 1919 World Series. "I played to the best of my ability. I feel that every man on our club did the same, and there was not a single moment of all the games in which we all did not try. How anyone can say differently, if he saw the Series, is a mystery to me!"

By the end of January, Comiskey realized he would have to raise his minimum figures on players' salaries. The contracts were being returned to his office, unsigned, almost as fast as they were being dispatched. Some of the demands for increases seemed preposterous. Chick Gandil's, for example. Gandil was asking for $10,000! Cicotte, Weaver, Jackson, Risberg, all unsigned. Even Dickie Kerr was giving him trouble: one year in the majors and a holdout already.

Comiskey called Gleason in Philadelphia. He needed him in Chicago to help straighten out the salary disputes. Gleason, who was close to the ballplayers, could be induced to play the salary game from Comiskey's side of the desk.

The National Baseball Commission met again, this time in Chicago. Business had been extremely good in 1919. It would be better in 1920. In the interest of stability, the great schism over the Carl Mays case was healed and peace was established. With the cost of living rising, the owners decided that it was time to raise the price of bleacher seats to a half-dollar.

In the Chicago *Herald and Examiner,* George Phair commemorated the passing:

> *Goodbye, dear pal, farewell for aye,*
> *Your life was long and sweet;*
> *And now you're dead as Barleycorn,*
> *Old two-bit bleacher seat!*

Garry Herrmann resigned as National Commissioner, leaving John Heydler of the National League and Ban Johnson of the American to tussle over a new appointee. Since no one was mutually satisfactory, the post was left open. Profession baseball would move into the 1920 season without a national commissioner. . . .

Comiskey watched February slide into March, all too aware of a larger list of holdouts than he had ever known. On February 14, for example, the A.P. reported the following: "SAVANNAH, GA.—Joe Jackson said today that he returned his White Sox contract unsigned, and would quit baseball unless his salary demands were met. He has business connections here."

The first batch of rookies and pitchers were already arriving at Waco, Texas, training camp, but the only infielder signed was Eddie Collins. It was increasingly clear that nothing could be accomplished through the mails. Harry Grabiner was dispatched to Savannah to get Jackson's signature. Comiskey himself would go West with Tip O'Neill to sign Gandil, Risberg, and Weaver.

Harry Grabiner was good at his job. In annual negotiations with the ballplayers, he could boast he had been responsible for saving Comiskey many thousands of dollars. His attitude was direct and inflexible, and he could rely on the rigid policy of his boss to back him.

Grabiner had never visited Jackson before, but, then, this year everything was different. There would be a special kind of fencing around that bothered the road secretary. He had never liked Jackson much. The Southerner would stare at him with those dark brooding eyes, never letting go of him, following every move he made. Grabiner habitually spoke rapidly, and Jackson always had trouble following his words. The Secretary found himself shying away from him during the playing season. Grabiner could not figure an illiterate man. What went on up there under the derby? He seemed, at times, like a big dumb dog; at other times, more like a fox.

Jackson's wife, Katie, was something else again. She was bright and capable. She did her husband's reading and writing for him. And, Grabiner presumed, his thinking. He hoped that she would not be home, but it was she who greeted him at the door. She bade him enter and sit down. She was sorry, but Joe was at the shop. At the shop? Grabiner asked. Yes, Joe had started up a new business, a valet service, right here in Savannah. She was careful to add that it was doing just fine.

That amused the White Sox Secretary; most ballplayers wanted to be businessmen, but they didn't know which end was up. Without baseball, Jackson was nothing. Grabiner believed that. He had to; it was his biggest argument.

When Jackson arrived an hour later, Grabiner asked Joe if he would drive him to town as he needed some smokes. They could talk business on the way. Jackson was obliging. In the car, he had some pointed questions to ask: Why hadn't Mr. Comiskey answered the letters he had sent? Why hadn't he been allowed to tell his story about the $5,000 he had been handed? Grabiner told him he knew about that money, and that Mr. Comiskey had fully appreciated Jackson's efforts. They had been working on the case all winter. It was all right for Jackson to keep the money. He assured the ballplayer that he was in no trouble, that the whole thing would be safely wrapped up in a few more weeks. He intimated that Comiskey had the goods on three of the players: Cicotte, Gandil, and Williams.

Then he drew Jackson's contract from his brief case, revealing the good news that it included a susbstantial raise. Comiskey would pay him as much as $9,000 a year—if he agreed to sign for three more years. Jackson objected; he didn't think he ought to do that. He'd had a fine year in 1919, hitting .354, second only to Cobb. He knew he'd have an even better year coming up. He figured he should be worth more money in 1920. And, in 1921, maybe much more. Why should he be tied to one figure like this?

Grabiner argued that the club took a chance on him, too. Suppose he had a real *bad* year? Suppose he got a few sprains and sat out half a season? Suppose anything at all; it's always a gamble. At least this way he'd be guaranteed a three-year income. And when the Secretary strongly urged Jackson to sign, there was more than advice in the tone of his voice. He added that these were troubled times with a number of White Sox players, and perhaps the best way for Jackson to show his reliability was to come to terms with Mr. Comiskey's generosity.

When the car stopped in front of the Jackson home, Grabiner handed the player the contract and a fountain pen. Jackson stared at the lengthy printed pages until he found the figures. He could read those all right, but he was terribly unsure of himself. He held the fountain pen, but didn't use it. He said that his wife always read his contract before he signed it. He felt he ought to have her read this one, too. Grabiner talked fast again. It was the usual contract except for the size of the salary and three-year agreement. Jackson asked about the ten-day Clause, which allowed the club owner to fire a player on ten days' notice. It was designed to protect the owners in the event of a player's injury as well as incompetence. In return, it afforded the player no protection at all. Jackson said he did not want to sign a three-year contract under which he could be fired with ten days' notice. Grabiner laughed nervously, assured him that the ten-day clause was not included this time.

The ballplayer stared at him, shrugged, then pressed the contract form awkwardly against the side of the car, and attacked the dotted line with Grabiner's fountain pen.

Harry Grabiner could put another notch on that pen. The contract would be sped to Chicago with the illiterate scrawl of the great hitter on the proper line. A half page above it, in small print, a paragraph read as follows:

> The club holds in reserve the right to terminate for cause, all obligations as stipulated above, ten days immediately following its notification to the signee. . . .

Chick Gandil drove a big new car out to Pasadena where the Chicago Cubs were in spring training. Many of them were his friends and they were surprised to see him. How come he wasn't down in Texas, working out with the White Sox? Newspapermen, eager for a possible story, gathered around as Gandil explained that he had sent his contract back to Comiskey. Not enough dough. He was going to manage a club in Idaho and get more than Comiskey ever paid him. Besides, his wife didn't like the East. The wet, chilly weather made her uncomfortable. She got too many colds.

A reporter commented that Gandil was not alone in his contract trouble. Did he know that Risberg was also holding out? Gandil replied that he had heard something about it. He added that he wasn't much surprised.

Buck Weaver finally signed a three-year $7,500 contract in early March and immediately reported to Waco, Texas. In Risberg's absence, Kid Gleason shifted the third baseman back to shortstop, working Fred McMullin at third. Weaver did not respond well to the change. He had never felt confident at short, for all his potential brilliance. He started to mishandle routine ground balls, to throw badly to first.

Risberg's lengthy holdout annoyed Weaver. He began to suspect that he'd settled for too little money. Then, too, there was a strange uneasiness about this year's club . . . a kind of hangover from the World Series. It was almost as if the five winter months had not separated the players. Weaver felt like an outsider. The cliques that had split the 1919 team were spliting this one, only more so. Even without Gandil, there was a grim, hostile feeling.

By the end of March, Weaver's depression had increased. He started making plans, figuring out how he could get himself transferred. He knew the Yankees wanted him. Colonel Ruppert was spending a lot of dough building a club. Weaver could get maybe $10,000 with the Yankees. He recalled how, last fall, he had played exhibition ball with Babe Ruth, and Babe had never stopped complaining about the Boston Red Sox being a lousy outfit. It was a way of getting Harry Frazee's goat, a technique Ruth had learned from Carl Mays. With hindsight now, Weaver realized that both of them had managed to get themselves sold to New York.

On March 26, the New York *Times* reported that: "Buck Weaver, Chicago White Sox infielder, left training camp today in Waco, Texas. He is asking for a new contract, expressing dissatisfaction with his salary. He was also quoted as saying he would ask for a transfer to New York."

When Comiskey read this, he immediately made contact with Weaver, and bluntly told him there would be no sales, no trades, no new deals. He was to get back into uniform immediately or he would never play baseball again . . . anyplace!

On April 1, New York *Times* concluded the story: "Weaver rejoins Sox and will play out his contract."

Swede Risberg came to terms with Comiskey two days before the season opener. Now, with the exception of Gandil, the entire 1919 club had returned. There was no mention of the 1919 World Series by anyone. If the seven ballplayers who had participated in the fix remained quietly apart from the others, there was nothing particularly noteworthy about it: there had always been cliques on this ball club. They were all too busy getting into shape to bother with matters over which they had no control. Besides, they were all playing to higher salaries, and could look forward to another pennant. Nothing else was their business.

Gleason, too, said nothing. Comiskey would watch from the grandstand, quick with his opinions on everything. But it wasn't until they were about to break camp and head North that the Old Roman suggested privately to Gleason that he keep a close eye on the seven.

Gleason agreed. He could understand why Comiskey hadn't thrown the whole thing out in the open and questioned those boys: everybody wanted a winner.

5

Meanwhile, there was contract trouble with an infielder of the Chicago Cubs Baseball Club. The ballplayer was Lee Magee, who finished the 1919 season with Chicago after signing a two-year contract with them. However, just before the 1920 season began, the Cubs had notified Magee of his unconditional release. For reasons not disclosed to the public, Magee found himself unable to make a deal with any other club. The doors of professional baseball were beginning to shut on players who had been involved with gamblers. The National League had a rather noncommittal method of easing undesirable ballplayers out without explanation. There was a clause in its constitution granting the League the right to pass on the desirability of any player.

Magee, of course, knew the reason: he had been named in connection with Hal Chase's gambling maneuvers. The rumors that surrounded the 1919 Series were starting to force the hands of baseball's power figures.

But Magee was not the kind of man who was willing to be victimized. Defiantly, he hired a lawyer and challenged the National League Commissioner, John Heydler, to do battle. It turned out to be a fruitless gesture for Magee, but it stirred up enough action to frighten Heydler and all of baseball's officialdom. The ensuing trial revealed that Magee, along with Chase, had been involved in betting against his own club in 1919. The jury decided against Magee who was promptly chased out of baseball forever. If he knew anything about the 1919 Series, it never came out at the trial. Significantly, the Chicago Cubs's attorney, Murray Seasongood, scrupulously avoided bringing that matter up.

It was the first public exposure to crookedness in baseball. To many, it seemed to threaten exposure of any number of other, comparable incidents. But baseball was not so inclined. Once again, business was booming. Attendance figures for 1920 were soaring higher than 1919.

Baseball Magazine had a curious word for it all, and in the process took another random pot shot at its favorite enemy, Hugh Fullerton: "Magee, after all, has not hurt the game in which he will no longer have a part. The greater harm was done by sensational writers like Hugh Fullerton, men for whose actions there was not the slightest excuse."

The logic of this tack was, at best, devious. The editorial casually dismissed Magee as a crooked ballplayer, but condemned Fullerton for trying to expose him.

The owners, meanwhile, began to attack the disease by picking a few pimples. Plain-clothes men circulated around notorious gambling centers at various ball parks. Ban Johnson announced that the American League had engaged a specially trained squad of detectives. To make a public show of their efforts, forty-six petty gamblers were arrested at one game. They were fined $1 each and told to keep away from the bleachers.

Chicago *Tribune* sportswriter, Jim Cruisenberry, made mockery of this whole procedure: There was a time when some of the bleacherites "would stake nickels or dimes on batters as they stepped up to the plate. 'A dime he does!' or 'Five he don't!' Detectives in the bleachers have arrested a number of these boys. But the big gamblers were still operating in the boxes almost directly behind the players' bench. . . ."

Actually, as everyone knew, nothing had changed from the previous year. Rumors had remained rumors over the winter. There was, however, one important difference: the gamblers had something big to hold over the seven players. If there was any doubt as to the extent of their power, that doubt was quickly dispelled. Their persistent aim was to control key ball games at the most advantageous odds. Their weapon was blackmail.

Opportunity presented itself quickly as the season opened. The White Sox got off to a rousing start. Cicotte was hot again. Williams even hotter. Red Faber had regained his strength and was destined for a great season. Dickie Kerr was even sharper than he had been in 1919. Jackson was hitting .400 and leading the league. Buck Weaver was close behind. The great ball club moved to Cleveland for a long series after winning six straight games. The odds, of course, were strongly in favor of the White Sox.

At this point, the good gentlemen from St. Louis seized the moment and took control. Joe Pesch and Carl Zork, Attell's partners of the year before, made contact. The contact man was Fred McMullin. The instructions were familiar enough: they were to lose the first game at Cleveland.

Immediately, the odds shifted, just as they had before the opening game of the past World Series. And once again, the betting skyrocketed, the odds ending up at 6–5, with Cleveland favored.

It was a close ball game, with Chicago leading 2–1. White Sox pitcher Red Faber was having a great day. He seemed unbeatable; it was going to be up to the fielders to take his victory away from him. They did, in the eighth inning. A fly ball was hit over Jackson's head in left. Swede Risberg went out to receive Jackson's throw and make the relay throw in. Risberg threw so badly that neither Buck Weaver nor Red Faber, who was backing up, could get their hands on the ball. The run scored, tying up the game, which Cleveland went on to win in the ninth.

The pattern was repeated periodically throughout the summer. The ballplayers accepted the action as a matter of course. They were paid off in small sums on no definite basis; a few hundred here, another few hundred there. (There is no record of these figures.) If they remained loyal to these commitments, it was less out of greed than out of fear. Gamblers had an ominous way of keeping their victims in line by emphasizing the need for both allegiance and silence. In a way, this simplified the problem for the ballplayers: it was a lot easier to accept dirty money if you were going to be butchered for turning it down.

Newspaperman Jim Crusinberry of the Chicago *Tribune* was not blind to the state of affairs; he had heard enough talk and seen enough devious action to guess the truth. There was even something special about the way the seven "suspected" ballplayers formed a separate faction on the club, even more isolated than in 1919. On road trips, they were always by themselves, eating apart from the others. There was a solemnity about them that was certainly not typical of their volatile personalities.

Cruisenberry had revealed all this to the *Tribune* sports editor, Harvey Woodruff. But what was there to print? The tale of a suspicion? Another few words of hearsay? Woodruff told him to stay with it, in hopes of coming up with something solid—a real exposé based on legitimate evidence.

Late in July, there was a moment that seemed like an opening: Cruisenberry was in a New York hotel room with Ring Lardner, idling away a wet afternoon. The White Sox and Yankees had rained out.

The phone rang. It was Kid Gleason.

"Come over to Dinty Moore's." Gleason spoke quietly. "I'm at the bar with Abe Attell. He's talking, and I want you to hear it. I won't let on that I know you."

Lardner and Cruisenberry agreed that Attell would not recognize them. It took them only a few minutes to get to Dinty Moore's. A great sporting hangout, it was a likely place for Attell and Gleason to have encountered each other. The two writers ambled up to the bar, casually ordered a drink and listened. Gleason began pumping the Little Champ for their benefit.

"So it was Arnold Rothstein who put up the dough for the fix . . . ?"

Attell nodded. "That was it, all right. You know, Kid, I hated to do that to you, but I thought I was going to make a bundle, and I needed it. . . ."

When Cruisenberry returned to his hotel, he immediately sat down to write the story.

Lardner laughed. "Who do you suppose is going to print that?"

Cruisenberry quickly learned that Lardner was right. In the office of the *Tribune,* Woodruff canceled the story. Attell, the editor noted for Cruisenberry's benefit, had access to powerful attorneys, all very adept at libel suits.

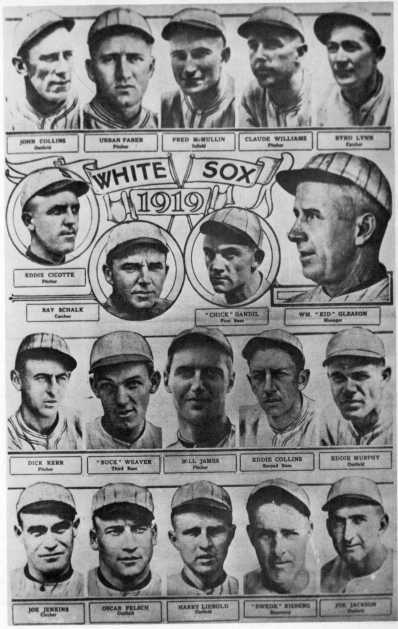

George Brace Photos

Claude "Lefty" Williams
George Brace Photos

Fred McMullin
George Brace Photos

Charles "Swede" Risberg
George Brace Photos

"Shoeless" Joe Jackson
George Brace Photos

George "Buck" Weaver
George Brace Photos

Oscar "Happy" Felsch
George Brace Photos

Eddie Cicotte
George Brace Photos

Arnold "Chick" Gandil
George Brace Photos

William "Kid" Gleason
United Press International Photo

Charles Albert Comiskey *Culver Pictures, Inc.*

Byron Banfield Johnson
United Press International Photo

Ring Lardner *Culver Pictures, Inc.*

Judge Kenesaw Mountain Lan
United Press International Photo

Arnold Rothstein
The New York Daily News *Photo*

William Fallon
United Press International Photo

Joe Jackson (*right*) and Hartley Replogle
United Press International Photo

William Thomas "Sleepy Bill" Bu

Chicago Historical Society

Billy Maharg
United Press International Photo

Abe Attell "The Little Cham
Brown Brothers

York Times.

WEDNESDAY, SEPTEMBER 29, 1920. TWO CENTS

EIGHT WHITE SOX PLAYERS ARE INDICTED ON CHARGE OF FIXING 1919 WORLD SERIES; CICOTTE GOT $10,000 AND JACKSON $5,000

Yankee Owners Give Praise to Comiskey And Offer Him Use of Their Whole Team

Following the announcement from Chicago yesterday that Owner Charles A. Comiskey had suspended two star pitchers, two regular infielders, his two leading outfielders and one utility player, Colonels Jacob Ruppert and T. L. Huston, owners of the New York Club, put at Comiskey's disposal the entire New York American League Club.

It is not likely, however, that the offer will be accepted. The reason advanced for the unusual offer is that such a grave and unforeseen emergency requires an unusual remedy. An American League rule prevents the transfer of a player from one club to another after July 1 without the asking of waivers, which would give any club in the league an opportunity to get the player. This is the technicality referred to in the message.

The telegram from the Yankee owners to Comiskey read as follows: Mr. Charles A. Comiskey, Chicago, Ill.,

Your action in suspending players under suspicion, although it wrecks your entire organization and perhaps your cherished lifework, not only challenges our admiration but excites our sympathy and demands our practical assistance. You are making a terrible sacrifice to preserve the integrity of the game. So grave and unforeseen an emergency requires unusual remedies.

Therefore, in order that you may play out your schedule and, if necessary, the world's series, our entire club is placed at your disposal. We are confident that Cleveland sportsmanship will not permit you to lose by default and will welcome the arrangement. We are equally certain that any technicality in carrying it out can be readily overcome by action on the part of the National Commission.

(Signed) JACOB RUPPERT,
T. L. HUSTON.

COMISKEY SUSPENDS THEM

Promises to Run Them Out of Baseball if Found Guilty

TWO OF PLAYERS CONFESS

Cicotte and Jackson Tell of Their Work in Throwing Games to Cincinnati.

BOTH ARE HELD IN CUSTODY

Prosecutor Says More Players Will Be Indicted and Gamblers Brought to Task.

Every major American newspaper headlined the great scandal.

To Gleason, who never saw in print his attempt at exposure, the suppression only added to his confusion. Previously he had deferred to Comiskey's wish to keep the scandal quiet. Now having given futile voice to his own urge to air the whole mess, he could well wonder whether the truth about the Series would ever come out and just how long anyone could ask him to remain silent.

Meanwhile, the Chicago White Sox continued to win enough ball games to stay on top—or close to it. They jumped in and out of first place like a fast-moving yo-yo. The Cleveland Indians were showing more power than they had in years. The Yankees, bolstered by the incredible Babe Ruth, kept close behind the leaders. By August 15, it was a wide-open pennant race. The interest it generated was phenomenal. All around the league attendance at ball games in 1920 almost doubled the surprisingly high figures of 1919.

For the gamblers, conditions were never better. As long as they could keep the White Sox from breaking loose, as long as they could get them to throw key ball games, holding the final pennant victory in doubt, they could reap a rich harvest. They had driven the ballplayers to the point where they could play ball with one eye on the scoreboard, checking inning-by-inning scores of Cleveland or New York. If Cleveland was winning, the White Sox would turn on the pressure to win. If Cleveland was losing, the White Sox would follow suit.

Charles Comiskey, during this period, found himself helpless before the fantastic profits of the 1920 gate receipts. Any residue of anxiety about the preceding World Series was smothered under this unprecedented pile of money. If Cicotte and Williams blew up in key innings, they also won over 20 games each, some of them brilliantly. And Jackson, the amazingly colorful Shoeless Joe, was having his greatest year since he came to Chicago, battling for the American League batting crown with a .385 average. The dirty rumors of last fall had been buried in the excitement of the pennant race. Comiskey counted his money and let them lie.

Bancroft Johnson, however, was not so inclined. Though he had refused to participate in Comiskey's abortive effort at exposure on that anguished night after the first World Series game in Cincinnati, he had since changed his tune. By now, the American League President had absorbed enough information to realize its significance. When he sensed how it might be used against his adversary, Charles Comiskey, he plunged into a thorough investigation of the 1919 Series and all its ramifications. As a result, by late August, he was also aware of the continued corruption of the White Sox during this 1920 season.

It was a situation loaded with high explosives. The problem was not a new one, but it was certainly a dangerous one. At the moment, Johnson chose to play it safe. If there was to be an explosion, he would be ready for the cleanup that followed. He would step in with the power of his position and root out the evils of professional gambling in baseball. That was, indeed, a stand both righteous and selfishly gratifying: Comiskey would be destroyed in the process.

On August 30, 1920, the White Sox arrived in Boston for a crucial three-game series. Though they had lost two games to the Yankees in New York earlier in the week, they were still a half game in first place over Cleveland. The Red Sox, enfeebled by years of dissension and the recent loss of Mays and Ruth, seemed no match for the pennant winners from Chicago. In the first game, however, the Red Sox shut them out 4–0, Lefty Williams taking the loss. In the second game, Cicotte held a 1–0 lead until the third inning when Jackson errored and two runs scored. In the seventh inning, Cicotte blew completely and the White Sox lost, 7–3. Boston *Globe* sportswriter Jim O'Leary spoke ominously to a friend: "Why, they're playing just like they did in the World Series!" "Brick" Owens, umpiring behind the plate, noted that Cicotte would show good stuff for several pitches, then, with two strikes on the hitter, he'd groove one with nothing much on it. He had never seen so many base hits with two strikes on the hitters. And he had never heard a catcher tear into a pitcher the way Schalk tore into Cicotte. Then, in the third game, Boston knocked them out of first place. The White Sox had lost six games in a row!

Immediately upon return to Chicago, Captain Eddie Collins presented himself to Comiskey. His contention, though recounted with anger, was simple enough: the Boston series had been sold out! Comiskey heard him out, neither shocked nor dismayed. This was tired information to the Old Roman, another chapter in the endless story. He looked at Collins in complete futility, knowing there were no foolish platitudes he could possibly toss at this brainy pro. All he could do was thank him for coming in. He would take no action.

6

Then, on August 31, seemingly from out in left field, the snowball of exposure started rolling. In the National League, the Chicago Cubs were hosts to the last-place Philadelphia Phillies in a routine end-of-season ball game. In the locker room under the stands, Chicago pitcher Claude Hendrix was relaxing before warm-up time while the Cubs took batting practice. In the grandstands above, a few thousand people were slowly drifting in, die-hard baseball fans who had little else to do. Upstairs in his executive offices, President William L. Veeck was completing some correspondence when a telegram was delivered to him. He interrupted his work to read its startling message:

DETROIT: COMMISSIONS OF THOUSANDS OF DOLLARS BEING BET ON PHILLIES TO WIN TODAY. RUMORS THAT YOUR GAME IS FIXED. INVESTIGATE.

MITCHELL B. STEVENS

Veeck was thoroughly baffled. Why should there be any gambling interest in this totally insignificant ball game? Especially as far away as Detroit, strictly an American League city. The suggestion of a fix shook him up, doubly so when similar telegrams and phone calls followed. What did it all add up to? A gambler's plot to get him to change pitchers? Why? To reshift the odds? Or had they gotten to Hendrix, the scheduled pitcher? A hurried phone call to Detroit informed him that there *was* a tremendous amount of money getting down on the Phillies today: the odds had shifted from 2–1 on the Cubs to 6–5 on Philadelphia!

Veeck was sufficiently alarmed to take precautions. The Cubs were battling for a spot in the first divisions, and every game mattered. He discussed it with his manager, Fred Mitchell. They decided to use their ace, Grover Cleveland Alexander, who had already won well over 20 games this season. As an added inducement, since Alex would be working ahead of his usual turn, Veeck offered him a $500 bonus if he won. He also requested that nothing be said to anyone.

Despite this, the Cubs lost, 3–0.

Veeck was worried. He had been through one serious incident with the Lee Magee affair earlier in the year. Another such incident now was going to hurt. The problem was how to take investigatory action without stirring up trouble. He had learned this procedure well by observing his fellow Chicagoan, Charles A. Comiskey.

Immediately after the game, Veeck asked the Burns Detective Agency to trace the telegrams and phone calls. Whatever happened, he specified, all this was to remain confidential. When a Burns official suggested that secrecy in this case might conceivably hamper the investigation, Veeck remained adamant: he simply did not want any of this to leak out.

On the morning of September 2, however, a letter arrived at the sports desk of the Chicago *Herald and Examiner*. It was postmarked Detroit, September 1. It read in part: ". . . The [Detroit] hotel lobbies were crowded with gamblers wanting to bet any amount of money on the Phillies, despite unfavorable odds. Conditions were so openly rotten that I was prompted to write as I do. Every fellow mixed up with baseball gambling hung around the tickers chuckling over the returns of that game. . . ."

The sports desk saw the potential scoop and went into action. They began a quick, intensive investigation. Two days later, on the fourth of September, they ran a front-page exposé:

BARE BASEBALL SCANDAL.
$50,000 BET ON CUBS AND PHILLIES
SURE-THING GAME!

The publicity jolted Veeck and threatened all of baseball. He told the press: "The charges that there were 'fixed' players on the Cubs came as no surprise to me. If I had any regret at their publication at this time, it is merely that investigations which were being made might be hampered by publicity."

But, like all baseball owners, exposure frightened him. Any such incident was explosive and had to be kept under control.

It was, perhaps, indicative that his investigators seemed to be getting nowhere. Or so he told the press. The Burns operatives had not been able to locate any of the people whose names had been given them.

Veeck then announced that he was asking the Chicago chapter of the Baseball Writers' Association to assist him. The entire membership was appointed a Committee of the Whole, Sam Hall of the Chicago *Herald and Examiner* to be Chairman. All expenses incurred by them would be paid by the Cubs. Veeck's challenge to the Committee was properly noble, and had the familiar ring of a Comiskey dictum: "Were the reflection on the Cubs the only matter entering this affair, I would not call for such assistance. But it is more serious than that. Baseball is much greater than the mere standing of the Cubs, and there must be no question as to its honesty. If your investigation develops that there is one man on the team who has done a single dishonest act, you will have rendered a service so great that its value cannot be estimated."

But the baseball fans of Chicago had had it. In the span of the past two seasons, they had heard enough stories of corruption to shatter their equanimity thoroughly. Now, finally, they wanted to see the fire that burned so well hidden below.

Like others who cared, newspaperman Jim Crusinberry was sick of the inaction. Driven by his own knowledge of the truth, he had to make some kind of move. He called on Fred M. Loomis, a prominent Chicagoan. Loomis was a successful businessman and an avid baseball fan. Crusinberry felt that perhaps a public statement by such a man might stir things up. Loomis agreed. He suggested that Crusinberry write a letter to be made public over Loomis's signature. The letter, he insisted, must be angry:

"Up to this time, baseball has been accepted by the public as the one clean sport, a sport engaged in by men, both owners and players, whose honesty and integrity have been beyond suspicions or reproach. At this time, however, it occurs to me that the game must be cleaned up at once . . . if baseball is going to survive. . . .

"It makes no difference who is hit in the investigation, from the president of either major league down to the clubhouse bat boy in the minors. The game must be protected.

"I am an intense lover of the game. . . . Just what is going to be done to clarify this situation which seems so badly confused? There is a perfectly good Grand Jury located in this county. The citizens and taxpayers of Illinois are maintaining such an institution for the purpose of investigating any alleged infraction of the law.

"Those who possess evidence of any gambling last Fall in the World Series must come forward so that justice will be done in this case where public confidence seems to have been so flagrantly violated."

The letter was published on the front page of the Chicago *Tribune* Sports Section. The response was immediate, far beyond even Cruisenberry's expectations. Illinois State's Attorney Maclay Hoyne sensed the public pressure and was forced to respond to it. Though mindful of his meeting with Comiskey, he had his own fences to mend. He was up for re-election in the Democratic primary a few weeks ahead. He could not afford public disfavor. Furthermore, Chief Justice Charles MacDonald of the Criminal Courts Division, an ambitious man, was clearly eager to ride an investigation for whatever it was worth. Hoyne had no choice but to give him the green light. The Grand Jury would be summoned.

On September 7, 1920, when the Chicago White Sox and Cleveland Indians, battling for the American League pennant, won morning and afternoon games respectively, the Grand Jury of Cook County, Illinois, convened. Judge MacDonald presided, and opened the proceedings with a lofty charge that a coterie of gamblers and bookmakers had fixed the Cubs-Phillies game of August 31; that these unscrupulous men were "besmirching the national pastime"; that even outside the ball park, through the operation of baseball pools in which the dimes of children were being swindled, their power was constantly growing, etc., etc.

As an added project, he recommended that the investigation include the possibility that the 1919 World Series might not have been played on its merits.

The enthusiastic members of the jury responded with a rousing cheer. Harry H. Brigham, President of the North American Can Company, was elected foreman. They were scheduled to sit for approximately three weeks. The prospects were completely nebulous. No one —either jury member, the Judge, the State's Attorney, Ban Johnson, Charles Comiskey, or any other baseball player or potentate—had the slightest notion of what would result.

And, for a while, it appeared that nothing would. The public had long since become inured to such inaction. It was more rewarding to follow the excitement of the brilliant American League pennant race, and watch the even more dramatic home-run-hitting spree of the amazing Babe Ruth, now approaching the unheard of total of 50!

On the morning of Friday, September 10, the Wall Street firm of W. E. Hutton and Co., a New York Stock Exchange brokerage house, received a startling "flash" over its private wire from Cincinnati: there had been a train wreck. Babe Ruth and several other leading members of the New York Yankees had been seriously injured while en route to a crucial series at Cleveland. Details would follow.

A few minutes later, several other brokerage houses received similar reports—from Chicago, Pittsburgh, and Cleveland. This time, however, instead of a train wreck, an auto was involved. Immediately, of course, the odds on the coming game shifted heavily against the Yankees.

Sometime later, though too late to rectify the unbalanced betting that resulted, Colonel Huston, part owner of the Yankees, denied the entire report: "Sure-thing gamblers started these vicious stories. Unfortunately, this is something baseball authorities have no way of stopping. I want to say, however, that there has not been a suspicion of anything wrong (with the coming New York-Cleveland series), no matter what one may think about betting on baseball. . . ."

No one, however, mentioned the possibility of tracing who had been responsible for initiating the completely false report.

The Grand Jury ignored the whole thing. Judge MacDonald hinted at the possibility of a "great gambling trust, covering the entire country, designed to exploit the national game by all devious methods known to crooked bookmakers. I want to invite all persons knowing of baseball pools, lotteries, and handbooks to appear before the Grand Jury. I desire that this investigation be widened to include all baseball gambling and not the one particular instance recently charged."

Noble as this may have sounded, it distracted attention from both the 1919 Series and the alleged Cubs-Phillies fix.

Assistant State's Attorney, Hartley Replogle (State's Attorney Maclay Hoyne was busy seeking re-election in the Democratic primary), added another layer of confusion: he was inclined to view the whole Cubs-Phillies scandal as merely a frame-up among a group of Detroit gamblers. In short, it never really happened at all!

Ban Johnson followed with a pompous statement that the American League would ask the Congress of the United States to enact a law making all betting on baseball a penitentiary offense. "Only in this way could baseball gambling be eliminated." American League officials did not elaborate on how such a law might be enforced.

To the average baseball fan, it all seemed like the same old evasive hogwash. It was not a time for faith in the governmental process. People read reports that the Republican Party was "buying the presidency" under Warren Harding's white plume. On September 14, the State of Maine went for Harding with a landslide. It was announced that 80 per cent of the new women's vote was directed against the League of Nations. The Senator from Ohio foresaw his triumph in November. "Maine is taking the lead in declaring for an American unmortgaged to the Old World." His reasoning was valid enough; Americans wanted to be left alone, uncommitted to anything.

The Chicago Democrats went to the polls for their primary elections on September 15. It was a frightening demonstration of the city's political climate. There were several killings, shootings, kidnapings, sluggings, riots, robberies, and a brutal attempt to steal a ballot box—all at the polls. Among the local incumbents, State's Attorney Maclay Hoyne was voted out of his job. He packed his bags and took his wife to New York. He wanted a vacation while he was still on the Illinois payroll.

It was a moment Ban Johnson had been hoping for. He had failed to see the reality of the World Series fix a year ago, but he saw it clearly enough now. His hatred of Comiskey had cleared his vision. He saw this Grand Jury as a tribunal that would lead to the destruction of his enemy and clean up baseball in the process.

Johnson was a mighty man, not afraid of scandal or exposure. He had long since seen Maclay Hoyne as another enemy, a man not eager to push this investigation to a decisive conclusion. Besides, Hoyne was Comiskey's friend. Johnson, as a result, had remained in the background. But now, with Hoyne gone and the Grand Jury floundering, he saw his chance. He marched into Judge MacDonald's chambers and laid it all out on the line.

The President of the American League could give the Judge information that would set the Grand Jury snowballing down a mountain. Johnson began with a list of thirty names, many with specified contacts and involvements with gamblers. Get them to start talking and others would follow. One name leads to another, one story opens the door to another and so develops, compounds, multiplies. That is the way of inertia in such an investigation.

He told the Judge he wanted indictments. If the Grand Jury came through, the Judge would make a big name for himself. Johnson reminded him that there was talk of forming a new baseball Commission. Who knew but what the Judge might not be an ideal man for such a post—and with Johnson's power behind him . . . ?

Judge MacDonald knew a friend when he saw one. He called in Hartley Replogle and they went to work.

On the following day, Monday, September 21, Assistant State's Attorney, Hartley Replogle, announced that subpoenas had been sent out to scores of baseball personalities—owners, managers, players, writers, gamblers, etc. The Grand Jury would hear them all. He declared that there certainly would be indictments; on the basis of preliminary investigations, he was convinced that witnesses were ready to talk.

Among the first to testify was Charles A. Comiskey. His text was rich with glimpses of his nobility as a loyal baseball man, but poor on evidence. In effect, he did nothing more than admit that he, too, had heard suspicions of foul play in the 1919 World Series . . . but he had not pursued them. He added, "At no time since the playing of the World Series did I have any co-operation from Johnson or any member of the National Commission in ferreting out this charge of crookedness. Johnson now says that an official investigation was made. If so, it was made unbeknownst to me, my manager, or my ballplayers. The result of such an alleged investigation has never been communicated to me nor to the American League. . . ." Then he said in stentorian tones, "If any of my players are not honest, I'll fire them no matter who they are, and if I can't get honest players to fill their places, I'll close the gates of the park that I have spent a lifetime to build and in which, in the declining years of my life, I take the greatest measure of pride and pleasure."

If the Grand Jury was moved, Ban Johnson was livid. He followed with a stinging charge that the Chicago White Sox were still under the control of the gamblers who threatened the players even now with exposure unless they acceded to demands. "I have heard," he said to the press, "that the White Sox would not dare to win the pennant this season!"

Comiskey raged at this statement in what was the first round of a newspaper tirade: "It was a terrible thing to report the blackmail of my players by gamblers just before they went into a series against Cleveland, a club in which Mr. Johnson has financial interests!"

On that day, some two hundred miles from the Grand Jury room, the White Sox opened the crucial three-game series with the Indians and trounced them, 10–3, moving back ½ game from first place.

Johnson returned Comiskey's fury: "This is not a time for quibbling and side issues. The integrity of professional baseball is on trial. I am amazed that the newspapers should give ear and voice to the vaporings of a man whose vindictiveness toward the President of the American League [himself] has been so long and so thoroughly known." To prove his dedication to clean baseball, Johnson got on a train for New York City; there he would find the gambler Arnold Rothstein and get the true story of the scandal.

There were other reports that the noted showman and song writer, George M. Cohan, had been somehow involved. At his office, 227 West 44th Street, off Times Square, Cohan told reporters: "I don't know anything about the World Series, so it would be foolish of the Grand Jury to call me." When asked if he lost $30,000 on the White Sox, he replied: "The only thing I have to say is that I have never lost any money on baseball."

On September 24, a Cleveland recruit, Walter "Duster" Mails, shut out the White Sox 2–0 on three feeble hits, keeping the Indians 1½ games in first place. In New York, Babe Ruth blasted his fiftieth and fifty-first home runs, propelling fans into a wild hysteria.

In Chicago's Criminal Courts Building, the Grand Jury quietly heard New York Giant pitcher, John "Rube" Benton. He told how "Buck" Herzog of the Cubs and Hal Chase had offered him $800 last September to throw a game to the Cubs. He had indignantly refused the bribe, then won the game. The report had reached the ears of John McGraw, but there had been no investigation, and the matter had been dropped. Following that, Benton insisted that he knew nothing about any other frame-up in baseball.

Buck Herzog, called from a road trip to testify, completely denied the allegation, attributing the story to an old grudge, dating back to 1915 when he was playing-manager over Benton with the Cincinnati Reds.

The door opened a little, however, when Charles Weeghman, former owner of the Cubs, came to testify. He had spent part of his 1919 summer up at Saratoga, New York, a sporting playground of the rich where the new war-millionaires played the horses by day and the roulette table by night. Arnold Rothstein's luxurious "The Brook" was a meeting place of the most illustrious. Weeghman told how he had met his "old friend" Monte Tennes, from Chicago there. Tennes was the notorious Chicago gambler who, on Attell's advice, had bet heavily on Cincinnati. "He told me the Series had been fixed. This was in August, mind you. Seven White Sox players had agreed to lay down. He mentioned their names and said the tip was straight. But he didn't want it because he liked baseball and didn't want to go in on such a crooked deal. I understand that in spite of the tip, he bet thirty grand on the Sox!" Then, incredibly, Weeghman told the Grand Jury that he didn't remember whether or not he'd told this story to National League President, John Heydler. He found it so preposterous that he could hardly credit it. The matter, he apologized, must have slipped out of his mind.

The Assistant State's Attorney did not press him. If there was any significance in a baseball club owner being an "old friend" of a leading Chicago gambler, no attention was paid to it. The next move belonged with Monte Tennes himself. If Weeghman had been naïve and garrulous, Tennes was cynical and secretive. The code of professional gamblers permitted no exposures, no testimony, no admissions. He spoke the evasive language of gobbledygook. "I know nothing of fixed games. I never told Charley Weeghman about any fixed games. I believe he must have misunderstood. Of course we talked baseball. One would have to talk baseball with Charley. I told him I intended betting on the White Sox. I bet on them. I lost my bet. And I made no cry of fraud."

George M. Cohan, meanwhile, apparently changed his tune. He responded to the Grand Jury call and testified that he, too, had heard some reports. It was also true, he added, that he had taken advantage of them and bet against the White Sox in those first two games. But, he insisted, that was all he knew.

From New York came an AP report on Ban Johnson. "I found the man Arnold Rothstein and after a long talk with him, I felt convinced he wasn't in any plot to fix the Series. He did admit to me that he'd heard of the fixing, but in spite of that, declared he had wagered on the White Sox. . . ." The white knight of the American League had stormed the bloody bastions only to end up in bed with the enemy. But Johnson was undaunted. He kept on gathering information. . . .

The testimony continued in this endless, inconclusive vein. It appeared that the Grand Jury was becoming something of a hearing room for vituperative baseball men who exposed only their personal grudges. The public grew disgusted. Further complaints were noised about concerning the manner in which the investigations were taking place. It was rumored that Replogle would be replaced for his failure to expose anything, that the whole thing was just another whitewashing of a potential baseball scandal. Somewhat less than candid, National League President, John Heydler, kept the whitewash nice and clean: "Every championship game in the National League in 1919 and 1920 was played completely on its merits," he told the papers. "I challenge any of these muckrakers, either inside or outside the ranks of professional baseball, to prove otherwise!"

Muckraker Harry Brigham, Foreman of the Grand Jury, snapped back to reporters: "Chicago, Cincinnati, and St. Louis gamblers have been bleeding and corrupting ballplayers. We are going to the limit in these inquiries, and I am shocked at the rottenness so far revealed!"

Whatever rottenness was revealed by the parade of witnesses, no indictments seemed in the offing. The hand of the law remained gentle. Nor were there any real exposures made to the public. Newspapers reported what was handed to them. Reporters kept long vigils outside the jury room, flashing pictures of the comings and goings of the vast range of baseball personalities, pumping them with questions, but only getting innocuous answers. They protested the secrecy. Why was everything going on behind closed doors? The investigation had not begun in this fashion. Chief Justice MacDonald had pledged open hearings. Newspapermen, who felt they had done much to bring about the whole investigation, resented Replogle and his pious statements about legal traditions and Grand Jury secrecy. Would Replogle be replaced over this very question?

Then, on Thursday afternoon, September 24, the cat finally stuck his neck out of the bag. New York Giant pitcher Rube Benton returned to testify, admitting the fact that he knew more than he had indicated on his previous visit. Replogle refreshed his memory with affidavits from two ballplayers of the Boston Braves, Arthur Wilson and Norman Boeckel, stating that Benton had revealed to them that Hal Chase had tipped him off about the White Sox losing the first and second games of the Series, and the entire World Series as well, and that Benton had won $3,800 on the tip.

Benton, though denying his own betting, was prepared to admit his knowledge of the fix. He told how he was in the room of another Giant pitcher, Jean Dubuc, at the Hotel Ansonia, a week or so before the Series. A telegram arrived from Bill Burns advising Dubuc that the White Sox would lose the Series. Benton also knew that Hal Chase had received several such telegrams from Burns. Chase, he declared, had won over $40,000 on Cincinnati! Benton described a meeting with a man named Hahn, a betting commissioner in Cincinnati, who had told him that several White Sox had been in on the fix, that they had gotten $100,000 from a Pittsburgh gambling syndicate. He recalled the names of Gandil, Felsch, Williams, and Cicotte. He had heard that there was "a gambling clique in Pittsburgh of professional bookmakers who advance money to major league ballplayers to bet on games they play in. . . ." Benton suggested that the Grand Jury would do better to call in Cicotte to tell them about all this. Cicotte would know what it was all about. . . .

The Grand Jury was impressed. They felt they were on the brink of important revelations. They voted to extend their sessions indefinitely—then adjourned until Tuesday morning.

7

Eddie Cicotte, along with the others, heard of Benton's testimony a few hours after he had given it. Everything that leaked out of the Grand Jury room was beginning to make news. Big news. What started out as nothing, another legal palaver of liars and lawyers, was suddenly turning into a monster.

Cicotte's uneasiness was compounded by the presence of a tall stranger, always hanging around. Cicotte would see him at his hotel, then again around the ball park. He was there with a smile, an offer of a cigarette, and finally a few innocent questions. In time, Cicotte learned the truth: the man was a detective, working for the American League—or, more accurately, Ban Johnson. He told Cicotte how much he already knew about him—and he knew everything.

A fatalism had settled in Cicotte. Now it turned to a sense of imminent doom. The fun had gone from playing ball. Gone was that wonderful stirring excitement of walking out to the mound for a clean new game. Gone was the sense of power when he blended his delicate skills to sneak a kunckle ball by a big swinger. He no longer walked to the mound in keyed-up suspense, nor felt any challenge. He pitched with the residue of his talent and whatever day-to-day fabrication of spirit he could generate. Mostly—from the day he had sewed that $10,000 into the lining of his jacket—he had felt like a tired, dirty, punch-drunk fighter.

Over the long 1920 season, the seven ballplayers had not talked about the fix. They hung around together, the same tight clique, but the 1919 World Series was never mentioned. In silence, they hoped that the memories would somehow disappear. Cicotte knew it wouldn't work. This was most apparent with this detective hanging over him.

On the morning of September 25, Cicotte read a statement that Ray Schalk was going to testify when the Grand Jury reconvened on Tuesday. "It's up to the ballplayers to protect the sport," Schalk had said. "If they're gonna drag me into this mess, I'm going before the Grand Jury and tell all I know. I'll mention the names of the men on my own team!"

On that afternoon, Lefty Williams pitched his twenty-second victory of the season, taking Cleveland 5–1. Joe Jackson homered, pushing his batting average up to a phenomenal .387.

The Grand Jury received an anonymous letter saying that Williams's wife had been in a Chicago poolroom last year, on the morning of the second World Series game, placing large bets against the White Sox.

Charles Comiskey watched his team climb back to ½ game behind the Indians. Still raging at Johnson, he defiantly declared that if the White Sox won the 1920 pennant, he would use every member of his ball club in the Series, whatever the suspicions against them.

But the truth was, it had gone beyond a question of suspicions. The whole mess was about to explode. It was, as Replogle told him, "purely a matter of time."

The real question at this point was just how much time? In the view of the tight pennant race and the clear-cut possibility (even probability) of another White Sox victory, perhaps it would be desirable to delay the Grand Jury investigations for a few days? It was a question worth asking.

Judge MacDonald summoned Replogle and Comiskey to answer it.

Comiskey and Alfred Austrian discussed it first, privately. The problem had frightening ramifications. Comiskey wanted that pennant. He thrived on pennants. His pride was once again at stake. This was the meat of his life. The fans of Chicago had topped all previous attendance figures, demanding another pennant.

But Austrian didn't see it that way. The dangers, here, were all too obvious. If Comiskey won the flag, then what? Would the Grand Jury again postpone any exposure until after the World Series? And if the whole scandal should explode before—or even after—the Series, then how would it look? If before, could the World Series be played?

With a decimated Chicago ball club? The bull-like figure of Ban Johnson loomed over them. The answer became glaringly apparent: the risks of delay were simply too great. The problem could no longer be related to the pennant race: it went beyond it. The entire structure of professional baseball was going to take a solid thumping. Comiskey had to keep his hands as clean as possible. There must be no pettiness or compromise attached to the reputation of the Old Roman.

Leading sportswriter for the Philadelphia *North American,* Jimmy Isaminger, knew of Billy Maharg for some years back. He had seen him box, a tough, burly middleweight who could take a lot of punishment. Maharg had fought around Philadelphia, but never showed very much, never got very far. He was a likable boy with a broad, open, friendly face. It was always easy to make him laugh. When Maharg fought, Philadelphia boxing fans always seemed to root for him.

Isaminger had another picture of Billy Maharg—also as a base-ball player. In fact, Isaminger had reason to believe his real name was not Maharg at all. It was George Frederick Graham—or Maharg spelled backward, if you will. "Peaches" Graham, the ballplayer, had been a catcher in the big leagues for about ten years, ending in 1912. He had caught his last season with the Phillies, a year in which he became friends with a young pitcher named Grover Cleveland Alexander.

This peculiar switch of names did not disturb the newspaperman. There was nothing particularly mysterious about a duel athlete maintaining separate identities for whatever reason. Maharg—or Graham —had simply never been important enough to merit any investigation. Until now, Isaminger thought. He had heard Maharg's name in connection with the World Series fix. What was Maharg doing these days? A few telephone calls supplied the answer. Maharg was working at a Ford assembly plant in North Philly in a routine semiskilled job. Then if the man had been involved in the fix—and Isaminger was prepared to believe he had been—he hadn't come out of it rich.

If not rich, then perhaps bitter. . . .

Isaminger decided to play a hunch. He would go out to the Ford plant and see if he could locate the ex-boxer-ballplayer.

On Sunday, at Comiskey Park, the White Sox battled to climb back into first place in the closest three-way pennant finish in years. Chicago novelist James T. Farrell was a nineteen-year-old boy at the time. Years later, he recalled his experience on that day:

I had a box seat for the game of Sunday, September 26th. It was a muggy, sunless day. I went to the park early and watched the players take their hitting and fielding practice. It looked the same as always. They took their turns at the plate. They took their turns on the field. They seemed calm, no different than they had been on other days before the scandal talk had broken. The crowd was friendly to them and some cheered. But a subtle gloom hung over the fans. The atmosphere of the park was like the muggy weather. The game began. Cicotte pitched. The suspected players got a hand when they came to bat. The White Sox won easily. Cicotte was master of the Detroit Tigers that day. One could only wish that he had pitched as well in the 1919 Series.

After the game, I went under the stands and stood near the steps leading down from the White Sox clubhouse. A small group always collected there to watch the players leave. But on this particular Sunday, there were about 200 to 250 boys waiting. Some of the players left. Lefty Williams, wearing a blue suit and a gray cap, was one, and some of the fans called to him. A few others came down the steps. And then Joe Jackson and Happy Felsch appeared. They were both big men. Jackson was the taller of the two and Felsch the broader. They were sportively dressed in gray silk shirts, white duck trousers, and white shoes. They came down the clubhouse steps slowly, their faces masked by impassivity.

A few fans called to them, but they gave no acknowledgment to these greetings. They turned and started to walk away. Spontaneously, the crowd followed in a slow, disorderly manner. I went with the crowd and trailed about five feet behind Jackson and Felsch. They walked somewhat slowly. A fan called out:

"It ain't true, Joe."

The two suspected players did not turn back. They walked on slowly. The crowd took up the cry and more than once men and boys called out and repeated:

"It ain't true, Joe."

This call followed Jackson and Felsch as they walked all the way under the stands to the Thirty-Fifth Street side of the ball park. They left the park and went for their parked cars in a soccer field behind the right field bleachers. I waited by the exit of the soccer field. Many others also waited. Soon Felsch and Jackson drove out in their sportive roadsters, through the double file of silent fans.

I went back to the clubhouse. But most of the players had gone. It was getting dark. A ball park seems very lonely after the crowd has cleared away. Never was a ball park lonelier or more deserted for me than on that September Sunday afternoon. It was almost dark. I went home. I sensed it was true. But I hoped that the players would get out of this and be allowed to go on playing.

George Buck Weaver was twenty-nine years old, but he had the lean, trim type of build that never changes. He was considered to be the most beautiful third baseman in the game. They said of him that he was good for at least another ten years. To opposing ball clubs, it was a frightening thought, for Buck was becoming a better ballplayer with each passing year.

Weaver was born in a small mining town in Western Pennsylvania. His father was employed in the ironworks. It seemed almost inevitable that the son would follow. In 1910, he was playing semi-pro ball when a team of barnstorming big-leaguers came through. A scout named Mike Kennedy of the Phillies spotted him, signed him to a contract for $125 a month. For Weaver it was a fortune. It meant the end to a probable mining career.

In 1912, he was sold to the White Sox, and joined them at spring training in Waco, Texas. He had Kid Gleason, then a coach, hit grounders to him at shortstop. When he missed one, he would call to Gleason to hit harder. Gleason would smash grounder after grounder at him, and every time that Weaver missed, he hollered for more power. It was the way he liked it, the tougher the better. He played shortstop that year, hit a feeble, .224, made a million errors. "Error-a-day Weaver" the fans called him. Yet there was something brilliant about him that kept him in the line-up. He loved to play ball. He never stopped playing ball from the moment he put on spikes. He was like a big kid on the field, laughing it up all the time. He said of himself: "When I broke in, I was like a lot of other ballplayers: didn't take the work seriously enough. I liked to play, but didn't make a study of the game like I should've done. Too careless . . . made a lot of wild heaves."

He had a bad year. "I couldn't hit 'em high. I couldn't hit 'em low. I couldn't hit!" he said.

At the time, he was a right-handed hitter. Then, one winter he was visiting Oscar Vitt, the great Detroit Tiger third baseman. Buck went out to help chop wood. He noticed that when he chopped from his left side, he always hit the grove in the wood, but when he swung right-handed, he missed. When he went home, he started swinging a bat lefty, in front of a mirror. He became a switch hitter.

Immediately, his hitting improved. And with it, his confidence. He was shifted from shortstop to third base, a spot that suited his style and temperament. He stopped throwing wildly and seldom made an error. He played very shallow at third, defying any hitter to drive one by him: his hands were so quick, it seemed impossible. The great Ty Cobb gave up trying to bunt against him. Said Cobb, "I'd see that filthy uniform standing there, the funny face grinning at me, and I wanted to lay one down that line more'n anything in the world. The s.o.b.'d throw me out every time!"

Gleason coached him through these developing years, worked hard with him. He loved Weaver, loved the relentless, joyous drive to win. Gleason made him into a fine .300 hitter, a long way from that .224 in 1912. He called Weaver a "fighting wolfhound who inspires the others. Off the field, he's just a quiet, mild, peaceful boy. Weaver loves to play ball. Why, he's got a smile on his face all the time, no matter what is happening. Even if he's fighting with an ump, he's grinning all the time!"

Buck Weaver hadn't smiled much since the investigation began. Today, he had looked at the gray, sodden sky and wondered if it was going to rain. He had gone to the ball park without eating. Feeling hungry at gametime, he had gobbled down a candy bar. This turned out to be a mistake, for it unsettled his stomach. But he had played hard against Detroit, trying to climb out of the doldrums. The fact that Cicotte was pitching hadn't helped. He never knew when Cicotte was going to win a ball game any more. He wished he could hit against him. He liked to hit against the little roly-poly pitchers.

Detroit had been no competition, a 5–1 breeze. Sometimes Weaver wondered how other clubs ever beat the Sox. There were other times when he wondered how the White Sox ever managed to get through nine innings together. The answer, of course, was that they got paid to do it. Without the dough, they'd probably be out there killing each other. Risberg and Eddie Collins, Williams and Schalk, and big, tough Gandil. Weaver would never forget last July when Gandil had tangled with Tris Speaker at first base. Speaker had torn into Gandil while the entire White Sox infield gathered around. Nobody stopped them; they all wanted Gandil to get his lumps.

For better or for worse, this was Weaver's ball club. It had been the only club he'd known for nine big-league seasons. No matter how much he wanted out, he tried not to let it bother him. Each year, he'd played his heart out. Every game was THE game. Every swing was real. The old, worn piece of dirty leather on his left hand was a tool of his greatness, and he slapped it, fondled it, oiled it with genuine concern. Relentlessly he would concentrate on every pitch. Life was this momentary thing, over and over again. He would set himself, loose, yet alert, sharp as a tack. Nothing else mattered but the round white ball and that split second when it moved at him, sometimes with the speed of a bullet. He loved it. He loved the quickness of his body, his instinct to lean one way or the other in anticipation of a hit at him. He was twenty-nine years old and this year had been his best. He had ignored all the tensions, all the squabbles, all the rumors. He had tuned himself only toward making himself the greatest. He could tell himself that he'd succeeded. As a hitter, he'd jumped 30 points higher than he'd ever hit. Up to .333. And there was no third baseman anyplace in the world like George Buck Weaver.

But he was tired after the Detroit game. The muggy weather had been wearing. The dreariness of the locker room got him down. It was as if they were all a bunch of second division losers. He hurried with his shower. He wanted to get over to Ma Cuddy's Tavern for a beer.

When he got there, he saw a reporter waiting for him. Reporters annoyed him. They no longer wanted to talk baseball. They all wanted to talk about the scandal. Weaver was out there playing baseball, and these guys acted like the ball game was in the Grand Jury room. Weaver didn't realize how wrong he was: the ball game *was* in the Grand Jury room.

"Hey, Buck, lemme buy you a beer!"

"No, thanks."

"You know the story about you they got in the Grand Jury?"

Weaver knew. There was a rumor floating around about how McMullin had delivered a package to him before the World Series.

"I don't care none."

"They're saying McMullin brought you money——"

"Look, I didn't get no money. Not from nobody!"

"They're saying there was witnesses. This package——"

"A package. So what! I got lots of packages. All the time. Especially in the Series. People send me presents. All ballplayers get presents, more or less. See this shirt? A present. Neckties. I get silk neckties, maybe ten or twelve each year. You know that? Fans send me neckties. Does that make me a crook?"

"Then you didn't get any package from McMullin?"

"No! I suppose before this investigation is over they will have every ballplayer in both leagues branded as a crook."

"Well, you gotta admit they've got some evidence of business being done——"

"Look, I'm gonna go before that Grand Jury on my own and cut loose with a lot of stuff from the shoulder——"

"They say you haven't spoken to Eddie Cicotte since the Series last year. It's common talk. Do you mind saying for publication why you're sore at him?"

"I won't answer that question in the papers. If the Grand Jury asks me that question, I might or might not answer. I'm a long way from being a squealer."

The reporter was writing in his notebook. Weaver turned away, aware that he shouldn't have said anything to these birds.

"Lemme alone," he grunted.

8

On the following day, Monday, September 27, 1920, the Philadelphia *North American* ran a story that startled millions of readers: "The Most Gigantic Sporting Swindle in the History of America!" Jimmy Isaminger reported his interview with Billy Maharg.

"We were all double-crossed by Abe Attell," Maharg asserted, "and I want everybody to know the truth. I guess I'd better get to the start: I am a friend of Bill Burns, the veteran southpaw. After quitting baseball, Burns, who is a Texan, bought oil leases and cleared over $100,000. In the middle of September last year, I received a wire from Burns in New York. I hopped a train and met Bill at the Ansonia. . . ."

Maharg related the story of his involvement in the fix, exactly as he had experienced it. Isaminger's article concentrated on five major points of Maharg's experience:

1. The first, second, and final games of the Series were "thrown" by eight members of the White Sox.

2. The offer to "fix" the series was volunteered to Bill Burns and himself by Eddie Cicotte.

3. The ballplayers were promised $100,000 to lose the Series, but actually received only $10,000.

4. Abe Attell manipulated the fix, but betrayed them all.

5. He and Burns lost every cent they had betting on the third game, which they thought was fixed like the first two.

"Then I took my medicine and came back to Philadelphia and went to work," Maharg concluded. "This is the first time I ever opened my mouth on the subject."

On that afternoon, the White Sox played their last home game of the year. Dickie Kerr shut out Detroit, 2–0. Weaver, Jackson, and Eddie Collins combined base hits to win the game. Significantly, Cleveland also won, holding onto their ½-game lead.

Before the game had finished, the Maharg story was repeated in Chicago afternoon papers. Several copies were waiting for the players as they filed into the locker room. They gathered around to read them. Nobody said a word. Joe Jackson, the illiterate, glanced at the faces of his cohorts, dressed hurriedly, and went out to get drunk. Happy Felsch rushed out after him. He, too, wanted to get drunk.

Another story, prominently displayed on an inside page, seemed inconsequential: a "mystery woman" had been uncovered by the State's Attorney's office. She was believed to have vital information to give the Grand Jury.

Eddie Cicotte returned to his hotel, only to face the tall detective with the smile and soft-spoken manner. Cicotte wanted to run away and hide. The detective told him there was no way to hide from what was going to happen to him. Everybody knew that evidence was piling up. The Grand Jury already had more than enough for indictments. The thing to do was to come clean. That would help Cicotte and everyone else. The State always takes care of its witnesses. Besides, Cicotte would feel better if he talked. . . .

Cicotte turned and went up to his room.

The following morning, Charles Comiskey came early to his office at the ball park as he always did. But this day would be different. He had nursed this problem for a full year, and now the end was near. That much was apparent. He had not been able to separate himself from it. He had twisted and turned, attacked and retreated, shouted and bluffed. He had prepared himself as cleverly as he could to face any eventuality. On this morning, however, all these tactics provided no ease for his anguish.

Kid Gleason was waiting for him, ready for the funeral. "Commy, do you want the real truth? I think I can get it for you. Today."

"How?" Comiskey asked. The question choked him.

"Cicotte. I know he's ready to break down. He's weak. I've seen him stewing with this all summer." Then he paused before asking. "Shall I get him?"

Comiskey sighed. Well, there it was. Finally, there it was. The end of his pennant hopes, the end of his ball club. The end of God knows what else!

What was he supposed to do? Now that he faced the real issue, he wasn't any more confident of decision than he ever was. It crossed his mind that maybe there was a way of stalling this thing for a while. . . .

"Go get him," he mumbled finally. Then he turned to call Alfred Austrian.

Gleason found Cicotte in his hotel room. He told him that Comiskey wanted to see him. Cicotte nodded. He didn't bother to ask the manager what it was all about.

Together they went downtown to the law offices of Alfred Austrian. On their arrival, Cicotte was asked to wait in the reception room. The pitcher sat there alone for over twenty minutes while his hands grew clammy with sweat. Then a secretary asked him to follow her into one of the inner rooms. Cicotte entered, but found this room empty as well. He sat there for another twenty minutes. By that time, he was shaking, sick with guilt and hopelessness. When he was finally led into Austrian's office, he was a beaten man. He confronted Comiskey, Gleason, and Austrian. They did not need to ask him a question. He crumbled into a chair and broke down.

"I know what you want to know—I know . . ." he sobbed. "Yeah —we were crooked—we were crooked. . . ."

Comiskey could not face him. He didn't want to hear the words that would trigger his own destruction.

"Don't tell me!" he snapped. "Tell it to the Grand Jury!"

At 11:30 A.M., the Criminal Courts Building was crowded with reporters and the usual band of baseball buffs and curiosity-seekers. Cicotte, escorted by Alfred Austrian and two bailiffs, pushed their way in. Cicotte walked stiffly through the gantlet, a smile frozen on his face. He ignored the flood of excited questions. At first, it was believed that the pitcher had come to clear himself of the charges. Someone shouted at him: "Hey, Eddie, you gonna get an immunity bath?" Cicotte seemed not to hear. He merely held his smile and moved on, Austrian's hand tight on his arm. He was led to an empty office on the sixth floor. Austrian introduced him to Hartley Replogle.

"This is the man handling the Grand Jury investigations, Eddie. He has the goods on you. Come clean with him and he'll take care of you."

A few more comforting words were spoken to him as a sheet of legal print was placed before him. It all looked complicated and legalistic.

"Sign it," Replogle said. Cicotte hesitated. "Don't worry," Replogle encouraged him. "We'll see that you'll be all right."

Cicotte signed. Since he wasn't up to reading the paper, he did not know it was a waiver of immunity.

They took him to another room, Judge MacDonald's chambers. The Judge looked him squarely in the eye. "Are you going to tell us everything, Cicotte?" The pitcher nodded. "We want to know about the gamblers. . . ." Cicotte swallowed thickly, nodded again. The Judge then instructed Replogle to indict him. The word had Cicotte worried. He turned to Replogle and asked, "What's that mean? Don't this go—what you promised me?" Replogle reassured him everything was going to be all right.

Then they took him down to the Grand Jury room. He had acted totally without benefit of counsel.

The members of the Grand Jury sat breathlessly still as the ballplayer began talking. "I don't know why I did it . . . I must have been crazy!" He had trouble finishing his first words; his voice was all choked up. "Risberg, Gandil, and McMullin were at me for a week before the Series began. They wanted me to go crooked. I don't know. I needed the money. I had the wife and the kids. The wife and the kids don't know about this. I don't know what they'll think." He stopped, suddenly buried his head in his hands. For a moment, it seemed as if he could not go on. When he raised his head, his eyes were wet with tears.

"Before Gandil was a ballplayer, he was mixed up with gamblers and low characters back in Arizona. That's where he got the hunch to fix the Series. Eight of us, we got together in my room three or four days before the Series started. Gandil was master of ceremonies. We talked about it, and decided we could get away with it. We agreed to do it.

"I was thinking of the wife and kids. I'd bought a farm. There was a four-thousand-dollar mortgage on it. There isn't any mortgage on it now. I paid it off with the crooked money. I told Gandil I had to have the cash in advance. I didn't want any checks. I didn't want any promises. I wanted the money in bills. I wanted it before I pitched a ball. We talked quite a while about it. Yes, we decided to do our best to throw the games at Cincinnati.

"Then Gandil and McMullin took us all, one by one, away from the others and we talked turkey. Gandil asked me my price. I told him $10,000. And I told him $10,000 was to be paid in advance. It was Gandil I was talking to. He wanted to give me some money at the time, the rest after the games were played and lost. But it didn't go with me. Well, the argument went on for days, the argument for some now, some later. But I stood pat. I wanted that $10,000 and I got it.

"The day before I went to Cincinnati I put it up to them squarely for the last time that there would be nothing doing unless I had the money. That night I found the money under my pillow. There was $10,000. I counted it. I don't know who put it there. It was my price. I had sold out 'Commy'. I had sold out the other boys. Sold them for $10,000 to pay off a mortgage on a farm and for the wife and kids . . . $10,000 . . . what I had asked, cash in advance, there in my fingers. I had been paid and I went on. I threw the game."

The Grand Jury questioned Cicotte in detail as to the manner in which the games were thrown.

"It's easy. Just a slight hesitation on the player's part will let a man get to base or make a run. I did it by not putting a thing on the ball. You could have read the trade mark on it the way I lobbed it over the plate. A baby could have hit 'em. Schalk was wise the moment I started pitching. Then, in one of the games, the first I think, there was a man on first and the Reds' batter hit a slow grounder to me. I could have made a double play out of it without any trouble at all. But I was slow—slow enough to prevent the double play. It did not necessarily look crooked on my part. It is hard to tell when a game is on the square and when it is not. A player can make a crooked error that will look on the square as easy as he can make a square one. Sometimes the square ones look crooked.

"Then, in the fourth game, which I also lost, on a tap to the box I deliberately threw badly to first, allowing a man to get on. At another time, I intercepted a throw from the outfield and deliberately bobbled it, allowing a run to score. All the runs scored against me were due to my own deliberate errors. In those two games, I did not try to win. . . .

"I've lived a thousand years in the last twelve months. I would not have done that thing for a million dollars. Now I've lost everything, job, reputation, everything. My friends all bet on the Sox. I knew it, but I couldn't tell them. I had to double-cross them.

"I'm through with baseball. I'm going to lose myself if I can and start life over again."

Cicotte testified for two hours and eleven minutes. He sobbed bitterly through much of his testimony. Part of the time, he was barely audible. The jury listened raptly, deeply moved by his anguish. There was not one moment during which the Jury pressed him in order to elicit further evidence. By the time they recessed for lunch, Cicotte had exhausted himself.

Judge MacDonald, however, was not satisfied. He was looking to break down the door that would expose the whole frame-up. He wanted to catch all the big boys involved and run them through his mill. He wanted evidence, not a statement of *mea culpa*. He wanted Cicotte to tell him of meetings with Arnold Rothstein *et al,* of a well-integrated, highly organized plot, naming names and dates and places. He wanted to lead the Grand Jury to a spread of indictments that would bunch them all into one big net, an ironclad case for the State to prosecute.

But Cicotte had failed him. For gamblers, Cicotte had mentioned Burns and Maharg. Did Cicotte expect the Judge to believe this whole project was manipulated by those two punks? He accused Cicotte directly: "I thought you were going to tell us about the gamblers!"

Cicotte had nothing to say about gamblers. He insisted that this was all he knew. He had told them enough to reveal the plot, hoping, thereby, to satisfy their need for exposure and his own need for expiation. For his own protection—and that of his wife and children—he told them no more.

Ray Schalk, White Sox catcher, spent most of the morning outside the Grand Jury room, waiting to testify. He did not know what was keeping them. Then he heard that Cicotte was inside.

Schalk's first encounter with Cicotte had been back in 1912. Cicotte was already a veteran when Schalk first came to Chicago, a small, baby-faced twenty-year-old who might have passed for sixteen. At training camp, down in Texas, Schalk was resting a sprained ankle, watching the proceedings from the grandstand. He saw Cicotte talking to a park policeman, pointing in his direction. The policeman then came over to the stands and told him to move out. "No kids allowed here, sonny!" Schalk had protested, trying to convince him he was a big-leaguer. The policeman grabbed him by the arm, with some sardonic wisecrack about his being the President of the United States, and threw him out. Schalk looked back, hoping for the support of the others, but all he saw was their laughter, especially Cicotte's.

Schalk looked forward to the day when he could be a major-league manager. From his earliest awareness of his own talent, he decided that that was right for him.

Comiskey appreciated ballplayers like him, the smart, aggressive, willful men. He didn't like Comiskey, but he always tried to stay on his side. Comiskey was cheap. Comiskey underpaid him. Every year, Schalk hated to face signing that skimpy contract and the cold-turkey dictums of Harry Grabiner. But he never argued salary. He never wanted Comiskey to think he wasn't loyal.

When the Grand Jury convened, he faced the question as squarely as he could: What should he do? He didn't relish the prospect of talking, but what else could he do? If he didn't talk, could he be punished as an accomplice? Was it still worse to be a stooly? What, in the long run, was best for himself?

Then he heard the excitement as the door of the Grand Jury room opened. In a moment, the news was out: Cicotte had confessed!

Schalk turned and quickly left the building. He felt no great sense of relief, even though this took the onus off him. He merely wondered about what was going to happen now.

He was mobbed by reporters. "What were you going to tell them, Ray?"

"We're still in a pennant race. But at the close of the season, I'll have plenty to tell."

"How about reports that *this* season's games were fixed?"

"I won't say anything at all now!" Schalk snapped, and walked away.

9

After leaving Comiskey Park following Monday's ball game, Joe Jackson had gotten himself good and drunk. If he was going to be confused, he figured he might as well be confused and drunk. When he awoke on Tuesday morning, he was confused and hung-over. The Sox had the day off. He thought maybe he'd call Lefty Williams and go to a movie. Nothing much else was happening. But he knew that this was crazy; trouble was brewing all over the place, bubbling over the rim of the pot. Sooner or later, he'd have to do something.

He missed his wife, Katie, who was home in Savannah. He needed someone to talk to. Katie would tell him what to do. He knew he was in trouble, serious trouble.

He reached for the phone and called the Criminal Courts Building, asked for Judge MacDonald. The Judge was in session with the Jury and could not be reached. He spoke briefly to the bailiff and told him who it was. In a few minutes, the Judge was on the phone.

"This is Joe Jackson, Judge . . ."

"What is it, Jackson? Are you ready to talk?"

"Look, Judge, you've got to control this thing . . . whatever they're digging up, I can tell you, I'm an honest man!"

"I can tell *you,* Jackson, I know you are not!"

Jackson heard the phone go dead. That worried him. He went downstairs for coffee and ran into Risberg and Felsch. The word was out that Cicotte had gone over and was spitting up his guts. So that was how the Judge knew so much. Jackson started to sweat. Risberg studied him. "Just keep your own mouth shut, that's all, Joe," the Swede barked. "I swear to you, I'll kill you if you squawk!"

Jackson spent the rest of the morning kicking himself around his room. Finally, too desperate to do otherwise, he called Judge MacDonald again. This time, the Judge did not hang up on him. He asked Jackson to come over and tell his story.

Before he got there, Jackson fortified himself with another coating of alcoholic armor. The rube from Brandon Mill, South Carolina, knew he was walking into a den of lions. He wanted to make the feast as painless as possible. Like Cicotte, it never occurred to him to get his own lawyer.

And, as with Cicotte, Alfred Austrian was waiting for him. He took Jackson into a vacant office and talked to him like a Dutch uncle. He asked him if he was going to confess? Jackson mumbled his innocence. He had nothing to confess. He merely wanted to tell what he knew. He repeated that he'd wanted to talk right from the start. He had tried to get to Comiskey after the Series. He even had his wife write letters.

Austrian shook his head. He told Jackson it would go bad for him to lie about anything. Cicotte had already told them the whole story. To deny his involvement would prejudice the Grand Jury. Did Joe understand that?

Sure, he understood. But he had to stay out of trouble. That's what mattered to him. He just didn't want to get into trouble. Austrian assured him he would be safe if he told everything he knew. That was the only way to protect himself. It was the honest way, to make a clean breast of it. The State was only interested in clearing out the gamblers, not the ballplayers. This was the way to clean up baseball. Joe's confession would help the State. They would all appreciate his co-operation. This way, he would never be prosecuted. The only way he'd be used would be as a witness.

Jackson finally agreed. He would talk. Just as long as nothing would happen to him.

Austrian put a large sheet of paper in front of him, handed him a pen. He pointed to a line on the bottom, told him to sign his name. Jackson hesitated; he didn't want to sign anything. Austrian told him not to worry. His signature was not going to change anything. The Grand Jury wanted it from all witnesses. Again, Jackson was too confused to argue. He was batting in another man's ball park. He signed.

Then Austrian, with the waiver of immunity in his brief case, took him downstairs to Judge MacDonald's chambers.

Hartley Replogle sat through the meeting in Judge MacDonald's chambers and said nothing. The events of the past few weeks were coming to a climax; the headlines would be big and shocking; the confessions would lead to new exposures. He had reason to feel excited over the leading part he had played. But this was saddening. These confessions rocked him. He looked at Jackson, pathetic and helpless. Replogle had seen him play ball a number of times, responded to the incredible power of the man at the plate. Now, with a shirt and a tie on, the ballplayer was nothing. Red-eyed, unshaven, smelling of alcohol, the great man on spikes was just another frightened pigeon in the Judge's chambers. Jackson sat there dumb and helpless, and they did what they wanted with him.

To Replogle, the players were victims. The owners poured out a stream of pious, pompous verbiage about how pure they were. The gamblers said nothing, kept themselves hidden, protected themselves —and when they said anything, it was strictly for cash, with immunity, no less. But the ballplayers didn't even know enough to call a lawyer. They only knew how to play baseball.

The Judge was stern with Jackson. He warned him not to deceive the Jury about anything, for if he did, they could get him for perjury. Jackson promised. He would tell what he knew. They took him downstairs to the Jury Room, Replogle leading the way. The great ballplayer approached the crowded corridor and seemed to shudder. Replogle patted him on the shoulder, trying to reassure him. He saw the battery of newspaper photographers with their harassing flash bulbs. He called to them to back away, to leave Jackson alone. But they set up a wall in front of the doors and began the agonizing process of picture-taking. Jackson hung his head, covering his face from the brilliant flashes of light. Then he suddenly exploded. He began cursing them, cursing gamblers, cursing baseball, cursing the whole damn world. He charged through the crowd like a plunging fullback, ironically seeking sanctuary in the Grand Jury room.

After they swore him in, he began talking. They asked him questions, leading into the story of the fix. He told them of the gradual feeling-out by Gandil and Risberg. They'd been at him for days. They could make some big dough. They would give him $20,000 for helping out. It was easy; all he had to do was go along with it; let a ball drop a few feet in front of him; don't hit the big one with men on. He could look good and still play badly. Twenty thousand dollars.

Finally he'd agreed, but he got only $5,000—$5,000 in a dirty envelope, delivered to his room by Lefty Williams. He'd get the other

$15,000 after the Series—after he had delivered the goods. He took Lefty's word for it.

Then, after the Series, he'd protested to Gandil and Risberg about that. He wanted the rest of his dough. If not, he was going to squawk. They told him: "You poor simp, go ahead and squawk. Where do you get off if you do? We'll all say you're a liar. Every honest ballplayer in the world will say you're a liar. You're out of luck. Some of the boys were promised more than you and got less!"

Jackson rambled on for almost two hours. He told the Jury how he hadn't played good baseball, despite his incredible .375 World Series average, and record 12 base hits. The Judge thanked him for his testimony. He came out smiling. The Jury had made him feel honest again. "I got a big load off my chest!" he told the two bailiffs beside him.

Again Replogle was protective. "Leave him alone," he demanded of the reporters. "He's come through beautifully and we don't want him bothered."

But Jackson still felt like talking. It was as if he had to pour it all out; his confusion, his anger, his bitterness, his fear. "They've hung it on me. But I don't care what happens now. I guess I'm through with baseball. I wasn't wise enough, like Chick, to beat them to it. But some of them will sweat before the show is over." Jackson was like a little boy, hitting wildly back at the big adult world. "They" were all the people who were causing his troubles: the legal machinery of Cook County, Illinois; the reporters; the club magnates—all lumped together into one word. His admiration went to Gandil, the man who got away with it.

Then he added, "Now Risberg threatens to bump me off if I squawk. That's why I've got the bailiffs with me. I'm not under arrest yet, and I've got the idea that after what I told them, old Joe Jackson isn't going to jail. But I'm not going to get far from my protectors until this thing blows over. Swede is a hard guy."

10

Charles Comiskey did not hear either Cicotte's or Jackson's confessions. He remained in his office at Comiskey Park all day, inaccessible to all but a few friends. Harry Grabiner was there to handle a sudden flood of sympathetic messages. A few matters, however, required the Old Roman's attention. Notably, the suspension of the eight ballplayers. Comiskey dictated the telegram that went out to them—and, of course, to the public:

CHICAGO, ILL. TO CHARLES RISBERG, FRED McMULLIN ETC.

YOU AND EACH OF YOU ARE HEREBY NOTIFIED OF YOUR INDEFINITE SUSPENSION AS A MEMBER OF THE CHICAGO AMERICAN LEAGUE BASEBALL CLUB. YOUR SUSPENSION IS BROUGHT ABOUT BY INFORMATION WHICH HAS JUST COME TO ME, DIRECTLY INVOLVING YOU AND EACH OF YOU IN THE BASEBALL SCANDAL NOW BEING INVESTIGATED BY THE GRAND JURY OF COOK COUNTY, RESULTING FROM THE WORLD SERIES OF 1919.

IF YOU ARE INNOCENT OF ANY WRONGDOING, YOU AND EACH OF YOU WILL BE REINSTATED; IF YOU ARE GUILTY, YOU WILL BE RETIRED FROM ORGANIZED BASEBALL FOR THE REST OF YOUR LIVES IF I CAN ACCOMPLISH IT.

UNTIL THERE IS A FINALITY TO THIS INVESTIGATION, IT IS DUE TO THE PUBLIC THAT I TAKE THIS ACTION EVEN THOUGH IT COSTS CHICAGO THE PENNANT.

> CHICAGO AMERICAN LEAGUE BB CLUB
> BY CHARLES A. COMISKEY

In the short span of the preceding eight hours, the Old Roman appeared to have suffered a physical collapse. His huge frame, normally erect, slumped dejectedly. For a man who had carried his sixty years lightly, he suddenly seemed terribly old.

Later in the day, Harry Grabiner brought in a telegram he thought his boss would want to see:

PHILADELPHIA, PA. I ACCEPT YOUR OFFER TO TELL WHAT I
KNOW OF THE CROOKED WORLD SERIES OF 1919 AND WILL GO TO
CHICAGO AND TESTIFY PROVIDED YOU HAVE A CERTIFIED CHECK
FOR $10,000 WITH HARVEY WOODRUFF, SPORTS EDITOR OF THE
CHICAGO TRIBUNE, TO BE TURNED OVER TO ME AFTER I TESTIFY.
PLEASE ANSWER.

BILLY MAHARG

Grabiner stood there while Comiskey read it. Of one thing Grabiner felt certain: Comiskey had no intention of paying $10,000 to
Maharg or, presumably, to anyone else. It had occurred to him earlier
that the one man who might legitimately claim the reward was Cicotte!
If Grabiner enjoyed this little irony, he kept it to himself.

Comiskey tossed the telegram on his desk and shook his head.

Kid Gleason looked at his boss and felt frightened for himself.
There was something so monstrous about this business, he sensed his
inability to cope with it. He had been in baseball all his life; nothing
else mattered to him. He hadn't made a lot of money like Comiskey.
He had only his talent as a baseball manager to sell. But this was his
ball club, too. He had a right to say that he helped make a great
pitcher out of Cicotte. He developed Lefty Williams. He had nursed
Happy Felsch into a superb outfielder, some said even better than Tris
Speaker. And above all, he'd created in Buck Weaver the best-hitting
and -fielding third baseman in the game. Out of his efforts, then, a
great team had emerged—only to sell out. It was something he would
never be able to understand.

He left Comiskey's office to face the reporters. "I'm going to take
my ball club to St. Louis for a three-game series with the Browns.
That's all that's left—three games. We'll do what we can to win the
flag. . . ."

He wanted to leave, but the reporters kept pumping him with
questions. What did he think of the confessions?

"This thing is good for baseball. I'm glad it came to a head. Now
it will all be cleared up."

Gleason had to say that. It was what Comiskey had told him to
say.

The official baseball world turned a shocked face for the world to see. It was as if they never dreamed that such a thing were possible. "It takes my breath away!" said Ban Johnson to the press. "I'll have to have more time to think it over. . . ."

Colonel Jacob Ruppert, part owner of the New York Yankees, was quick to endorse the indictments. He added that no World Series should be played if the Sox should win the pennant. But a few hours later he saw an opportunity for a grandiose gesture and quickly reversed himself. He wired Comiskey and released his message to the press:

YOUR ACTION IN SUSPENDING THE PLAYERS NOT ONLY CHALLENGES OUR ADMIRATION BUT EXCITES OUR SYMPATHY AND DEMANDS OUR IMMEDIATE ASSISTANCE. YOU ARE MAKING A TERRIBLE SACRIFICE TO PRESERVE THE INTEGRITY OF THE GAME. THEREFORE, IN ORDER THAT YOU MAY PLAY OUT YOUR SCHEDULE, AND, IF NECESSARY, THE WORLD SERIES, OUR ENTIRE CLUB IS AT YOUR DISPOSAL.

It was, in fact, a useless offer. The rules of professional baseball clearly stated that a player had to be part of his team before August 31 in order to play in the World Series.

Harry Frazee of Boston followed Ruppert. He said it was the duty of every club in the American League to give one of its players. The Red Sox would make their offer immediately.

Comiskey released his own statement through Harry Grabiner: "We'll play out the schedule if we have to get Chinamen to replace the suspended players!"

11

Abe Attell had reason to be worried. All of a sudden, too many things were happening. His name was repeatedly plastered all over the papers. He hadn't had as much publicity since he'd been featherweight champion of the world. This was more than he'd bargained for. It made him look like some sort of crook. Then, this morning, the early knock at the door. That was always bad news. Didn't they know how he hated to get up before ten? A message for him. Maclay Hoyne, the D.A. from Chicago, staying at the Waldorf Astoria, wanted to see him.

Attell hurried across 47th Street and Broadway en route to Lindy's. It was where the Times Square crowd hung out, and the Little Champ was accustomed to conducting a good part of his business there, as well as much of his social life. He saw a number of his friends smoking cigars in front of the shrine. He was hoping he could find his lawyer, William J. Fallon.

There was nothing particularly unique about the greeting he received from the boys in the street. That is, until the big glass door of the restaurant opened and a man stepped out to join them. He was an old friend of Attell's, but he wasn't feeling friendly. He had lost $2,000 on the Series. He simply walked up to Attell, drew back his big right fist, and smashed the ex-featherweight champion of the world squarely in the mouth. Attell saw the punch coming, but too late to roll with it. It sent him reeling to the street. He was still a young man. It was eight years since his retirement, but he had not gained a pound. He always stayed in good shape. But this time, he didn't get a chance to show it. The others broke up the fight before it got going—perhaps out of sympathy for the assailant.

Attell was left fuming. They calmed him down with a warning: there was bad talk going around town. A few heavy World Series losers were really looking for him. One of them, it was said, was not averse to a little gunplay. . . .

Inside Lindy's, a reporter spotted him holding a bloody handkerchief to his face, and followed him to the men's room.

"Who hit you, Abe—and why?"

"I ran into a door."

"Sure. A door with knuckles."

"Look, wise guy—I know what you're thinking. But it ain't right. Put this in your paper. That punk from Philly is a rotten liar!"

"Who, Billy Maharg?"

"Yeah. Him. You know what? Arnold Rothstein is the man behind these stories. And I am surprised at this because I've been a good friend of Arnold's. He is simply trying to pass the buck to me.

It won't go. A.R. is trying to whitewash himself. Nobody can pass the buck to me. That Philly guy's story of the fake telegram and all the rest is all bunk!

"I have done many things for Rothstein. When he didn't have a cent I fed him and boarded him and even suffered a busted nose defending him from a bootblack in Saratoga. We've not been on the best of terms for the last year, but I didn't think it would end up this way.

"Well, I'm retaining a lawyer to take care of my interests, and in a day or so, I'll tell what I know of this thing and it will shoot the lid sky high!"

William J. Fallon, the famous New York lawyer, was not at Lindy's. Fallon, referred to as The Great Mouthpiece, was more or less permanently retained by Arnold Rothstein. And though Abe Attell was smart enough to seek shrewd counsel, he was not smart enough to realize that in a clash of interests between these two clients, The Great Mouthpiece would show deference to The Big Bankroll. But then, Rothstein had arranged it all that way. Fallon was to take care of Attell, seemingly as an act of friendship. Fallon didn't care, so long as Rothstein paid the bill.

Fallon had read Maharg's statement, and was fully aware of Attell's problem. But when Abe recounted his recent skirmish, including what he had told the reporter, Fallon exploded. It was stupid for Attell to talk, especially to the press. But to Attell, it was either his neck or Rothstein's. He would prefer to let A.R. take care of himself.

Fallon had one thing on his mind: keeping Attell away from the Chicago Grand Jury. Every time the Little Champ opened his mouth, it brought that subpoena closer to him. Fallon already knew how much Rothstein would hate that. Put a man like Attell on the stand and anything could happen. Fallon never had met a shady character who wasn't terrified of a courtroom.

He told Attell to keep out of sight. From then on, Fallon would do the talking.

Fallon's picture of the problem was clear enough. There was nothing particularly strange about it, except perhaps from the publicity point of view. Professional baseball was a national institution (unlike A.R.'s other involvements, such as horse racing, bootlegging,

ouses, money-lending) and the public press liked to play
it came to baseball. Fallon had to keep Rothstein's reputation clean, if such a thing were possible.

Rothstein was not at home. His wife, Carolyn, was. Fallon told
her what to say when the reporters came—and he was certain they
would. She should tell them that Maharg's story was essentially correct . . . viz., that Arnold had nothing to do with the World Series
fix.

Fallon then turned to the principal matter of the moment: Maharg. That man had to be silenced. Not because he was full of
dangerous information. It was simply better policy to cut off the
flow of evidence as quickly as possible. A question of inertia: body in
motion tends to remain in motion. If Maharg sang to the Grand Jury,
ten other punks might want to sing, too. If Maharg suddenly decided
not to, twenty other punks would get the message.

Fallon got on the phone and called a friend of his in Philadelphia. . . .

In Lufkin, Texas, Arnold "Chick" Gandil was languishing in a
county hospital, having just been operated on for appendicitis. He
had sold his new home in Los Angeles three weeks before, settling for
a $6,100 price, though it had cost him considerably more. This had
been his wife's doing. She had been eager to return to her home in
Texas. Gandil had submitted, bought a new car, and had driven her
and his daughter down, nursing a bellyache all the way. The news reports of the last two days had not made him feel any better. He gave
his doctor a statement for the reporters outside his room: "It's a lot
of bunk. Nothing to it. They're trying to make a goat out of somebody. And I'm telling the world, that somebody won't be me!"

12

Claude "Lefty" Williams had spent part of the previous evening with
his friend, Joe Jackson. The other part, he had spent with his wife.
Together, they decided that he should do what Jackson had done.

The logic was simple enough: there was no longer anything to be gained by silence. The telegram of suspension lay on the table. Perhaps, as Jackson had said, their statements would put them in a favorable light with the law. If Williams was skeptical about that, it was also true he had nothing better to go on. He was twenty-seven years old with a well-trained left arm. He wanted to be able to use it for another ten good years.

He dressed quickly and went downtown to Alfred Austrian's office. He told the lawyer he was ready to talk.

Austrian was very pleasant with him. He told Williams how sorry he was about all this, and how much he had admired his great pitching skill. Williams was shy in the face of this imposing man. He had been with the White Sox for five years and had never met Austrian before this. Nor had he seen anything quite like this elaborate office. He nodded his thanks and tried to smile. When he asked if it might not be a good idea if he got himself a lawyer before he talked, Austrian quickly advised him not to. "There are times when you can get along better without one. Of course, if you want one . . ." Williams hesitated. Austrian leaped into the breach by assuring him that it really wasn't necessary. After all, the State's Attorney's office had promised to take care of Cicotte and Jackson. They would treat Williams the same way.

Austrian then suggested that perhaps it would be wise if Williams made his statement right here. The atmosphere in the Grand Jury room was, at best, rather disturbing and certainly not conducive to clear thinking. It would, of course, be necessary to repeat it for the Grand Jury, but then it would not be jumbled by all the pressures and questions imposed on him. Williams agreed.

"My name is Claude Williams. I am the same Claude Williams who lately has been a member of the Chicago American League Baseball Club. I am making this statement of my own free will and volition. . . ."

Austrian then proceeded to ask him questions. A stenographer took it all down.

Q: I want you to mention the names of the gamblers, the places, the times, and everyone you talked to about the whole subject.

A: This situation was first brought up to me in New York. Mr. Gandil called me to one side, out in front of the Hotel Ansonia, and put this thing to me. . . . After coming back to Chicago, I was called down to the Warner Hotel where the eight members that are named —not eight, I will take that back: I will name them for you: Eddie Cicotte, Chick Gandil, Buck Weaver, and Happy Felsch, and two fellows introduced as Brown and Sullivan.

Q: They were the gamblers?

A: They were supposed to be the gamblers, or fellows that were fixing it for the gamblers—one of the two, they didn't say which.

Q: Sullivan was from Boston, wasn't he?

A: They didn't say. They said they'd come from New York. They introduced themselves as Brown and Sullivan from New York.

Q: And you would know them if you saw them?

A: I would, sure. I would know them.

Q: Go on.

A: I was informed that whether or not I took any action, the games would be fixed.

Q: Who informed you of that?

A: Chick Gandil.

Q: Right then and there?

A: No, not right then and there. Just right after that. Just as I got in the hall. So I told them anything they did would be agreeable to me: if it was going to be done anyway, that I had no money. I may as well get what I could. I haven't seen those gamblers from that day to this. We were supposed to get—Gandil told me we were supposed to get . . . what was it? . . . I was supposed to get ten thousand dollars after the second game, when we got back to Chicago, but I did not get this until after the fourth game; and he then said the gamblers had called it off: and I figured then that there was a double cross someplace. On the second trip to Cincinnati, for the sixth and seventh games, Cicotte and I had a conference. I told him we were double-crossed and I was going out to win if there was any possible chance. Cicotte said he was the same way. Gandil had informed me in Cincinnati (before the Series began) that Bill Burns and Abe Attell was also fixing where we would get one hundred thousand dollars, making twenty thousand dollars more. That I never received.

Q: You had a meeting in Cincinnati with the ballplayers? Where was that?

A: That was in the hotel.

Q: Who was there?

A: In Chick Gandil's room? We never had a meeting. We just went up there. We just dropped in one at a time; there was Buck Weaver, Eddie Cicotte, Happy Felsch, and myself.

Q: Was Weaver there?

A: Yes.

Q: And what conversation did you have there?

A: We asked him [Gandil] when he was going to get the hundred thousand that Burns and Attell was supposed to give us. He says 'They are supposed to give me after each game, supposed to give me twenty or thirty thousand dollars after each game,' which, if they gave him that, I know nothing of at all.

Q: When did he say you would get some money?

A: He didn't say. He didn't make no statement. I was supposed at first to get so much, get ten thousand dollars after the second game [Williams lost it 4–2]. I didn't receive it until the fourth game. I got only five.

Q: Did you ever ask Gandil or anyone else——

A: (interrupting) I never even talked to Gandil from that day to this.

Q: Did you ever talk to any of the other ballplayers?

A: I never talked to no one.

Q: I mean about it.

A: I never talked to no one.

Q: Did any of the other ballplayers talk to you about it?

A: They never mentioned it to me.

Q: Do you know how much Weaver got?

A: I could not say.

Q: Did he tell you how much he got?

A: He never did.

Q: Or Felsch?

A: None of the boys ever told me a word of what they got— whether they got a penny or not.

Q: Did you know what games the Sox were to lose for all this money they were getting?

A: Why, they were supposed to lose the first two to Cincinnati, and I never did hear whether they were to lose or win the one with Kerr [third game].

Q: Now, is that all you know about the whole thing?
A: That is all I know.

If Williams was less than completely honest, it was only on the last question that he might have been challenged. Why had he done so badly in the first inning of the last game? What was the nature of the gamblers' approach to him, that they should know in advance that he would have a disastrous first inning? Like Cicotte, he spoke guardedly about events involving the gamblers. If Austrian had any indications of foul play—and he certainly must have had suspicions since Maharg had referred to it specifically—he never pursued it. Even in the Grand Jury, the pitcher was not challenged on this score.

Williams left the Criminal Courts Building and stepped out into the sunshine. It was clear and pleasantly cool. He was glad to be alone. He walked for a while, then took a taxi back to his apartment. There, he ran into Byrd Lynn, the second-string catcher and ex-roomy. The two friends stopped and stared at each other. It was Lynn who finally offered his hand. Williams accepted it and tried to smile. But suddenly tears started rolling down his cheeks. They shook hands; then Lynn, all choked up, backed hurriedly away. They did not say a word to each other at this meeting or ever again.

Williams went upstairs to his wife. He began to wonder seriously what was going to happen to him.

13

The Chicago *American* had on its staff one of those very young newspapermen who could qualify as reporter-at-large. Harry Reutlinger was a warm, witty cynic who learned to come up with remarkable stories that his colleagues would never dream of getting. On this sunny morning, he sat in the newspaper offices reading the stories of the World Series scandal. Somehow, they made little sense to him. The facts, as reported, did not jell. They appeared to be slapped together by hearsay and smatterings of conversations, either over-heard or gathered on the run. After reading several papers, Reutlinger noted discrepancies in their treatment of the same basic story. The Joe Jackson confession, for example, was quoted four different ways by four different papers. What had he really said? And what was the real story behind these ballplayers?

To Reutlinger, what was clearly lacking was a simple, solid inter-view. A full, rich, uninhibited statement by one of those boys who could spill out what was on his mind. The trouble was, this news-paperman knew little of the baseball world. But such a problem never stopped him. He walked over to the Sports Desk and asked one question:

"Who is the dumbest guy of those eight players?"

The reply, after a brief hesitation, was Felsch.

Reutlinger asked, "The one they call 'Happy'?"

"That's right," was the reply.

Reutlinger smiled. He sensed he was already on the right track. "Where does one find this happy chap?" he asked further.

"The Warner Hotel," he was told.

Less than an hour later, he knocked on Felsch's door. Under his arm was a bottle of good Scotch whisky, wrapped sloppily in a copy of the morning *American*. Felsch smiled. He was in his bath-robe, and had been soaking a swollen big toe.

Reutlinger smiled back. "Hap," he said. "I can cure that bad toe." And he withdrew the wrapping from the bottle of Scotch. "All we need is a couple of glasses. . . ."

Felsch was too friendly a man not to warm up to a person like this. Reutlinger, himself, delighted in talking to the ballplayer. He told Felsch he was a writer. He wanted to understand what went on with this rotten scandal. He thought the public would like to know. By God, why shouldn't Felsch tell his own story?

For the life of him, Felsch couldn't figure out why not. He began to spill it all out:

"Well, the beans are all spilled and I think that I am through with baseball. I got my five thousand and I suppose the others got theirs, too. If you say anything about me, don't make it appear that I'm try-ing to put up an alibi. I'm not. I'm as guilty as any of them. We all were in it alike.

"I don't know what I'm going to do now. I have been a ballplayer during the best years of my life, and I never got into any other kind of business. I'm going to hell, I guess. I intend to hang around Chicago awhile until I see how this thing is going to go. Then, maybe, I'll go back to Milwaukee."

The smile that gave him his nickname faded as he considered his prospects.

"I wish that I hadn't gone into it. I guess we all do. We have more than earned the few dollars they gave us for turning crooked. All this season the memory of the World Series has been hanging over us. The talk that we threw games this year is bunk. We knew we were suspected and we tried to be square. But a guy can't be crooked part of the time and square the rest of the time. We knew that sooner or later somebody was going to turn up the whole deal.

"Cicotte's story is true in every detail. I don't blame him for telling. He knew the Grand Jury had a case against him and there wouldn't have been any object in holding out. He did the best thing to do under the circumstances. I was ready to confess myself yesterday, but I didn't have the courage to be the first to tell. I never knew where my five thousand came from. It was left in my locker at the clubhouse and there was always a good deal of mystery about the way it was dealt out. That was one of the reasons why we never knew who double-crossed us on the split of the hundred thousand. It was to have been an even split. But we never got it.

"Who was responsible for the double cross I couldn't say. I suspected Gandil because he was the wisest one of the lot and had sense enough to get out of baseball before the crash came. But I have heard since that it was Abe Attell. Maybe it was Attell. I don't know him, but I had heard that he was mixed up with the gamblers who were backing us to lose.

"I didn't want to get in on the deal at first. I had always received square treatment from 'Commy' and it didn't look quite right to throw him down. But when they let me in on the idea, too many men were involved. I didn't like to be a squealer and I knew that if I stayed out of the deal and said nothing about it they would go ahead without me and I'd be that much money out without accomplishing anything. I'm not saying this to pass the buck to the others. I suppose that if

I had refused to enter the plot and had stood my ground I might have stopped the whole deal. We all share the blame equally.

"I'm not saying that I double-crossed the gamblers, but I had nothing to do with the loss of the World Series. The breaks just came so that I was not given a chance to throw the game. The records show that I played a pretty good game. I know I missed one terrible fly ball, but you can believe me or not, I was trying to catch that ball. I lost it in the sun and made a long run for it, and looked foolish when it fell quite a bit away from where it ought to be. The other men in the know thought that I had lost the ball deliberately and that I was putting on a clown exhibition. They warned me after the game to be more careful about the way I muffed flies.

"Whether I could actually have gotten up enough nerve to carry out my part in throwing the game I can't say. The gold looked good to all of us, and I suppose we could have gone ahead with the double cross. But as I said, I was given no chance to decide. When we went into that conference in Cicotte's room, he said that it would be easy for us to pull the wool over the eyes of the public, that we were expert ballplayers, and that we could throw the game scientifically. It looked easy to me, too. It's just as easy for a good player to miss a ball as it is to catch it—just a slow start or a stumble at the right time or a slow throw and the job is done. But you can't get away with that stuff indefinitely. You may be able to fool the public, but you can't fool yourself."

Reutlinger then asked him: "How did Cicotte get ten thousand dollars?"

"Because he was wise enough to stand pat for it, that's all. Cicotte has brains. The rest of us roundheads just took their word for the proposition that we were to get an even split on the hundred thousand. Cicotte was going to make sure of his share from the jump off. He made them come across with it.

"I'm going to see Buck Weaver and get him to go over to see the State's Attorney with me. I'm going to get through with all of this. It will be a load off my mind to tell everything I know. It's been hell for me. I have a bad foot—the big toe is all smashed and it kept me awake all night. And then on top of that came this action by the Grand Jury.

"As for hiring a lawyer and putting up a defense in this case, I haven't made any plans. I haven't talked to anybody about this case but you, and I want to see Weaver and Williams before arranging for a defense.

"I got five thousand dollars. I could have got just about that much by being on the level if the Sox had won the Series. And now I'm out of baseball—the only profession I knew anything about, and a lot of gamblers have gotten rich. The joke seems to be on us."

Harry Reutlinger was moved. How much of Felsch's story was honest and accurate, he had no real idea. What evoked his admiration was the genuine remorse and lack of self-pity. Felsch was guilty, yet he had pride in himself. The entire confession was devoid of anger or bitterness. He had simply done a bad thing and was ready to take the consequences. If he admired Cicotte for his good sense in getting paid in advance, he did not really believe that Cicotte was anything but an idiot like himself. Reutlinger had seen enough of America to know that the written rules were rigid and righteous, while the real rules were often wide open and dirty. Such he assumed, were the rules of baseball itself. You played hard and got away with as much as you could, legal or otherwise. Wasn't Ty Cobb supposed to be the greatest of them all at that game? It was all Felsch ever knew, he guessed. To the people of America, professional baseball was clean and honest and Reutlinger had been naïve enough to believe that himself, though he'd never given it much thought. Now he sensed that it never really had been, that Felsch and the others had taken no real departure from the only reality they knew. Not that it could be justified or excused. It was, at best, stupid and downright dishonest. But it opened the door to an examination of just how dishonest the men who ran this great national pastime must be. Felsch had said, "I had always received square treatment from 'Commy' and it didn't look right to throw him down." Reutlinger knew what that meant: square treatment from Comiskey was merely honest exploitation. Felsch and the others must have hated Comiskey for their own assortment of reasons, for a decent man would not betray another without some basic cause for bitterness. Call that Reutlinger's law; he saw in Felsch's defense of his boss only the honest desire not to hide his guilt.

What struck Reutlinger was that Happy Felsch was completely without basic evil. He wasn't even a dishonest type. He would never steal a dime from you, even if you left him alone with an unlocked safe. He would probably stake you with his last five dollars. He had merely been sucked into a plot for some easy money in a society that thrived on the worship of it. The cruel irony was that the unseen men who used him—the gamblers—had gotten rich on his broken back.

"The joke," as Felsch so artfully put it, "seems to be on us."

Reutlinger went back to his office and reread the reports of Cicotte's and Jackson's confessions. He compared them with Felsch's. The conclusions were dismaying. He was struck by the almost incredible lack of organization that surrounded the entire fix. One ballplayer did not know what the other was doing. Jackson, for example, said that the third game was fixed, but that they won it anyway. Williams did not even know. No one checked on the distribution of the money. They never sought to confer with one another except in rare, isolated instances. They had maintained a more rigid silence within their own group than did the gamblers with those outside the fix. If Williams knew little of the inner workings, Jackson seemed to know less. Felsch could offer no report as to what happened. But most of all, Reutlinger could not understand the curious ignorance as to where the money went—the whole reason for the frame-up. It was as if these four men wanted to pretend that the whole thing was not really happening at all. They simply resigned themselves to what they called the "double cross" and let the Series and the money slip away from them. They were "roundheads," as Felsch described them, passive participants in their own destruction. They had spoken a halfhearted "yes" to the persuasive Gandil, and then let happen whatever might happen.

IV **THE IMPACT**

"Never bet on anything that can talk!"

Nick the Greek

1

The Hot Stove league has opened
Ahead of time this year;
'Twill be the hottest season
Of all its long career.

George Phair
Chicago *Herald and Examiner*
September 29, 1920

As the impact of the confessions sank in, the American people were at first shocked, then sickened. There was hardly a major newspaper that did not cry out its condemnation and despair. Henceforth, the ballplayers involved were called the Black Sox. But the scandal was a betrayal of more than a set of ball games, even more than of the sport itself. It was a crushing blow at American pride. The year before, America had won the war in the image of nobility and humanity. "Saving Europe from the Hun" was a sacrificial act. Our pride in victory was the essence of American pride in itself. Baseball was a manifestation of the greatest of America at play. It was our national game; its stars were national heroes, revered by kids and adults alike, in all classes of our society. In the public mind, the image was pure and patriotic. The game had become part of our culture, intruding on our very speech patterns: "He began life with *two strikes* on him. . . . I'll take a *rain check* on that lunch. . . ."

Now, suddenly, that pride was shattered. The National Pastime was nothing more than another show of corruption. To a kid—as to many adults—it seemed terribly indicative. If baseball was corrupt, then *anything* might be—and probably was. If you could not trust the honesty of a big-league world series, what *could* you trust?

There is no way to gauge the extent of the damage on the American psyche. It is impossible to add up bitterness like a batting average. How great was the layer of cynicism that settled over the nation? How many kids developed tolerance for a lie, for a betrayal, for corruption itself?

The scandal touched all strata of American life. Newspapers dramatized its destructive effect on children, but adults, even intellectuals, sensed its cutting impact. Ring Lardner, for one, was deeply hurt by this full, final realization of his worst suspicions. His adoration for the White Sox disintegrated; his love for professional baseball began to fade with it. In time, he stopped reporting baseball, even stopped going to ball games. The scandal scarred him, leaving a wound that would remain tender for the rest of his life. Significantly, he never wrote a column on the fix or a word about any of its participants. The disillusion, however, was undoubtedly a contributing element to Lardner's bitter portrayal of sporting figures in his later short stories.

There was something almost prophetic about the scandal. The 1920's, a decade of unprecedented crime, corruption, and immorality, were just beginning.

"Say it ain't so, Joe . . . say it ain't so." It was like a last, desperate plea for faith itself.

A week later, Chicago kids were hollering derisively: "Play bail!" in lieu of the usual cry to begin a game. . . .

The fans were angry, and in their anger, they did not seek solutions or explanations. They cared less about retribution for the eight men who had sold them out than the ugly fact that the thing had happened at all. If the spokesman for the owners tried to isolate the scandal (clean out the dirty players and baseball will be pure again), the fans were not buying it. You simply could not convince them that Jackson, Weaver, Cicotte *et al* were a combine of evil. It was somehow vaguely understood that the problem was bigger than that.

The owners panicked. The multimillion-dollar structure of organized baseball was on the verge of tottering. The recent history of the game had been too heavily loaded with inner turmoil, dissension, and power politics. The reputation of the business had hit bottom. The New York *Times* editorialized: "Professional baseball is in a bad way, not so much because of the Chicago scandal as because that scandal has provoked it to bringing up all the rumors and suspicions of years past . . . their general effect is to wrinkle the noses of fans who will quit going to ball games if they get the impression that this sort of thing has been going on underground for years."

There was another threat quietly lurking in the background, perhaps the most dangerous of all: the District of Columbia Supreme Court Decision of April, 1919, that marked baseball as a combination in restraint of trade, in violation of the Sherman Anti-Trust Act. The case in point involved the dissolution of the Baltimore Baseball Club in the recently disbanded Federal League. The decision loomed as a threat to the very structure of organized baseball. If it was permitted to stand, baseball would have to dissolve the National Commission; sever relations between the National and American Leagues; completely sever relations between the major and minor leagues; completely revise the contracts by which players were hired, eliminating the ten-day clause and the reserve clause itself.

This decision was now being appealed in the District of Columbia Court of Appeals. It did not take any great imagination to see how greatly the new baseball scandal might affect that Court's ruling.

It was an apt time for panic.

Albert D. Lasker was a prominent Chicago businessman and gentleman sportsman. He was a leading stockholder of the Chicago Cubs. A year before, he had offered a proposal to reorganize the National Commission. It was built on the principle that the game belonged to the public and must be governed by the public—not by the owners. The owners had all but laughed at such a proposal. Now, however, it could be pulled out of the drawer for serious scrutiny:

It became known as the Lasker Plan. To the public at large it seemed like an excellent idea, but wasn't it like putting a lock on the stable door *after* the horse was stolen? And just what difference did it make who was controlling baseball: if baseball really wanted to purge itself of corruption, the owners could have done it under any system.

Charles Comiskey, William Veeck of the Cubs, Barney Dreyfuss of the Pirates, and John McGraw of the Giants sponsored the plan. Comiskey's sponsorship was a logical step in protecting his reputation and preserving the game. It was noteworthy that the first objections should come, not from old baseball men like these, but from the millionaires who had only recently bought their way in. But then, they were the owners in Ban Johnson's camp, and Johnson was not a man to give power away to strangers. The rumors of a fresh war began to spread.

Immediately, however, important names were suggested to head the new Commission. They were among the most prominent people in America: General John Pershing, Senator Hiram Johnson, Judge Kenesaw Mountain Landis, Major General Leonard Wood. It ran like a Presidential nominating committee list for the Republican Party.

2

John Heydler, President of the National League, appeared to be an eager witness before the Grand Jury. He assumed the attitude that the 1919 scandal was something of a freak. It would never have happened, he said, but for the disorganization of the National Commission. If baseball had had a real governing body, the moment anything went wrong, the manager or club owner would have notified the tribunal and justice would have been quickly administered. The present governing body of the major leagues, he sang out, should be relegated to the scrap heap.

The ensuing applause for Heydler was something less than well deserved. It would be difficult to admire any baseball potentate who assumed the role of a bold and perspicacious man after so many years of equivocation. Jury foreman Harry Brigham had some thoughts on this: "Actually, I can sympathize with those boys [the ballplayers]. They were foolish, unsophisticated country boys who yielded to the temptations placed in their path by professional gamblers. There was no one around," he added significantly, "to keep those gamblers away. . . ."

The Jury voted indictments for the two gamblers mentioned by

Lefty Williams: Sullivan and Brown. Sullivan, the Jury was informed, was Joseph "Sport" Sullivan of Boston. The identity of Brown—the name, of course, that Nat Evans had taken—remained a mystery to everyone, exactly as Arnold Rothstein had anticipated.

Late that afternoon, Buck Weaver received a call from Alfred Austrian. The message was simple and direct: Austrian wanted Weaver to go along with the others and confess his involvement. Would Weaver come down to his office either that evening or the first thing in the morning?

Weaver's first reaction was one of fury. He wanted to tell Austrian to go to hell. He swallowed his anger, but declined the offer. He was smart enough to sense that Austrian was his enemy. He was finally and fully aware that he was in a real bind. He had been named by three confessors before the Jury. He would obviously be tied in with the sellout—unless he did something to prevent it.

Impetuously, he called the Assistant State's Attorney, Hartley Replogle. Replogle was sympathetic. Yes, he would listen to Weaver's story, but only if Weaver agreed to waive immunity and appear before the Grand Jury. Replogle assured him that the Jury would also be sympathetic.

Weaver hung up. The lawyers were all such agreeable fellows. They even sounded harmless. But the bodies were dropping like flies.

The shattered remains of the great Chicago White Sox reported at Comiskey Park for a practice session, but Gleason called it off. It was too cold out. Gleason talked to the players for a half hour and turned them loose. He spent the rest of the afternoon discussing with his coaches a makeshift line-up for the coming series with the St. Louis Browns. Mathematically, they were still pennant contenders. In fact, they could jump into the lead with one victory, if Cleveland should lose. But not one man in the park believed they could win it. Not even Gleason himself, for all his show of enthusiasm. The pall of defeat hung over them all. Whatever they felt about the eight men who had "sold them out," they were not pleased by the suspensions. It was too easy to count the money they stood to lose because of them.

The reporters who gathered around these loyal boys, however, did not see things that way. Or, at least, they so indicated in the words they wrote. The line was supposed to be one of hope and a promise of great new prospects. What does money matter when it comes to matters of justice? "You guys are pleased, now, aren't you? You're gonna win that flag without them, isn't that right? No more sellout! No more betrayal!"

Sure, the ballplayers nodded. They were delighted.

Then, as they were breaking up for the day, the locker room door opened and Eddie Cicotte walked in. He stopped, as if surprised that they were still there. This was clearly the last thing he wanted to face. For a moment, he just stood still, trying to decide whether to back out the door or go through with his mission. They all looked at him, then looked away. Cicotte walked directly to his locker as if he were the only man in the room. He took his glove and his shoes and dropped them into his bag.

The question must have occurred to many of them: Where would Cicotte get the chance to use them again?

Newspapers passed on to their readers a neat and simple package, explaining the World Series scandal. Eight evil men had betrayed the purity of the great national pastime. Now that they were exposed, everything was going to be fine. It was a tragedy that a man with the stature and dignity of Charles A. Comiskey should be so victimized.

The San Francisco *Call* headlined a story: "GRAND OLD MAN OF BASEBALL FEELS KEENLY THE INGRATITUDE!"

In New York, the *Evening Sun* lionized him: "It is said that Comiskey has more friends than any owner. In his dealings with the players, he has been like a father to many, the advisor to most, and the liberal square dealer to all. Ofttimes, some of Comiskey's men had cruelly taken advantage of his policy. They had cornered him when they knew he needed them and dragged unreasonable contracts from him. . . ."

"Save Commy" fan clubs were organized. Real baseball fans were urged to send telegrams and write letters in support of the noble hero, to show Commy that they stood behind his fight for honest baseball. It was reported that huge stacks of mail were already pouring in.

On September 29, newspapers supplemented their headlines of the revelations with several secondary stories: It was reported that a "mystery woman," Mrs. Henrietta B. Kelly of 3909 Grand Boulevard in Southside Chicago, the owner of a two-family house where several members of the White Sox were accustomed to staying, had "vital information" for the Grand Jury.

Then, too, in Beloit, Wisconsin, "because of the confessions of Cicotte and Williams, Mr. W. W. Chesbrough today refunded to John Keenan $10 which he had won unfairly. Chesbrough had bet on the Reds."

Meanwhile, Eddie Cicotte was reported missing. "He had checked out of his hotel in Chicago, allegedly to go home to Detroit. But his family said he was still in Chicago, for all they knew. He never told them he was coming home. The Detroit police said there was no sign of him, dead or alive, in that city."

In Philadelphia, Bill Maharg suddenly changed his tactics and clammed up. "As for the reward, that ten-thousand-dollar offer by Comiskey may be on the level, and it may be the bunk. Either way, I don't want it. I didn't talk for money. My idea was to show how nice a double cross was wrung up. People that know me know I wouldn't take that ten grand. And as for people that don't know me, I don't care what they think!' "

Apparently William J. Fallon had done his work well.

3

Illinois State's Attorney Maclay Hoyne had been vacationing in New York for almost two weeks. The Cook County Grand Jury investigation, he had thought, would wither on the vine. The surprising eruption that followed had caught him unaware. For one thing, it made him look bad, a kind of backhanded comment on his absence. He had lost control of his own administration, lame duck though it was; he didn't want his enemies to make political capital out of it.

When he read that the Grand Jury, led by the eager, impetuous Judge Charles MacDonald, was going ahead with indictments, Hoyne got his back up. "I have spent months looking into this matter," the New York *Times* quoted him. "I wired my office four days ago not to finish the investigation until I return." He doubted that any crime, as legally defined, had been committed within the jurisdiction of Cook County. Such indictments would only be thrown out of court. The only applicable Illinois law, as he saw it, was a misdemeanor . . . unless, of course (he added slyly), the players had actually taken part in the gambling. . . .

In the Congress of the United States, Representative Sidney Mudd of Maryland was incensed. If there was no law, by God, he would introduce one. Congress must make it a Federal offense to bribe ball-players and throw ball games. Since professional baseball was played in leagues that cover two or more states, it was therefore in violation of interstate commerce.

In Chicago, Judge MacDonald would have none of Hoyne's dilatory tactics. "This probe will continue without interruption. And I say this in face of the fact that Mr. Hoyne ordered the indictments held up until his return. The law adequately covers the crime com-mitted. Ballplayers and all others involved in crooked work will be indicted, prosecuted, and punished. The present Grand Jury will be reconstituted into a special body on Saturday and will continue its inquiry."

Alfred Austrian indignantly substantiated this. He quoted Section 46 of the Illinois Criminal Code:

"If any two or more persons conspire or agree together . . . with the fraudulent or malicious intent wrongfully and wickedly to in-jure the person, character, business or employment or property of another, or to obtain money or other property by false pretenses, they shall be deemed guilty of conspiracy."

To Austrian, it was a matter of law that men are responsible for the natural consequences of their acts "even though these conse-quences differ from the end sought to be accomplished. It goes with-out saying that the natural consequence of throwing ball games was to injure the business and property of Charles Comiskey." Austrian took pains to illustrate how the owner of the White Sox stood to lose a total of a half-million dollars because of the conspiracy. Comiskey owned players' contracts worth $230,000, now all but worthless. (For example, Mr. Veeck had been prepared to purchase Buck Weaver for $75,000. Weaver was no longer worth a dime.) The drawing power of the team and other losses of good will, Austrian estimated at a total of $300,000.

"It makes little difference that the case is unusual," he explained. "There is always a law that makes men responsible. Three hundred years ago it was held indictable to prevail upon a person to lay a wager on a footrace and then procure one of the racers to throw the race. This conclusion could only have been reached on the ground that there was a conspiracy between two persons to cheat a third."

Meanwhile, in New York, Maclay Hoyne talked with Hugh Fullerton and others familiar with baseball graft. Hoyne, bloated with new information, was hungry to re-establish his own power. To this newly ardent investigator, the world had become a sea of corruption. Its waters were about to drown them all.

"I have evidence, too," he declared with categorical pomp as he left for Chicago, "that the coming World Series between Brooklyn and Cleveland has also been tampered with!"

Hoyne was not being entirely honest with such a ringing cry. It was designed primarily to lend stature to his name, but it resulted in a lot of damage to others. It was, in effect, another shot into the bleeding hide of organized baseball. The sporting world jumped another fifty feet in the air.

The newspapers screamed with flaring headlines: "CHARGE NEW WORLD SERIES FIX!" Fans gagged on the concept of continued corruption. The attack on baseball began to resound even from the pulpits: Call off the World Series, then see if baseball can get straightened out!

Charles Ebbetts, owner of the Brooklyn Club, the National League pennant winners, would have none of it. He raced to the office of the Kings County District Attorney, Harry Lewis, and worked out a plan of action: there had to be an "investigation." Every possible taint must be removed from his ball club. He would march his boys in, one by one, and they would prove their innocence. Not only were they not involved in any fix, they had not even been approached!

The District Attorney co-operated. He immediately sent out a series of telegrams to Maclay Hoyne in Chicago, demanding the sources and nature of his information. The Brooklyn Grand Jury, meanwhile, was prepared to move with incredible rapidity.

The Cook County, Illinois, Grand Jury had, by this time, shot its wad, at least as far as the excitement of sensational revelations was concerned. After all, what could equal the confessions?

There remained the "mystery woman," Mrs. Henrietta Kelly. She told the Grand Jury she owned a pair of houses near Comiskey Park where a number of the players were accustomed to live . . . among them, Eddie Cicotte. She was prepared to relate how she had overheard Cicotte remark to his brother, Jack, just after the 1919 Series, "I don't care what happens any more, I got mine!"

It seemed like hollow testimony, following Cicotte's confession as it did, but Mrs. Kelly made the most of it. She later complained to the police that she'd been threatened: if she gave any more evidence of crookedness, she would "be bumped off!" The police were instructed to protect her.

On the same afternoon, some thirty miles away, the Chicago Cubs played an exhibition game in Joliet, Illinois, against a local semipro team. As the players prepared to be driven back to the hotel where they dressed, a crowd of fans gathered around the entrance to the field, to watch the departure. One car, in which several players were riding, was making its way cautiously through the crowd when one of the fans jumped on the running board, shouting wildly, "Here are some of those crooked ballplayers from Chicago. Let's get 'em!"

Infielder Buck Herzog, seated in the back, pushed the man off the running board, then leaped out of the car and jumped on him. They rolled in the dirt, pummeling each other with fists and elbows before an enthusiastic crowd. Herzog was more than holding his own when a friend of the fighting fan came out of the crowd brandishing a penknife and plunged into battle. Herzog raised his hand to ward off the attack, and took several slashes before he could properly defend himself. The fans then interceded, and the knifer fled the scene with his liberated friend.

In Cincinnati, the 1919 World's Champions, nine games out of first place in the 1920 race, were struck dumb by the Grand Jury confessions. Manager Pat Moran reported that it all sounded incredible. "They're great actors, those boys. They ought to be on the stage!" Third baseman Heinie Groh shook his head: "Cicotte put everything on that ball when he pitched to me. I found his delivery as hard to solve as any I faced all year!" Big Edd Roush the Reds' big slugger was just as baffled: "I can't yet see how they could play the way they did and throw the games. It is a mystery to me."

Cincinnati had won its first World Series after forty-three years of professional baseball—only to learn it was damaged goods.

Less than a week before World Series time, Charles Ebbetts anxiously told the Kings County Grand Jury of his ballplayers' innocence: "I will bank my reputation on the honesty of my team. Any man who becomes President of a ball club and holds that position for a number of years becomes a good judge of human nature. . . ."

Mr. Ebbetts's choice of words must have stung Mr. Comiskey's ears—unless, of course, human nature is different in Brooklyn than in Chicago. . . .

The Kings County D.A., Harry Lewis, was still sending telegrams to Maclay Hoyne in Chicago, requesting further information as to his charge of a bribery attempt on the Brooklyn Club. There had been no replies from Hoyne or his staff.

To certain old-time ballplayers, the revelations evoked interesting memories. Charles "Red" Dooin, formerly playing-manager of the Phillies, told the Associated Press how gamblers tried to bribe them to throw the last seven games of the 1908 pennant race to the Giants. "Those White Sox fellas were pikers to what we passed up. All we had to do was name a price. Why, the gamblers opened up a satchel, must've had over $150,000 in it, told our pitchers to help themselves. At the first game at the Polo Grounds, a big man handed me $8,000, told me there was $40,000 more waiting for me. I called big 'Kitty' Bransfield who threw him down the stairs!"

Horace Fogel, former President of the Phillies, added to Red Dooin's tale. He recalled how, in 1905, a group of New York gamblers, headed by little Tim Sullivan, approached Rube Waddell, star pitcher of the A's, and offered him $17,000 to stay out of the World Series against the Giants. He could invent his own excuse. Waddell, it turned out, did *not* play: he claimed that he'd hurt his pitching arm, stumbling over a suitcase on a train! According to

Fogel, Waddell was paid $500 in a Boston hotel, but was double-crossed out of the rest—even though the Giants won.

In Boston, a resolution was passed and duly noted in the local press:

> "RESOLVED: that the eight White Sox players be condemned and punished for this murderous blow at the kid's game; and be it further resolved that Ray Schalk and Dickie Kerr be commended for their manly stand against the Benedict Arnolds of baseball."
> *Roosevelt Club of Boston Newsboys.*

Buck Weaver had spent the last few days in terrible confusion. He had sought the advice of everyone from Hartley Replogle of the State's Attorney's office to Charles Comiskey himself, indicating his one wish to clear himself of any corruption. But they were all interested only in his confession of guilt. He had no money for high-priced lawyers, but there was little doubt in his mind that he needed one. He told reporters: "I've been wrongfully accused and I intend to fight. I shall be in major-league baseball next year, if not with the White Sox, then with some other team. They have nothing on me. I'm going to hire the best lawyer in Chicago to defend me, and I'm going to be cleared.

"Look, I know you have to put in local color in an interview. But print what I say, and don't say I'm prematurely aged over this thing. Don't say my shoulders are drooping, my head hanging, and my back humped. I'm no condemned criminal and I don't like being pictured as one!"

Weaver meant every word of it. He expected to be back in uniform in 1921. Then he went to a meeting with Swede Risberg, Fred McMullin, and Hap Felsch in Joe Kauffman's tailor shop, out at 33rd and Wentworth Avenue in Chicago. They planned to team up to defend their innocence.

Risberg, meanwhile, was angry at Jackson's accusation. "I never threatened him! I'm no slugger, although I'm able to take care of myself."

It was an understatement. Some years before, in an Oakland, California, bush-league game, Risberg disputed a third strike call by umpire Jake Baumgarten and knocked him unconscious with one solid right-hand punch.

"The Swede," as Jackson had commented, "was a hard guy."

Bill Fallon noted in the New York *Times,* that the reporters had visited Rothstein's home and spoken with "a member of the family." Carolyn Rothstein, apparently, had followed his instructions and added details of her own:

"You can say that Maharg's story is substantially correct. Arnold was never in on the deal at any stage. He told me that he was much surprised when the proposition was put up to him, and declared to Burns that he didn't think it could be done. He never sent any telegrams to Attell in Cincinnati during the Series, and if Attell says he received any money or telegrams from him at that time, it's a lie. Why should Arnold be sending telegrams when he didn't have a thing to do with the matter?

"I had heard long ago that Abe Attell had been bragging to friends how the deal was put over. He should keep on bragging now."

Fallon smiled. The story amused him. But when he read on, another story did not. "HOLD GAMBLERS PLAN NEW SERIES FIX!" This one hurt. He knew what the public would be saying: Arnold Rothstein was at it again.

He put in a call to A.R. He thought it was time for a meeting.

If Hugh Fullerton was distressed at the Grand Jury revelations, he could, at least, feel a sense of relief at having been right as well as courageous. In the past year, he had suffered considerable abuse from the more conservative commentators. *Baseball Magazine,* in particular, continued to vilify him. He could hardly be blamed, then, for taking some small advantage of his vindicated position. He sat down and wrote a stinging letter to the editor:

Editor, *Baseball Magazine.*
Dear Sir:
    Several months ago you printed several scurrilous and untrue stories concerning me. . . . In view of recent developments, do you not think it your duty to print in an equally prominent space an apology and a retraction. I suggest this before proceeding fur-

ther in this matter. I desire most of all to know who inspired this
attack against me. . . . In plain English, what person in organized
baseball ordered you to write it? I think that such a statement by
you at this time may have a bearing on the case now before the
Grand Jury in Chicago. . . .

Hugh Fullerton

The *Baseball Magazine* printed Fullerton's letter, but replied
with neither apology nor retraction:

"Fullerton had picked up an ugly story that was kicking around in
the gutter—a story that decent writers would refuse to handle—and
blew it up into a muckraking tirade against organized baseball. There
are two kinds of people in the world: one builds up, the other tears
down. Hugh Fullerton, of course, belongs to the latter. . . ."

The editor chose to keep up his abuse: "Was the public investigation hastened by what he did?" And it answered protectively: "It
was not."

And again: "If the public investigation for which he clamored
had been conducted last Fall, would the lid have been blown off?"
The answer was a hypothetical evasion: "Probably no."

The reply was a triumph of hypocrisy; for the magazine had constantly resisted any such investigation, even denied the need for it.
There are, indeed, Fullerton later commented, two kinds of people
in the world: one sees the truth, the other doesn't.

4

Joseph "Sport" Sullivan was at the Boston ball park on that Wednesday afternoon, September 29, when he learned that Lefty Williams
had named him before the Illinois Grand Jury. In less than an hour,
he was on a train, en route for New York. He wanted to be where the
power was. While on the train, he picked up a New York newspaper
and was staggered to read Abe Attell's statement implicating Arnold
Rothstein as the father of the whole plot.

If Attell could play this kind of a game, why not Sullivan?

He checked into the Hotel Ansonia and presented himself at Lindy's restaurant. Twenty minutes after his arrival, a reporter was at his table, asking him questions. Sullivan grimaced in artificial anger. "They've indicted me and made me a goat, and I'm not going to stand for it. I know the whole history of the deal from beginning to end. I know the big man whose money it was that paid off the White Sox players—and I'm going to name him!" He was ready to admit—proudly, in fact—that he'd made a bundle on the Series. But there's no crime in that, is there? I've been instructed by my lawyer in Boston, William J. Kelly, to go to Chicago, if need be, to clear my name."

Boston papers, meanwhile, had elaborated. The gambler known as Brown was also believed to be a Bostonian, a friend of Sport Sullivan's, having attended the Series and stayed at the Blackstone Hotel in Chicago with him. Sullivan, the papers said, was a leading Boston gambler, famed for being George M. Cohan's betting commissioner during the great 1914 Series when the Braves upset the vaunted Philadelphia A's in four straight. Sullivan had taken the underdogs for Cohan and won him a small fortune. In 1919, when Boston gamblers who had backed Chicago at 10–7 learned that Sullivan was again on the short odds, they panicked and hedged their bets.

It was also noted that Sullivan had no criminal record in Boston. However, he had, for a time, been barred from sections of the ball park where gamblers congregated. Several years back, the police had wanted him for questioning in connection with a number of auto thefts, but Sport had conveniently skipped town for the duration of the investigation.

Sullivan was just finishing his meal at Lindy's when someone else had learned of his arrival—and heard the nature of his statements. A messenger sat down beside him, quietly told him that as soon as he was through eating, Mr. Fallon would like to see him—at 355 West 84th Street.

Sullivan knew that address. It was Arnold Rothstein's.

Fallon was annoyed. Rothstein had called him that morning, angry at Attell's incriminating statements. Now this big dumbhead from Boston was compounding it. Fallon knew what Sullivan was up to:

tinhorn characters always played their trump cards first. Sullivan wasn't going to Chicago to talk. He merely wanted to indicate a show of strength lest A.R. get the idea he could be pushed around.

Rothstein's spacious apartment was uncommonly pleasant. Looking out on the Hudson, it got the full light of the afternoon sun and was furnished with darkly upholstered, old-country furniture.

The only view the four men present appreciated was that of money. They were Rothstein, Fallon, Attell, and Sullivan. The problem they had to face, Fallon began, was to work out some sort of *modus operandi*. They were all in this together, facing a common enemy: the Grand Jury of Chicago. It was damn stupid of them to be clawing at each other. If they played this hand together, with Rothstein behind them, Fallon could promise them they'd all be free and clear. As he saw it, the Grand Jury indictments would hold up, and subpoenas would be sent out almost immediately. The three of them would then be extradited and forced to testify. And that, he emphasized, must be avoided at all costs. . . .

How? Simple enough: they would leave the country. Immediately. Sullivan would go to Mexico. Attell to Canada. Arnold would take his wife to Europe. And just to keep it all friendly, Arnold insisted on picking up the tab. Fallon nodded at Attell and Sullivan: a little vacation with pay, as it were.

Agreed?

They all exchanged glances and finally nodded. Rothstein had already reached into his pocket and withdrawn that ever-ready bank roll.

5

When State's Attorney Maclay Hoyne returned to Chicago, he immediately reviewed the testimony of the Grand Jury and reversed himself, now convinced that conspiracy charges would stand up against the ballplayers indicted. In effect, he indicated he had never

thought otherwise. He also agreed with Judge MacDonald's statement that he had been misquoted by the New York *Times*.

He told the Grand Jury that he had amassed a huge quantity of
information in New York, not yet crystallized into evidence. He still
had men there working on the matter, following all leads. When he
was specifically asked about his statement that the coming World
Series was also being tampered with, he requested that the Grand
Jury refrain from questioning him at this time. He would have more,
and better, information later. "Safety first is my motto when you are
battling a gambling syndicate with a million-dollar bankroll."

The Grand Jury assented. They would have to suspend further
investigations anyway, since the 1920 World Series was about to
begin.

Meanwhile, the decimated Chicago White Sox went to St. Louis
for an all but hopeless final three-game stand. The fans of St. Louis,
long since out of the pennant race, responded to the plight of this
once-great ball club. They cheered their arrival, draped a garland of
flowers on the fiery Ray Schalk in a special ceremony before the game.
It was almost as if they wanted their own club to lose. It didn't. The
Browns won, 8–6. Two days later, the season ended with the White
Sox in second place, two full games behind the Cleveland Indians.

Afterward, Kid Gleason sat in the lobby of St. Louis's Planters
Hotel and cried the blues: "I'd like to quit today and go home for
good. I'd like to get away from baseball forever. . . ."

Back in Chicago, newspapers exaggerated stories that Comiskey
was close to a physical collapse. He was inundated with barrels of
telegrams and letters from old friends and well-wishers: ex-baseball
greats who knew what he meant to the history of the game; Chicago
kids, who knew only that they loved baseball and Comiskey had
given them the best; Hollywood movie stars who wanted to show their
fans that they were as American as any of them and loved baseball;
Chambers of Commerce. It seemed almost as if the victim was not
baseball, not the fans, not the kids, but the Old Roman himself.

Comiskey played the role in a dignified mantle. As the season
ended, he dictated a letter to the ballplayers who had remained loyal:
"If it could be possible, I regret more than you do the occurrences
of the 1919 World Series. As one of the honest ballplayers of the
Chicago White Sox, I feel you were deprived of the winner's share

of the World Series receipts through no fault of yours. I do not intend that you, as an honest player, shall be penalized for your honesty, or suffer by reason of the dishonesty of others. I therefore take pleasure in handing you $1,500, this being the difference between the winning and losing players' shares."

The text of letter was, of course, released to the press.

To the fans, it was a touching and sentimental gesture—a gesture of nobility worthy of page one, which was exactly where it was displayed. An artful, tactical maneuver for the preservation of the Comiskey image, it was also, to the ballplayers, found money. They did not protest that the actual difference between the winning and losing shares was not $1,500, but something over $1,900. They released their own letter to the press: "To the fans of Chicago: we the undersigned players of the Chicago White Sox, want the world to know the generosity of our employer, who of his own free will, chose to reimburse us with the difference . . ." etc.

It all seemed like one big happy family.

A few days before the scheduled opening of the 1920 World Series, the Kings County, New York, Grand Jury questioned a dozen members of the Brooklyn Baseball Club as to possible contacts with gamblers. Their answers were simple and direct: they knew absolutely nothing that could in any way be considered even suspicious. District Attorney Harry Lewis, having heard nothing further in response to his telegrams to Maclay Hoyne, gave them a clean bill of health. The World Series could begin without taint.

6

In New York County, District Attorney Edward Swann had not been having a successful term of office. Members of his own political party were beginning to mark him "lousy." He desperately needed something to bolster his fading status. He saw in the baseball scandal a chance to get himself into the political arena, even if he had to fight lions. If the conspiracy had been conceived and managed in New York, and if

New Yorkers were injured by the conspiracy, surely, then, there was cause for legal action on his part. He put his staff to work, ready to tangle with anyone, including the heavyweight Arnold Rothstein. But he read the public press and settled for the featherweight Abe Attell.

Attell seemed to be nowhere in sight. He was rumored to be in Atlantic City. Swann soon found that he had to be content with The Great Mouthpiece himself. Fallon had nothing but contempt for Swann, for the law, and for the truth. "Abe Attell is innocent," he was quoted as saying. "Any statement in the public press or elsewhere purporting to come from him are false. He will not submit himself to unwarranted questioning. If there is any legal demand for his appearance, he will go before a court or a Grand Jury."

Swann immediately asked the New York Grand Jury to subpoena Attell. "Attell was seen in New York a day or so ago with Sport Sullivan, another gambling manipulator of the fix!" But to what avail if Attell could not be found? To embarrass Fallon? Fallon, of course, was not one to be embarrassed. He told reporters of the New York *Times:* "Attell has not been in touch with Sullivan. He doesn't even know Sullivan!"

In Boston, meanwhile, Sullivan's lawyer, William J. Kelly, played the same game as William J. Fallon. "The statement that Mr. Sullivan intended to expose certain people in New York is absolutely untrue, for the reason that, having had no participation in any such affair, he could make no statement implicating anyone!"

And so the war of idle words went on. To a credulous newspaper reader, the whole world was innocent.

On October 3, Fallon announced in New York that he had spoken with Mr. Kelly, and at Mr. Kelly's request, had agreed to assume the role of counselor for Mr. Sullivan.

District Attorney Swann got angry. He demanded that Fallon produce both Attell and Sullivan immediately, but this was clearly disintegrating into a losing battle. "Fallon," he told reporters, "is up to his old tricks . . . the disappearing witness. . . ."

There was also a conflicting report that Attell had been worked over by the gambling underworld. Attell's statement of intent to squeal did not sit pretty with them. Swann had heard talk of a meeting in the back room of a Times Square saloon where Attell was warned to keep his mouth shut. Had they gone further than a threat?

Swann pursued another tack. "There definitely was a 'master-mind' who fixed the 1919 Series. A major New York gambler had a sucker list of wealthy—but not wise—men whom he persuaded to bet huge sums on Chicago." But when Swann tried to reach these men to get them to talk about the action, to name names, they all refused. They would rather suffer the loss of the money, even if a conspiracy to defraud them was involved, than suffer the indignity of being exposed as suckers.

Fallon had to laugh. It struck him as significant that somehow Rothstein's name had remained unmentioned through all of this.

If Fallon was laughing, Rothstein was not. One of his World Series "suckers" had succeeded in turning the tables on him. A wealthy stockbroker found a way to get even: he had seen to it that Rothstein was tipped off to a supposedly red-hot stock, expected to rise 20 points inside of a week. Rothstein accepted the tip and invested $200,000. But instead of going up, the bottom fell out. The broker, as it turned out, had sold short.

Swann's investigators caught up with the gambler Nick the Greek in New York. Nick, who had bet heavily on the Reds on Rothstein's advice, put on a sad face. "Truth of the matter is, I lost. The White Sox is my favorite team. I dropped a few bucks, that's all, because I was broke at the time. I'm through betting baseball from now on. I'll stick to craps. It's the safest game for gamblers these days."

Meanwhile, in the 1920 World Series, the Cleveland Indians, led by player-manager Tris Speaker, whipped the Brooklyn Robins, five games to two. Outstanding in the victory was Cleveland second baseman Bill Wombsganns' unassisted triple play. It was also noted that there was almost no betting on the outcome of the Series.

Up in Montreal, Abe Attell was growing tired of hiding in his hotel room, seeing the same movies. The lure of a sporting event was irresistible. Even the farce of a professional wrestling match was worth the risk of exposure.

Significantly, the Little Champ was recognized at ringside. Wire services relayed the discovery to American newspapers.

"Yeah, here I am and here I sit!" Attell told them with a cocky grin. "They can't touch me here!"

But even as he said this, the wheels of betrayal were turning—along the New York Central Railroad. Arnold Rothstein was not sailing to Europe as he had pledged. He and his lawyer were speeding to the city of Chicago and its Grand Jury room. The Big Bankroll and the Great Mouthpiece were going to smother the Little Champ.

It was all Fallon's doing. Rothstein, though aware of the potential advantages, was afraid of the dangers. To appear before the Grand Jury and subject himself to such a direct confrontation with the power of the State seemed like a blatant violation of his rule of thumb. Fallon, however, believed this very defiance would serve to work for Rothstein. Shrewdly, the lawyer sensed what bedlam would result from the gambler's very appearance: the harassing of relentless reporters and the blinding rush of newspaper photographers would "violate the privacy" of his client. He instructed Rothstein to act injured when that happened. All this, he guessed, would render him sympathetic.

If such a tactic tended to assuage Rothstein's anxiety, there was something more basic that encouraged him to go West. He wanted to meet Alfred Austrian. Now that the whole World Series case was out in the open and subject to litigation, sooner or later he knew such a meeting would be necessary. It was another Rothstein rule of thumb to accept the inevitable and cope with it as soon as possible.

In Chicago, then, the two New Yorkers stopped at Austrian's offices on arrival. The meeting, as Rothstein had anticipated, proved to be a significant one. Right off the bat, Rothstein announced that he needed a responsible Chicago attorney to represent his interests, and that it was Austrian he wished to retain. The Chicago attorney was somewhat staggered by this. Did not Mr. Rothstein realize that he was counsel for both the Chicago baseball clubs? How could he justify such a conflict of interests! The New York gambler wore the smile of the cynic. While he acknowledged that a year before they had been on opposing sides, their present positions were no longer in conflict. They were both, in effect, facing a common enemy: exposure. The answer, Fallon emphasized, was silence. Silence would protect Mr. Comiskey in the future, just as it had protected him through the recent highly profitable 1920 baseball season. . . .

It had long been clear to Fallon that Austrian and his client, Charles Comiskey, were going to be co-operative. That Comiskey, like all baseball men, hated this Grand Jury investigation, was as plain as the nose on the Old Roman's face. Baseball, like any other business, wanted to keep its problems from public scrutiny. The whole

concept of ballplayers consorting with such evil symbols as Arnold
Rothstein was an anathema to them. As a result, Fallon knew that
nobody here in Chicago would want to lay a legal hand on A.R. The
implication of bigness—and Rothstein meant bigness—placed too
great a burden on baseball to purge itself. In short, the less guilt, the
better . . . the less said, the better. Rothstein's vindication became essential to everyone, not only to Rothstein himself.

It made Fallon laugh how often things worked out so neatly.

But there were problems to be ironed out. What if there was extensive Grand Jury testimony that incriminated Rothstein? Wouldn't
they have to indict him? Fallon had long been aware of the necessity
of getting his hands on that testimony. And, once again, he found himself allied to the alleged enemy. It was all part of the same pattern, all
cut from the same cloth: if Rothstein was vulnerable, so was Comiskey. If Rothstein wanted that testimony, so, then, did Comiskey.
Austrian's approach was, perhaps, more specific. The signed confessions and immunity waivers he had done so much to obtain for the
Grand Jury now loomed as the rock on which the indictments rested
—and on which the trial would inevitably be based.

Somehow, they all had to get that testimony. It was a job for
which Fallon had an expert's background. But he was not unaware
that here he was in the presence of power. Austrian surely had access to easily pulled strings. Was he not friendly with Maclay Hoyne,
the State's Attorney himself? Wasn't Hoyne's entire administration
about to be replaced? It was, in effect, a perfect time to operate. . . .

As it turned out, Fallon was right about Rothstein's entrance to
the Grand Jury. The famous New York gambler was mobbed by the
press and all but savagely manhandled. By the time he managed to
work his way into the Jury room, he had successfully established his
pose as a visiting dignitary who had been rudely maltreated by the
local reception committee. He expressed himself as such to Judge
MacDonald and the members of the Jury. They could not but respond
with a sense of guilt, and treated him accordingly. For the first and only
time during its lengthy session, a witness was permitted the company
and support of his counsel during questioning. William J. Fallon accomplished this by holding that condition as the price of his client's
testimony. If they wanted Rothstein, they had to take Fallon with
him.

Rothstein was an affable, intelligent witness. He told the Grand Jury he had chosen to appear because he was "sick and tired" of all the rumors and allegations of his involvement. He wanted to set the record straight, personally, so that this august body might know of his innocence.

He then asked for and was granted permission to read a prepared statement:

"Abe Attell did the fixing.

"I've come here to vindicate myself. If I wasn't sure I was going to be vindicated, I would have stayed home. The whole thing started when Attell and some other cheap gamblers decided to frame the Series and make a killing. The world knows I was asked in on the deal and my friends know how I turned it down flat. I don't doubt that Attell used my name to put it over. That's been done by smarter men than Abe. But I wasn't in on it, wouldn't have gone into it under any circumstances, and *didn't bet a cent on the Series* after I found out what was under way. My idea was that whatever way things turned out, it would be a crooked Series anyhow, and that only a sucker would bet on it.

"I'm not going to hold anything back from you. I'm here to clear myself and I expect to get out of here with a clean bill of health."

Maclay Hoyne treated him like a friendly witness. His questions presumed Rothstein's innocence, spared him any possible show of embarrassment. It was, perhaps, indicative that Fallon's protective presence seemed completely unnecessary. In such an atmosphere, Rothstein became relatively garrulous. He spoke of his love for the game, his long-term friendship with and admiration for John McGraw, his warm (and successful) meeting with the American League President, Bancroft Johnson. To a total stranger in the room, he might have been a dignified young United States Senator whose motives had somehow been misunderstood.

Hoyne later declared: "I don't think Rothstein was involved in it!" This was supplemented by another legal mind, Alfred Austrian's: "Rothstein, in his testimony today, proved himself guiltless."

When Abe Attell read the Montreal papers on the following day, he bellowed in rage. Normally a fastidious man, this time he threw his clothes into his suitcase and caught the first train back to New York.

He, too, was going to Chicago "to set the world straight."

But significantly he called Rothstein as soon as he arrived in New York. Attell had been around long enough to know a few fundamental principles: there was no action by an opponent that could not be made to work for you. To a man like Rothstein, after all, everything was a tactic.

Rothstein was ready for him. He asked him to come right over.

When Attell arrived, Fallon was already there. It seemed almost as if they'd been expecting Attell that afternoon.

The Little Champ came out of his corner swinging hard. He accused Rothstein of selling him out. He wasn't going to be A.R.'s patsy, and he would spill everything to the Grand Jury.

Fallon interrupted and tried to calm him. "There no reason why you should go to Chicago . . . no reason at all."

Fallon's tone was so authoritative, Attell stopped punching.

"But now they're gonna indict me sure!" Abe cried.

Fallon shrugged. "They would've anyway. That's why Arnold's testimony won't matter. It won't change a thing!"

Abe saw the opening and threw a hard right. All that stuff would be used against him!

It was Arnold's turn. Typically, he reached into his pocket as he began talking. Immediately, Attell knew it was time for the making of a deal.

"Bill," Arnold was saying, "I want you to take care of the Champ. I want you to see to it that they don't extradite him. I don't want him in that Grand Jury room—and I don't want him on trial."

He handed Fallon $50,000 cash. Fallon nodded, stuffed the wad of folded bills into his pocket as if it were a dirty handkerchief.

Attell dropped his guard. The bell had just rung, ending the fight. He didn't question Rothstein's motives; he understood that A.R. would not want him to testify. That was enough for him. As for Fallon, Attell knew that the great man would figure out how to keep him away from Chicago. It was enough for Attell that Fallon had said, "Your troubles are over."

But there was no peace for Arnold Rothstein. Nassau County, Long Island, New York, had chosen this time to begin an intensive investigation into gambling activities in Long Beach, having discovered the corruption of several highly placed Nassau officials. Rothstein, owner of a Long Beach establishment, was subpoenaed.

It was the same old story to the Big Bankroll. They would hound him, keep him on the defensive, take up his time with interrogations and legal proceedings. While he had no fear of convictions, the intermediary harassment seemed too severe to justify the returns. He released to the press this near-incredible statement:

"I am leaving the world of the gamblers and fixers.

"From now on, I shall devote myself to my racing stables and to the real estate business. It is not pleasant to be what some call a 'social outcaste.' For the sake of my family and my friends, I am glad that chapter of my life is over."

The newspapers made much of the story: "ROTHSTEIN RESIGNS AS KING OF GAMBLERS!" At thirty-eight, they speculated, he had amassed a fortune of two million dollars. Actually, it was close to double that figure.

7

The good ship baseball lists to port,
Its ancient hull is leaking;
It trembles when the wild winds snort,
Its mast and spars are creaking.
The owners gather weak and wan
And gaze upon the weather;
They'll slap a coat of whitewash on
And hope it holds together.

George Phair.
Chicago *Herald and Examiner*
October 19, 1920

It remained essential that a move should be made toward the reorganization of baseball's governing body. Albert Lasker, proponent of the plan, continued to take the lead. He summoned a group of

powerful friends to a meeting in Alfred Austrian's office. William
Wrigley of the Chicago Cubs; Charles Comiskey and his club's secretary, Harry Grabiner; Horace Stoneham of the New York Giants
and his manager, John McGraw; the two New York Yankee owners,
Colonels Ruppert and Huston; and Harry Frazee of the Boston Red
Sox. It was decided that tactically it was best to start the ball rolling
through the National League. The reason for this was simple enough:
the American League was led by Ban Johnson.

A few days later, October 7, 1920, in New York, John Heydler
met with his eight National League club owners. They promptly
agreed to form a new governing body to run baseball. To effect this,
they dispatched a telegram to all the American League clubs, inviting
them to a joint meeting at the Hotel Congress in Chicago on October
18 "for the purpose of immediately forming plans for the future government and safeguarding of the national sport."

As predicted, Ban Johnson would have none of it. As soon as the
World Series was over (and the American League had won), he
declared his opposition: "It is my judgment that to hold such a meeting at this time is a mistake. The Cook County [Ill.] Grand Jury has
been reconvened and will continue its investigation. . . . Much important testimony will be presented which might weigh heavily in future deliberations of these self-appointed custodians of the game."
Then, with typically ornate phraseology: "It is not wisdom to pull
down an old house while you are still removing the furnishings."

Ban was a powerful man. He could take five loyal American
League clubs in any direction he chose to move: Philadelphia, Cleveland, Detroit, St. Louis, and Washington. St. Louis, for example, immediately announced it would not attend the meetings, and the others
followed suit.

Heydler, however, would not be deterred. The public, he declared,
was in no mood to wait. The meeting was held as scheduled, with 11
of the 16 major-league club owners present. The owners proposed a
complete reorganization of baseball with the National Commission
abolished and a civilian tribunal not financially interested in the
game in complete control. A follow-up meeting was to be held on
November 8 to actuate the plan. The five absent clubs would be invited and urged to attend. If they didn't, a new single league would
be formed under the plan, leaving out the dissenting five.

It was an ultimatum . . . a threat of war, softened, however, with a special plea for peace.

Johnson's reply came after a meeting of his group. He found the plan wholly ineffectual. The management of baseball properties in which large sums of money had been invested required the practical leadership of baseball men who knew the history of the game and all its players. The inherent dishonesty of some players, he said, was the cause of all the trouble.

Heydler shook his head in despair. (It was impossible to argue with Ban Johnson.) He dreaded the thought of another baseball war. But only the eleven clubs met again; they moved into action without the dissenting five. The problem of choosing a man to head the new Board of Control had been secretly resolved for some time.

That man was Federal Judge Kenesaw Mountain Landis.

Judge Landis's father had been a Union surgeon during the Civil War. During General Sherman's dramatic march to the sea, he was operating on a wounded soldier, on a table, under the shadow of a Georgia hillside. A cannon ball crashed against a huge rock, caromed and shattered the surgeon's leg. When his son was born, two years later, in Millville, Ohio, out of memory of that imposing moment, he named the boy Kenesaw Mountain, after the site.

Young Landis grew up in Logansport, Indiana. He failed algebra in high school and quit. He got a job as a newsboy through his older brother who worked on a local paper. He would get up at dawn, load up "like a pack mule," and sell papers. He graduated to clerking in a general store for $3 a week, then to a job as errand boy in a train dispatcher's office on the Madalia Railroad. He wanted to become a brakeman, to see something of America, but his boss turned him down.

He played amateur baseball, but his greater athletic skill was as a bike rider. What he lacked in speed, he made up with psychology. Once, before an important race in a strange town, he bought twenty medals, pinned them ostentatiously on his racing uniform, and appeared looking like a champion. He completely intimidated his rivals and won.

In time, he decided to study law in Cincinnati. A strange-looking "hay-seed" type, he failed to mix socially and was ostracized from fraternity life. Indignant at this, he organized the non-frat majority and got them to win school elections.

As a lawyer, he was something of a firebrand, the kind who takes into court a case that is normally settled outside. He was appointed Federal Judge in Illinois by President Theodore Roosevelt in 1905. He became nationally known when he forced John D. Rockefeller to come to Chicago to testify in a case against his Standard Oil Company on which Landis slapped a fine of $29,240,000!

Landis was no stranger to baseball problems. In 1914, he had presided over the legal battle that tore apart the major leagues when the newly formed Federal League pressed suit against their monopolistic power. Landis studied baseball history for weeks, but never rendered a verdict; this case, at least, was settled out of court.

To the frightened owners, Landis's appointment would lend great dignity, if nothing else, to baseball.

Having decided this, they began to draw up plans for a new twelve-team league; the twelfth club would be the first of five dissenters to apply. . . .

Johnson, meanwhile, remained irate. He led his contingent of "the loyal five" to begin forming plans for a new league of their own. This was nothing new to him: he had done it several times before.

The New York *Times* viewed it all with deep regret:

"If any more proof were required that the men financially interested in the game are incompetent to run their own business, the current baseball war which is about to break out supplies it. The 1919 World Series fix was bad enough, but next it appears that the men in control of the game had been unable to run down rumors. . . . This failure was alone sufficient proof that baseball needs the guardianship of bigger men from outside the game. . . . The obstacle to reorganization is Ban Johnson, once a brilliant and successful executive, who now seems to think that baseball exists for his own greater glory . . . he would rather ruin a business than lose his job."

It was true enough. On the day the editorial appeared (Johnson was in Kansas City at the meeting of minor-league executives, dissuading them from endorsing the Lasker Plan. "Keep non-baseball men out of baseball!" he roared.

The war clouds gathered with menacing persistence.

Fortunately, there were dissidents among "the loyal five." The eleven clubs that opposed Johnson had the money and power to destroy the others. The Lasker Plan did not seem an issue worthy of war and its consequent self-destruction. The dissenters sent word to Heydler that they would like to talk things over.

The armistice was agreed upon, curiously enough, on November 11. Baseball would retain its two-league organization. Landis was appointed sole arbiter, in lieu of a three-man tribunal, "if he could be induced to accept." A delegation of the owners hurried over to the Federal Courts to confront him with the decision. They found him hearing a case involving a $15,000 bribery on an income-tax fraud. They filed into the room, hat in hand, interrupting the proceedings. Landis banged his gavel, ordered them to be silent. When he was informed of their mission, he retired them to his chambers to wait. Forty-five minutes later, Judge Landis increased his income from $7,500 as a Federal Judge, a position he chose to keep, to $50,000 by becoming baseball's commissioner.

Ban Johnson said he was satisfied.

Meanwhile, the Illinois Grand Jury finally completed its investigation. On October 22, it handed down its final indictments, naming the eight White Sox ballplayers and five gamblers: Abe Attell, Bill Burns, Sport Sullivan, and one Rachael Brown; also the recently barred ballplayer of the New York Giants, Hal Chase. The indictments included nine counts of conspiracy to defraud various individuals and institutions in the State of Illinois. Its legal verbiage was so garbled that even the lawyers subsequently assigned to the prosecution of the case made little sense out of it.

8

On November 2, 1920, Warren G. Harding of Ohio was elected President of the United States by a landslide. At approximately the same time, there was a change of administration in the Illinois State's Attorney's office: Maclay Hoyne was replaced by the newly elected

Robert Crowe. As usually prevails, the retiring attorney's entire staff went out with him.

Before Hoyne left office, however, he had a mission to perform. Along with an assistant, Henry Berger, he went to the files in which the voluminous Grand Jury testimony was kept and brought the material to his office. Thereupon, he had his secretary make copies of certain portions.

The real purpose of this maneuver was plunder. Berger, already familiar with the material, knew exactly what to look for. Fallon had been explicit enough: if the name of Arnold Rothstein was mentioned in the testimony of a witness, Fallon wanted it. Berger ploughed through hundreds of pages, gathered enough to fill a brief case. Hoyne, meanwhile, had a simpler assignment: he lifted the confessions of Cicotte, Jackson, and Williams along with the waivers of immunity they had signed before giving testimony.

News of this tampering with the files was relayed to Hoyne's eager assistant, Hartley Replogle, also retiring. He immediately brought it to the attention of Judge MacDonald. Though there was nothing concrete in the report, the Judge was determined not to permit any interference. He stormed up to Hoyne's office and had the records impounded.

Hoyne feigned indignation. He claimed that he simply wanted copies of certain aspects of the testimony for his own records. He insisted that any retiring State's Attorney had a right to maintain such records of his term of office.

The new State's Attorney, Robert Crowe, dutifully ordered an investigation. When word of this reached Judge Landis, the new Commissioner declared that there'd better not be any tampering with evidence. If any of it was missing, he'd see to it that Federal action was taken!

There was, of course, plenty missing. A slew of vital papers, telegrams, and other communications could be found safely secured in the filing cabinets of Alfred Austrian's office. The Rothstein-Comiskey alliance had accomplished its first goal.

As for the copies of the testimony involving Arnold Rothstein, those portions were promptly handed over to William J. Fallon.

No "Federal action" was ever taken. In fact it was not until many months later that the theft was dramatically exposed.

To William J. Fallon, this change of administration had offered a golden opportunity. Henry Berger was out of a job, and Fallon needed a man intimate with the inner workings of the State's Attorney's office. It had not taken long for these two men to get together. Berger switched sides and joined the defense. Immediately Fallon and Berger met with George Gorman, the new assistant State's Attorney, assigned to prosecute the World Series case. Fallon always tried to encourage such preliminary meetings, for it afforded him an opportunity to size up his adversaries. He took pains to assure Gorman that he would present Abe Attell and Joseph "Sport" Sullivan at any forty-eight-hour notice, and would co-operate in arranging for a speedy trial. Gorman was gratified by this attitude. So gratified, in fact, that he did not demand that Fallon place bond for his clients.

Only the ballplayers were required to do that. They had had to put up $5,000 each.

Ban Johnson, meanwhile, dedicated himself to the prosecution. From American League funds, he appropriated $10,000—to assist the State's Attorney. Two notable lawyers were hired to work with George Gorman. James "Ropes" O'Brien, like Henry Berger, was formerly of Maclay Hoyne's staff. O'Brien's nickname referred to his success in securing convictions, sending several men to the gallows. During murder trials, O'Brien made it a habit to wear a bright red tie. The other was ex-Judge George Barrett, an old friend of Johnson's.

Charles Comiskey publicly protested—as he did all further actions by Johnson to dominate the prosecution. Comiskey declared that this should be his province: had he not suffered the most?

George Gorman was a worried young man. His first assignment— to prosecute the Black Sox case—was far from a rewarding one. For one thing, the line-up against him was more powerful than he enjoyed coping with. Fallon and a gathering battery of leading Chicago criminal lawyers in defense of the ballplayers—Ben Short, Thomas Nash, Michael Ahearn—were men who charged a fee of over $200 a day. Who, Gorman began to wonder, was paying them? Certainly not the ballplayers. Was it Rothstein? Comiskey? Then, too, the issues in this case were badly confused, the opposing forces very subtly muddied and vague. The entire baseball world was opposed to the

trial on principle, especially Comiskey, of course, who had the most
to lose.

The question of the law, itself, was a complex problem. It seemed
to Gorman that the nature of the indictments made it extremely difficult to secure convictions. Where was he going to find witnesses?
And how was he going to prove the conspiracy spelled out in the indictments? He was already aware that the signed confessions and
immunity waivers had been lifted, a loss that seriously complicated
the prosecution of the case. Would those confessions be admissible
without the immunity waivers? And who had them anyway, Comiskey
or Rothstein?

Gorman spent the fall ignoring the case and busying himself with
other matters. Members of his staff examined the indictments and
shook their heads dolefully. Some said that they did not think the case
would ever get on the calendar—and if it did, it would be impossible
to win.

If George Gorman kept stalling, Ban Johnson kept starting him up
again. It was not without reason that he had installed two attorneys
to work with the prosecution, at the expense of the American League.
He kept detectives digging up fresh information, talking to everyone
who knew anything. His drive was relentless: get that case ready for
trial!

As the winter turned into the new year, 1921, there had been no
apparent progress. Then Gorman announced a planned arraignment
by February 1, hoping that the trial could be wrapped up before the
baseball season began. It was, perhaps, his way of saying that if the
ballplayers should be acquitted, they could be ready to play again.
Cautiously Landis questioned this implication. Even if the ballplayers were acquitted, he explained, they would "not necessarily" be
reinstated.

9

An arraignment was held on February 14, 1921. The courtroom was
overcrowded with spectators. The ballplayers were present, but not
the gamblers. When Buck Weaver came in, there were rousing

cheers. To the defense, it seemed like a good omen. To Weaver, it was worth a jest: "They oughta build bleachers here and charge admission!"

Judge William Dever looked down from the bench and saw a powerful array of defense attorneys. One of them, James "Ropes" O'Brien, had suddenly—and curiously—shifted from the prosecution. They were four of the leading criminal lawyers in Chicago. The Judge smiled to himself, aware of his curiosity: he, too, wondered who was paying for all that high-powered legal talent.

Their opening move was a petition to Judge Dever for a bill of particulars, setting forth in detail the charges on which these boys were to be tried. Thomas Nash, counsel for Buck Weaver, followed with a request for a separate trial for his client. The Judge denied it. "Weaver was indicted for conspiracy, and must stand trial with the others."

Ben Short, another defense attorney, cut loose with a few introductory remarks for the benefit of all. "The magnates lead the public to believe the ballplayers got about $10,000 a year, and here we find out they get as little as $2,600. At the end of the season, they have nothing left but a chew of tobacco, a glove, and a few pairs of worn-out socks—yet the people have been pitying the poor magnates."

The first clash between opposing attorneys occurred when George Gorman attempted to read excerpts from Jackson's and Williams's confessions. It was a trial balloon, sent up by the State to discover if the defense was going to fight the admission of these confessions.

Ben Short and Michael Ahearn were on their feet immediately, shouting him down.

"Are you going to deny they confessed?" Gorman shouted back.

"Why don't you indict them for perjury, if that's what you're attempting to get at!" Ahearn roared.

"I want to tell you, you're running dangerously close to the border line on that very thing!" Gorman retaliated.

It was a prophetic opening salvo. The confessions would be a continued source of disputation throughout the trial. . . .

At the following session, Judge Dever agreed with the defense: the indictments were not clear. The State must furnish a bill of particulars by March 1, two weeks before the trial date.

George Gorman knew he was going to have trouble. It would be tough enough to face that battery of defense attorneys. And who was he going to use for witnesses? The only people who could supply evidence had been indicted. How could he expect to get them to testify against themselves?

Ban Johnson, meanwhile, had not been idle. If the prosecution needed more evidence, he would dig it out. If they needed a star witness, by God, he would get one for them. But, he realized, this would take time. Gorman was relieved. He wanted nothing better than to take time, unless it was to have the entire case dismissed. Gorman went to Robert Crowe, the State's Attorney, who offered a motion of *nolle prosequi,* requesting time to prepare new evidence: the work of the previous staff was incomplete. There were too many loose ends, too many indications of the corruption of witnesses. To effect this necessary delay, Gorman had to pull out his one remaining trump: he publicly announced that the original confessions of Cicotte, Jackson, and Williams, along with a slew of other valuable papers, vital to the prosecution, had disappeared from the files!

This announcement had a jarring impact on the Court. It was further noted that the Chicago *Tribune* had been approached by a New York agent, offering various documents for publication—at a stiff price. Fearing libel, the editor had rejected the offer.

But the exposure of this theft forced Judge Dever's hand: he had to grant the State's motion. He declared the entire case stricken from the call. This meant that the State would have to hand in new indictments. The case would have to be prepared all over again!

The ballplayers had spent the winter in limbo. They would be forced to do the same in the spring. It was already March 14. Spring training had begun, and there were renewed questions as to whether the eight ballplayers would be eligible. Landis's retort cracked like the snap of a whip. He had begun, it was said, to earn his salary. "Baseball can protect itself regardless: all the indicted ballplayers have today been placed on the ineligible list!" Comiskey saw the ball slipping from his hands. He didn't need Landis to bar his ballplayers: he could do it himself. Immediately he gave them their formal unconditional release, thus making them "free agents"—free, but impotent.

The gamblers, of course, had been "free agents" all along.

State's Attorney Robert Crowe, supervising the case, had been advised that the gamblers under the old indictments were not going to be submissive. In fact, they were so powerfully protected that the chances were very much against their even standing trial! Gorman refused to believe this. Fallon, himself, had been reassuring. Besides, was not the Illinois State's Attorney's office strong enough to contend with Fallon? Was Fallon bigger than the law?

Crowe knew the answer to that: he needed new victims. He had to have a few gamblers to prosecute. How would it look if there were only those ballplayers on the defense? If there had been a conspiracy, with whom did they conspire?

Once again, Ban Johnson came through for him. If the State needed gamblers, he would supply them. Crowe immediately reconvened the Grand Jury. . . .

The Grand Jury worked quickly and secretly. Within a week, there was a sudden and surprising declaration. Five new indictments were handed down, a completely new concept of the origin of the entire World Series scandal: Carl Zork of Des Moines; Benjamin Franklin, David Zelser, and the two Levi brothers, of St. Louis; all Abe Attell's partners at the Sinton Hotel.

Crowe crowed to the press: "I told you that the first investigation had been bungled, and that the real men behind the conspiracy had not been indicted. We have handled this investigation carefully. . . ."

The newly indicted Carl Zork, a shirtwaist manufacturer from Des Moines, indignantly pleaded total innocence: "I don't know what this is all about."

By the end of April, Gorman was ready to begin. He sent out warrants to arrest all the indicted ballplayers and gamblers. Hal Chase was picked up in San Jose, California. The eight Chicago White Sox players turned themselves in. It was feared that Abe Attell and Sport Sullivan were in Canada, trying to escape extradition. The gambler named Rachael Brown had not yet been found.

Curiously enough, Nat Evans was accidentally picked up in St. Louis as a suspicious character and arrested. But to local detectives he was only Nat Evans and was released on insufficient evidence. Sleepy Bill Burns, it was reported, had skipped to Mexico.

Actually Attell was not in Montreal this time; he was sweating in New York. But then, Fallon had told him not to worry. So when he was instructed to turn himself in (he refused to do that on principle), he allowed himself to be arrested in Times Square, by appointment, as it were. Requisition papers were immediately signed by Illinois Governor Small, to escort Attell to Chicago as a fugitive from Illinois justice. It was said in Chicago that Attell would tell all. It was once again assured that he would not fight extradition. George Gorman was relieved. He hungered to put Attell on the stand.

Attell was booked at New York's West Side Police Court. He gave his age as thirty-eight, his occupation as clerk, his address at 854 Seventh Avenue.

Then, Fallon went to work. He appeared in court before Magistrate Robert C. Ten Eyeck. "We admit that the prisoner is Abe Attell. But we will not admit that he is the Abe Attell mentioned in the Chicago indictment. The prisoner was not in Chicago at the time mentioned and knows nothing about the case. If the Chicago authorities send witnesses here who can prove that Attell is the man wanted, we will make no further objections to extradition."

Immediately, Gorman saw there was going to be trouble with Fallon. To combat this, he sent Sammy Pass, the Chicago manufacturer's agent and friend of the White Sox, to New York to identify Attell. Pass had been one of the complaining witnesses before the Grand Jury, having been suckered into bets with Attell amounting to $3,000.

Fallon knew all this, of course. He even knew what train Sammy Pass had taken to New York. And when it pulled into Grand Central Station, Fallon himself was there to meet it. He wanted to buy Sammy a drink. . . .

He bought him a lot more than one. To Fallon, whisky was the tonic of life. He never minded combining this kind of business with this kind of pleasure. He could even get to like his victims. He ended up asking Pass one simple question: "How much did the Series cost you?" A moment later, $3,000 changed hands.

On the following day, Samuel Pass testified that insofar as Abe Attell was concerned, this whole business was a mistake. He had never met this Attell, nor had he been suckered into bets with him before the 1919 World Series. It was someone else who claimed to be Abe Attell. He had come to New York because "I did not want to see an innocent man go to jail!"

To the Judge, there was insufficient evidence to cause Attell's extradition. He banged his gavel and dismissed the Little Champ. His troubles, as Fallon had promised him some months before in Rothstein's apartment, were over.

In Chicago, George Gorman's troubles were only beginning. A few days before, Hal Chase had been released in San Jose on the flimsy technicality that a proper warrant had not been sent. The State of California refused to extradite him and canceled his bail. Gorman could not help but wonder whether Fallon had arranged this also.

Then, too, where was Joseph "Sport" Sullivan?

Who—and where—was the man named Rachael Brown?

And what about Sleepy Bill Burns?

All around him, the rats were escaping from the traps and fleeing into the woodwork. He could almost hear them laughing at him.

Nobody was laughing at Ban Johnson. He was going to bring in a witness if he had to collar one himself. His first target was the Texan Bill Burns. Burns was a gambler. Like all gamblers in trouble, Johnson reasoned, Burns would run away or turn State's witness. The problem, then, was to find him. How does one find a rat like that? Texas was a big state.

Shrewdly, he headed for Texas by way of Philadelphia. He would find the rat with the aid of a rat-friend. Billy Maharg was not hard to find. He was still a ten-dollar-a-day worker at the Ford Assembly Plant.

Johnson made a deal with him: he would pay his Ford company salary and all expenses if he would go to Texas to find Burns. If he did, Johnson promised to keep Maharg from being indicted. Maharg agreed. Since he knew much of Burns's habits, having spent a year with him on a Texas ranch, he felt he could locate him. . . .

It took Maharg two weeks to track Burns down. He found him in a little border town called Del Rio, doing some languid fishing in the Rio Grande. Maharg told him that Johnson wanted to see him. He recommended that Burns talk to him, for Johnson seemed ready to make some kind of a deal.

It could be said that Burns even enjoyed the meeting, for it was Johnson (and a lawyer working for the prosecution, John Tyrrell) who were on the asking end, having come all the way to Del Rio to see him. Burns could sit back and listen: Just what did the President of the American League have to offer him?

The answer was simple enough: immunity. The State of Illinois needed a witness. All he had to do was tell his story, exactly as it happened.

Burns's first reaction was to cringe. He feared reprisal from the gamblers. The world of the stool pigeon was an eerie one. Johnson had to smile: and what was the world of the fugitive from justice; a paradise?

Burns still didn't like the deal. Why should he even appear at the trial? His information had it that none of the indicted gamblers were going to appear: their indictments could not hold up. Johnson was ready to wager him $100 that Burns's indictment would. He was also ready to wager him another $100 that they would get him extradited. Burns couldn't keep on running forever, now, could he?

This time, Burns smiled back: the word "wager" amused him, and the way Johnson threw the sum of $100 at him, as if it were some colossal figure. But in the end, he realized the alternatives: either he returned to Chicago as a defendant to stand trial with the others, or he testified for the State. Or, Johnson added, he kept on running.

He thought about it over night. The more he did, the less he felt the danger of gangster reprisal. After all, who would he be fingering? Abe Attell? One or two other minor punks? It wasn't as if they were going to jail as a result; they weren't even going to be there! Then, too, he saw himself getting retribution by his testimony. The ballplayers and gamblers who had crossed him up, failed to pay him for his efforts—this would be his way of getting even.

Johnson took Burns and Maharg back to Chicago. Maharg went on to Philly and the Ford Motor Company. Burns was bedded down in a small, out-of-the-way hotel, protected by American League detectives.

With a witness like Burns, the State was ready to begin trial.

V THE TRIAL

"Where is Arnold Rothstein? Why was he not indicted? Why were Brown, Sullivan, Attell, and Chase allowed to escape? Why were these underpaid ballplayers brought here to be the goats in this case? . . ."

A. Morgan Frumberg
DEFENSE ATTORNEY

1

The ballplayers had watched the spring pass them by, held in limbo by the tortuous deliberations of the law. It was a sloppy period for them in which the months of waiting seemed endless and without function. In April, the baseball world had begun its season without them, leaving them to stew in their guilt and loneliness. Except for Gandil, it was their first experience out of uniform and it brought home to them the full impact of their dependence on it. It wasn't only a question of their livelihood; no matter how often they talked of money, each of them knew what the others were really concerned with. They were ballplayers. That's all they were. Not pool-hall owners, or farmers, or garagemen, or businessmen. The center of their lives was their talent on spiked shoes. Without the demonstration of this, they were nothing. They noted the failure of the 1921 Sox to win ball games and tried to laugh about it, as if this was a backhanded testimonial to their prowess. But their bitterness had long since become overshadowed by their shame, and old enemies no longer seemed hostile nor the causes of their bitterness so sharp.

They tried to busy themselves, using their talent and renown as best they could. A Chicago investment broker, George Miller, put up money to back them in a semipro club named "The Major Stars." Its nucleus consisted of Jackson, Risberg, Williams, McMullin, Felsch, and Gandil. Cicotte, averse to placing himself in the public eye, declined to join them. As for Buck Weaver, his sole intent in life was to clear his name and return to baseball. He assumed an attitude of complete innocence and kept himself away from the others—especially those who had named him.

But even in semipro, there were obstacles. Local officials were pressured to oppose these games, for semipro baseball was primarily a Sunday activity. The concept of climaxing the Lord's Day with a ball game of confessed bribe-takers seemed like a travesty of morality. Besides, the local semipro association of clubs, had always been permitted to use Comiskey Park for special occasions. What would Comiskey say about this kind of competition? An emergency meeting was held, and it was decided that no club in the association would be permitted to play against "The Major Stars."

The result of all this was nothing more than an irritant to the ballplayers. If money could be made at such ball games, there were other community clubs ready to apply the American concept of justice: after all, these men were innocent until proven guilty. . . .

The ballplayers themselves clung to that concept. The more they were victimized by the stalling legal machinery of the State of Illinois, the more they felt purged of their guilt. Over the long months of waiting, their sensitive ears were filled with the scuttlebutt of the pending trial and what appeared to be their constantly shifting status. Rumors and opinions bounced them back and forth like ping-pong balls: They had a good chance. The State had no case. If it had, it would have prosecuted months before. Especially when the public resentment against the fix was at its peak. . . . Or, they were doomed. Ban Johnson would see to that. The delay enabled the prosecution to find Bill Burns and bring him to Chicago to testify as State's evidence. Besides, regardless of the waiting period, the American public would never stand for their acquittal. Not after those confessions.

But they came to realize that, for all the nerve-racking impact, time was working for them. If they were rattled by the muddiness of the law, they found reassurance in other forces that seemed to be on their side. Their lawyers were the best example of that. Ben Short, Thomas Nash, Michael Ahearn . . . they were powerful men, as prominent in the legal profession as the players were in baseball. They acted with vigor and inspired confidence. The ballplayers were told they had hired the best.

There was, however, something unbelievable about it. Who, actually, *had* hired them? In the days immediately after the indictments last October, there had been a number of legal confabs with several lawyers during which nothing had been settled. Only Weaver had gone ahead, retaining Nash to work for him. Over the winter, Short and Ahearn had come into the picture and a legal team had been formed. The ballplayers had made token payments; there had been no requests for more. As the months dragged on, the consciousness of the ever-rising fee due these high-priced men staggered the defendants—until it became clear that such payments were to be handled by others.

By "others," the ballplayers realized, the lawyers meant Charles A. Comiskey. When "Ropes" O'Brien suddenly "shifted" from the staff of the prosecution to the defense, the line-up became much clearer. This was Alfred Austrian's work—in behalf of his client. To the ballplayers, it meant only one thing: Comiskey wanted to get them off. He wanted them acquitted in a court of law and given a clean bill of health. The telegram of suspension had spelled it out: "IF YOU ARE INNOCENT OF ANY WRONG DOING, YOU AND EACH OF YOU WILL BE REINSTATED."

It was such a neat picture of mutual interests, so beneficial to all parties, that nothing else made sense. The lawyers supported this highly promising view of things. The ballplayers rallied their hopes and eagerly waited for the trial that would determine their fate.

2

On June 27, 1921, a major heat wave began in the Midwest. Temperatures rose to the high 90's and never seemed to waver. The trial began with it, and the courtroom was overcrowded with over ninety coatless spectators, adding to the discomfort of the small, stifling room. These were baseball buffs of all ages. They returned day after day, as wedded to the dramatics of the trial as any fan was to the World Series itself. There were many Chicago youngsters among them, repeatedly fighting their way into the courtroom to feed on the sight of their heroes in this bizarre setting. They would watch the action, unaccustomed to its rituals and traditions. They were more closely tuned to the flavor of Comiskey Park and brought with them the spirit of the grandstand. As a result, the bailiffs had a busy time trying to maintain order.

The presiding judge was Hugo Friend, a man who seemed no

older than the defendants. The ballplayers sat in small groups, separated from each other. In one section sat Cicotte, Jackson, and Williams. In another, Riseberg and Felsch. Gandil sat alone. When Buck
Weaver entered, he passed them all, acting as if he didn't even know
them. The word was out that the others were angry at Weaver for not
playing ball with them on The Major Stars.

Nobody seemed to care that Sport Sullivan, Abe Attell, Hal
Chase, Bill Burns, or the gambler known as Rachael Brown, were
absent. As for the indicted St. Louis shirtwaist manufacturer, Carl
Zork, this new star defendant of Robert Crowe and George Gorman
was said to be "too sick" to come to Chicago at this time. His attorney explained: "When I would question him, he would turn white
and cry and tremble, and it was impossible to continue a conversation." The State countered with an affidavit from Paul Richert of
St. Louis who swore he had seen Zork, perfectly healthy, on the streets
a few days before. Another gambler from St. Louis, Ben Franklin,
was also "too sick" to attend trial.

Gorman turned to the bench, insisting that these defendants be
present; it was virtually impossible to proceed without them. Judge
Friend agreed, warned the St. Louis lawyers that they must present
their clients or be held in contempt.

The defense opened with a motion to quash the trial, claiming
that the indictments were illegal under Illinois law. There were five
separate conspiracies charged in one indictment as laid out in the bill
of particulars:

1. A conspiracy to defraud the public.
2. A conspiracy to defraud Ray Schalk.
3. A conspiracy to commit a confidence game.
4. A conspiracy to injure the business of the American League.
5. A conspiracy to injure the business of Charles A. Comiskey.

Defense Attorney Ben Short charged that "the State has come into
court, limping and lame, and knows its case is a failure. If it wasn't
a failure, you'd have the real babies of this conspiracy here—the men
who made millions—and not these ballplayers who were reported
to get big salaries but most of whom got practically nothing!"

Gorman retorted, "We've got the real leaders!" Then he added guardedly, "All except those who are sick."

Short ridiculed him, his voice rising derisively: "You'll make a farce out of this if you can, won't you!"

Gorman snapped back, "There is nothing farcial about this conspiracy!"

After recess, the State submitted a list of witnesses it would call. They were familiar names, relatively insignificant to the prosecution of the case: Charles Comiskey, Kid Gleason, Garry Herrmann, John Heydler, Ban Johnson, Ring Lardner, etc. etc.

There was one name, however, that concerned the defense: William "Sleepy Bill" Burns.

A week later, on July 5, Judge Friend denied the defense's motion to quash the indictments, and the panneling of the jury began. On hand were 100 veniremen. Each side was awarded 120 peremptory challenges. Before they were through, over 600 prospective jurors were questioned.

The questioning itself was indicative. The State probed into the attitude of each venireman concerning the value he would attach to the testimony of a co-conspirator: Would the juror find fault with the Illinois law that a man may be convicted on the uncorroborated testimony of an accomplice? (Clearly the prosecution was going to rely on Sleepy Bill Burns.) These were supplemented by a barrage of such questions as: Do you know any ballplayers? Did you ever play semipro or pro ball? Did you see the 1919 World Series? Do you oppose Sunday baseball? Do you think baseball is an honest game? Do you bet? Do you bet in baseball pools?

It took three days to agree on four jurors. By July 12, there were still only four. The Judge grew angry. Unless more speed was shown, he would order night sessions.

The ballplayers watched and waited and wondered. Nothing seemed to be happening, yet the courtroom was never lacking in spectators. Even during the dull panneling sessions, the uniqueness of major-league ballplayers standing trial excited great curiosity. The crowds came and gaped at them, asked for autographs, encouraged them, treated them more like maligned heroes than criminals. Their spirits soared at this daily show of support and public approval.

One day, a group of loyal members of the White Sox paid a surprise visit. Kid Gleason, Dickie Kerr, Red Faber, and Eddie Collins filed in, and suddenly all proceedings stopped. It was as if the court sensed the dramatics of the moment in which these two rival groups, one a symbol of integrity, the other of corruption, were confronting each other in public for the first time. This, as it turned out, was true enough: the ballplayers had not faced each other since the previous September. The visitors sat down quietly before they became aware of the probing eyes upon them. In the now silent court, they sensed what was expected of them, but they did not know how to respond to it.

Then, from across the room, Swede Risberg called out jovially, "Hello, Kid, how's the boy?"

It was a clean, warm, friendly greeting, and Gleason responded in kind. "Pretty good, Swede—how's yourself?"

They shook hands warmly. "And there's old Bucko!" Gleason twinkled. "Stacking up pretty good, Buck?"

"Sure," Weaver began, but Faber and Kerr started to tickle him. Weaver was famous for his ticklishness. They showed more friendliness toward each other in those five minutes than in the entire two seasons past.

They kidded around and talked baseball for a few minutes. Then as the court came to order and the visitors filed out, Happy Felsch called after them, "Hope you win the pennant, boys!"

At the moment, the Chicago White Sox were battling to stay out of the cellar, seventeen games behind the lead.

This demonstration of compatibility and mutual concern was vividly reported by the press. The editorial angle attached to it was highly critical: If honesty in baseball was to be put on trial, the honest ballplayers ought to shun the enemy, not fraternize with them. A war on corruption must not be a friendly one; its symbolic rivals must not be indifferent to the right *vs.* wrong values they represent. The public, in short, must be convinced that the courts and baseball itself meant business.

Comiskey was immediately alerted to this criticism of his honest ballplayers. He called on Gleason to rectify the situation. The problem had only one solution: Gleason must simply deny any friendliness. The papers would print his denial. The story had been in error; they would retract. Nobody had tickled Weaver. Perhaps he'd been tickling himself. . . .

Gleason submitted to this charade, but the retraction was an empty one. It fell on deaf ears. The press, for all its moral protestations, was more inclined to feed its readers the corrupt angle. The wider its spread, the juicier the story—and, of course, the more righteous its indignation.

The whole thing was a tempest in a pot of tea. In the *Sporting News,* baseball's national weekly, the aging writer, John B. Sheriden, was a legitimately angry man: "I have seen prominent citizens rob a city blind and retain their positions of influence and honor. . . . But I have never seen the rich bribe giver punished by the majestic law. These things being so, it is not easy for me to feel so shocked at the fraternization of the White Sox with their former teammates."

The trouble was, America expected higher morals from ballplayers than they expected from businessmen—or anyone else, for that matter.

The defense attorneys were eager to interview Sleepy Bill Burns, and requested permission of the Court to do so. St. Louis second baseman Joe Gedeon, Risberg's friend, who had revealed his knowledge of the fix to Comiskey in hopes of getting the $20,000 reward, was also lined up as a prosecution witness and included in the request. The defense would confront them with Gandil, Risberg and company. The Judge acquiesced and compelled the State to produce the two witnesses.

Both Burns and Gedeon were uneasy. The thought of facing the players was unnerving. After all, they had all known each other first as ballplayers, and now two of them would rat on the others. Gandil was famous for putting his big fist through a heavy wooden door, and the Swede, as Jackson had put it, "was a hard guy." The two witnesses had no desire to sit in the same room with them, certainly not without ample protection.

There were several bailiffs present when the interview began. Along with their lawyers, Gandil, Risberg, and Cicotte walked into the Hearing Room. Burns and Gedeon looked up nervously. Then the Texan smiled sheepishly and drawled his greeting: "Well, hya, boys. . . ."

Surprisingly enough, the ballplayers smiled back, embarrassed by this strange, uneasy confrontation. Their involuntary reaction was not violent at all, but quite the opposite. The witnesses and their victims greeted each other like long-lost pals.

Burns relaxed. He could play his role with impunity now. He answered all of Defense Attorney Ben Short's questions with a single well-coached answer: "I do not care to discuss the case at all." Said Joe Gedeon: "I have nothing to say!"

It could be said that the defendants might have done better with less friendliness.

On July 15, the final four jurors were sworn in amid cheering from spectators and veniremen alike. The New York *Times* described the jubilation as "the kind which generally greets a 9th inning home-team rally." It had taken two weeks to fill this jury box. There were two clerks, two machinists, telephone repairman, stationary engineer, hydraulic press operator, foreman of a motor company, steel worker, salesman, florist, and foreman of a stockyards rendering plant—all men. All but two were married, their ages between thirty and forty-seven, most of them under thirty-six. All understood baseball, none had played semipro or pro ball, none claimed to be ardent fans. One of them, a machinist, said he was a White Sox rooter, but had bet on Cincinnati because he thought they were the better club.

On Monday, July 18, in a sweltering courtroom, George Gorman rose to make his opening remarks. He reviewed the story of the fix, sticking closely to the narrative as recounted in the Grand Jury confessions and repeated to the press. It was only when he started to quote Cicotte's confession that the defense rose to object. The ballplayers, it was announced, repudiated those confessions. There was to be no mention of them! The Judge sustained the objection.

Michael Ahearn punctuated his victory with appropriate baseball jargon: "You won't get to first base with those confessions!"

Gorman replied in kind: "We'll make a home run with them!"

"You may get a long hit," Ahearn conceded, "but you'll be thrown out at the plate!"

The spectators got a laugh out of the interchange; the eight ballplayers did not.

Nor did they laugh when Charles Comiskey was called to the witness stand, the first witness for the State. Led by Gorman's questions, he reviewed the high lights of his brilliant career in baseball. Then, suddenly Ben Short shot at him: "It's a fact, is it not, that you jumped from the National League to the Brotherhood (Players League) in 1890?"

It was a deceiving question, completely out of context, loaded with innuendo. It was asked in ignorance of baseball's and Comiskey's history. In the language of the baseball-oriented courtroom, Short had thrown him a "nasty curve." Had he been better informed, he would have seen the irony of his question: the lawyer for these eight exploited athletes was attacking the exploiter for his one significant action against the plight of the exploited.

Comiskey, having sacrificed himself for the good of the Brotherhood, as noted above, could only rage at the question. His face reddened as he leaned forward in his chair, shaking his finger furiously at Short.

"It is not true!" he shouted. "I've never broken a contract. Never! I haven't broken any or jumped any. You can't get away with that with me!"

"Well, you jumped from one league to another," Short shouted back.

"I went to the Brotherhood, but I never broke a contract. You can't belittle me. . . ." Comiskey seemed almost ready to attack.

"Well, you're trying to belittle these ballplayers. . . ."

Judge Friend took pains to quiet the stormy scene. If Comiskey's anger seemed out of proportion to the attack, no one made mockery of it. His sensitivities on the score were well founded.

Short proved to be a better-informed interrogator when he got on Comiskey's financial history. He tried to point out that the White Sox organization had made more money in 1920 than it had in any previous year. Gorman objected: Comiskey's finances were not relevant. Judge Friend sustained the objection. Short raged at this. "This man is getting richer all the time, and my clients are charged with conspiracy to injure his business!"

Again, objection. Again, sustained.

Short pursued Comiskey on his penuriousness: "Isn't it a fact that you only pay your players three dollars a day board——"

"Objection!"

"Sustained!"

In disgust, Ben Short released the witness.

The trial came alive on the following day. William Burns was called to the witness stand by the State. Though this move was no surprise to anyone, there was considerable tension in the courtroom as the witness was sworn in. The questioning began with Assistant State's Attorney, Edward Prindeville.

Burns was dressed in a dark green checkered suit and a lavender shirt, with a light bow tie. He was nervous at first, and wiped his face repeatedly with a large handkerchief. He revealed a peculiar habit of running his hands over the bald spot of his head. There were periods during the questioning when he couldn't seem to take his hand away from it. He would lean forward with his chin resting on his right hand. His voice was pitched low, too low, in fact. He was constantly, embarrassingly, reminded by the Court to speak up. After a few minutes, he requested and was granted permission to shed his coat.

Burns gave his address as San Saba, Texas. He was forty-one years old, married since quitting professional baseball in 1912 when he went into the oil business. He then told how he had visited New York in September of 1919, specifically to sell some oil leases. It was then he had bumped into Eddie Cicotte at the Hotel Ansonia. Prindeville asked Cicotte to rise so that Burns could identify him.

Eddie Cicotte slowly got to his feet and stared aimlessly at the witness stand. He kept his hands by his sides and waited obediently. Burns looked back at him but said nothing for a moment. It was as if he were momentarily lost in daydreams. There were seven other ballplayers and four gamblers, but to Cicotte, the lawyers were singling him out as if he were some special breed of criminal. He could guess why: the State was going to make him the number one target because it was he who had spit up his guts last September.

"That's him!" Burns finally spoke out, and Cicotte sat down.

"What did Cicotte say when you met him in New York?" Prindeville asked.

At this point, Michael Ahearn leaped to his feet. "Objection!" All eyes turned to him. "The prosecution has no right to relate any conversations with alleged conspirators before a conspiracy has been proved!"

The Judge nodded. "Sustained."

Prindeville shrugged, seemingly unconcerned. He assured the court that he would have no trouble proving this. Burns would be allowed to give this testimony later.

The questioning continued. Burns exposed the initial negotiations, contact by contact. He was led through a daily record of his meetings with Cicotte, Maharg, Chase, Attell, Bennett, and Arnold Rothstein at the Jamaica Race Track. Burns also told of his meeting with the players in Cincinnati at the Hotel Sinton, just before the game.

Q: Who was there?

A: There were Gandil, McMullin, Williams, Felsch, Cicotte, and Buck Weaver.

Q: How about Jackson?

A: I didn't see him there.

Q: Did you have any conversation with them?

A: I told them I had the hundred thousand dollars to handle the throwing of the World Series. I also told them that I had the names of the men who were going to finance it. I told them they were waiting below.

Q: Who were the financiers?

A: They were Arnold Rothstein, Attell, and Bennett. (This was either an incredible error by Burns, or an outright lie. To say that Rothstein was in the Sinton lobby was preposterous. Burns, significantly, never mentioned it again.)

He described how Attell offered them $100,000 to be paid in five installments, that Attell was representing Arnold Rothstein who was "a walking bank."

Prindeville looked at Cicotte as he asked Burns the next question. Those sitting close to Cicotte saw him redden.

Q: Did the players make any statements concerning the order of games to be thrown?

A: Gandil and Cicotte said the first two games should be thrown. They said, however, that it didn't matter to them. They would throw them in any order the financiers wished.

Then Burns turned from the lawyer and again stared at Cicotte, this time with his slow Texas smile. Involuntarily, Cicotte began a move to get to his feet, as if he was supposed to rise again. Burns was becoming adept at using timely pauses. "Cicotte said he'd throw the first game if he had to throw the ball clear out of the Cincinnati ball park!"

The courtroom broke into a wave of laughter. Cicotte winced. He had no recollection of saying anything like that. The eyes of everyone in the room were on him. Even the other ballplayers around him were laughing—especially Gandil who was laughing out loud. Cicotte was too embarrassed to do anything but force his lips into a stupid grin.

Burns began rambling on as to how Attell had refused payment after the first game and had gone back to the players to tell them this. Burns named Gandil as the spokesman for the players. Gandil fixed his eyes squarely, penetratingly, on Burns. Somehow, the witness appeared rattled and his voice dropped so low that Defense Attorney Ben Short broke in: "If it please the Court, the witness must speak louder!"

Burns snapped back. "I probably could if I were like you!"

Short scowled at him. "What are you, ashamed of your story?"

At which point, the Judge interceded and calmed them down. Gandil grinned in triumph. If nothing else, it was a pleasure to get Burns's goat.

Burns had always been afraid of Gandil, and had despised him. Now he was holding all the cards. If he played them right, he could enjoy his victory.

Prindeville asked when he had seen Attell again. Burns told of taking Gandil and Williams to meet Attell and Bennett, and of how Attell had showed them the telegram from A.R. in New York promising $20,000.

When Burns said that the players had objected to being paid on Friday because it was supposed to be bad luck, he got a big laugh.

Q: Did Gandil say anything?

A: Yes. He wanted to know if they were being double-crossed. I told him that I wasn't double-crossing them.

Q: Did you offer them any security?

A: Yes, I told them I'd give them an oil lease.

Q: Did you put it up?

A: No. Maharg advised me not to. He said Rothstein might double-cross us, and then I would be out. The ballplayers wanted to put my lease in escrow, but I refused.

Q: When did you see Attell next?

A: Immediately after the second game. Maharg was with me. We went to his room at the Sinton. Bennett was also there.

Q: Is Bennett in the courtroom?

A: He is.

The courtroom came alive, looking around in search of the mysterious Bennett.

Q: Do you see him?

A: Yes. He's behind that post. (Burns rose from his chair and pointed.) He's the man in that yellow shirt.

Judge Friend ordered the man so designated to rise and be identified before the jury. Max Lusker, attorney for the three gamblers, immediately leaped to his feet and protested. He was overruled. He then told the jury that the man so designated was not "Bennett" but his client, David Zelser! Burns, of course, had known this partner of Attell's only under the name he had assumed for the Series.

The State turned the witness over to the defense. James "Ropes" O'Brien plunged into attack. His aim was nothing more or less than an attempt at character assassination.

Q: Mr. Burns, how much money did you receive from Ban Johnson?

Gorman objected. Judge Friend sustained.

Q: Did you get five hundred dollars from Ban Johnson?

A: Yes, for my expenses for two months.

Q: How much of this went to your wife and how much did you keep?

A: (with a smile) I don't know.

Q: Had you any visible means of support during the last year other than Ban Johnson?

Burns replied that he had worked some in Mexico, where he had gone after he was indicted. At which, Defense Attorney Michael Ahearn broke in and snapped at him:

Q: I suppose you went to work for Pancho Villa when you were there?

A: (testily) No, I wouldn't work for Villa. And I wouldn't work for you, either, Mr. Ahearn!

Burns then explained his return in April to Del Rio, Texas, where Maharg caught up with him.

Q: What was your occupation then?

A: Well, fishing.

Q: What for—witnesses?

No reply.

Q: You knew you were coming under indictment when you came to Chicago?

A: Yes.

Q: Being under indictment didn't worry you, did it?

A: No.

Burns could smile. He knew he had had a real good day.

Refreshed by a night's sleep, he returned to the witness stand at ten o'clock in the morning. Assistant State's Attorney Edward Prindeville opened the testimony with a question about what happened in Attell's room after the second game.

Burns's fluent description of the rolls of money, "four to five inches thick," and of the suitcases stuffed with bills held the courtroom and particularly the players in a rapt silence. Then he explained how Attell and Bennett had claimed that all the money was tied up in bets. To Burns the important point was his own protest against the paltry $10,000 Attell finally handed over.

Burns told how he tossed it on the bed in Gandil's room and said $10,000 was all Attell would give. "Gandil asked: 'Are we being double-crossed?' And I said, 'No, you ain't.' "

Q: Was anything said about the game the next day?

A: Yes. Attell told me to ask the players to win the next game. He said: "Tell the Sox to win a game so we can get more money down." This would help shift the odds. The players said they would think about it.

They thought about it, all right, Burns explained. Gandil told him the next day that the third game would go like the other two. But it didn't. Gandil himself had batted in the winning runs. Burns related how he and Maharg had lost their shirts, and how Attell and Bennett said it was the same with them.

Q: What did you do then?

A: I asked Gandil about my part of the $10,000 I had given them.

Q: Did you say anything to him about the $20,000 that Attell offered?

A: No, he never gave me a chance. I asked him again about the money they owed me. I said, "I'll get my share or I'll tell everything."

Q: What did he say to that?

A: (indignantly) He didn't say anything. Just walked away from me.

Burns was on the stand for his own protection. But his threat of two years earlier was becoming a dramatic reality.

Then, once again, defense attorneys took turns badgering him, trying to break down his story. They never got to first base.

From New York, however, Arnold Rothstein released an angry statement to the press concerning Burns's testimony.

". . . I talked to Burns once in my life when he approached me in the matter of throwing the games. I didn't think he had a chance in the world and told him so, and added that even if he could assure me he could actually do it, I didn't want him to ever speak to me again as long as he lived. That was the first and last time I ever had knowledge of the situation until I heard my name being used out West [Chicago].

"Burns said I was waiting downstairs in the Sinton Hotel, Cincinnati, to join a conference between himself and the other ballplayers. I was never in Cincinnati in my life. At the time he mentioned, I was at the race track in New York. . . ."

If the Court wondered about Rothstein, there were others who wondered more about Attell. According to the State's own star witness, Attell covered the action of the fix like a giant octopus, with all eight tentacles reaching out for money. Where, then, was this little monster? Why wasn't he in court standing trial? The course of his escape was revived by the press. Somehow, they recalled, he had convinced a New York court that he was not the same Attell that the Chicago Grand Jury was looking for. Or, at least, Fallon had.

The New York *Sun* was bitterly derisive about it. "Is Abe Attell himself or is he somebody else? The good Abe Attell, one might al-

most call him the Dr. Jekyll Abe, thinks that somewhere in Chicago
there is another, a bad Abe, a sort of Mr. Hyde Abe, who goes
around fixing World Series games, and corrupting lily-white ballplayers who have wives and kiddies for whose sake they must become corrupt."

The little Champ could laugh. Nobody could hurt him nine
hundred miles from the battleground.

3

As the third day of testimony began, the State had good reason to be
jubilant. Burns continued to be a remarkably agile witness who, after
his initial nervousness, took to the business of testifying as if it were
his own particular cup of tea. He was amiable, quick-witted, and
pleasant. He became cordial even to aggressive defense attorneys who
constantly sought to trip him up. He seemed like a man without an
ax to grind, an honest witness who was there to put the truth of the
matter before the Court.

Then, too, Judge Friend came through for them. He ruled that
the State had proved a conspiracy had existed, and that testimony
could now be entered concerning actions that took place in New York.

When Burns resumed the stand for further questioning by the
State, the bailiffs had to struggle to keep the spectators in their seats.
Burns himself seemed the coolest person in the room. This was
merely a stage on which he was certainly the principal actor, a role
he was enjoying to the fullest.

Especially today. Today he was going to let loose with some
heavy artillery. He had waited hungrily for the moment . . . then it
came:

Gorman: Mr. Burns, I am going to question you now concerning
certain meetings you attended at the Hotel Ansonia in New York
City before the World Series. . . . When did you meet Cicotte in
New York prior to the World Series of 1919?

A: September 16.

Q: What did he say to you?

A: He said that the Sox would win the pennant, and that he had something good for me.

Q: Did he tell you what that good thing was?

Burns stared at the crowded court. The spectators leaned forward in their seats, waiting for him to come across.

A: No.

Q: When did you next meet him?

A: On the eighteenth.

Q: Who was present?

A: Cicotte and Gandil.

Q: Was anything said?

A: Yes, Gandil said: "If I could get $100,000, I would throw the World Series!"

He had taken his time spitting it out, and the crowd really came alive. There was an audible response, and all eyes shifted from him to Gandil. This was the first declaration that the ballplayers had initiated the fix, and not the gamblers. As it sank in, the effect was devastating. Even the Judge seemed jolted. Gandil sat there, wearing his same stone face. Burns thought: The sonofabitch—if he'd paid me off, none of this would have happened!

Q: And what did you say?

A: I said I would see what I could do.

Q: Was anything else said?

A: Well, Gandil said they would sure throw the Series if they won the pennant.

The courtroom reacted with a babble of shock. It was several moments before order was restored.

Joe Jackson sat through all this like a kid listening to a fascinating story he had never heard before. Somehow he'd assumed that it was the gamblers who had started it all. He had been following the proceedings with absorbed attention. As Burns had pointed out, he hadn't been at those meetings in Cincinnati. He had ducked them, an indication of his confusions about the fix. Now he was sitting there with Gandil, Cicotte, Risberg *et al,* all of them lumped together in one big, silent bunch. Was that the way they would be judged? He hated himself for having confessed. He had run scared and gotten drunk. Not so much because he had been stupid, but because he'd been weak. He had allowed himself to believe the lawyers' promise of protection. Now he had no choice but to rely on them. That, too, he hated. Because he couldn't understand all this. At recesses, he would nervously joke about his ignorance. "Hey, lawyer, who's winning?" he would ask Ben Short. His counsel would smile back and shrug. In a ball game, Jackson could always look at the scoreboard and tell. Here, the answer was a shrug.

The State was through with Burns and turned him over to the defense. Attorney Michael Ahearn stood before him a few moments later, and the badgering began in earnest this time. It led, however, only to Burns's further triumph.

Q: When you went to Cincinnati, *you* proposed the conspiracy to the players!

A: I did not.

Q: You talked of an offer of $100,000 made by Attell and Bennett.

A: That was the players' proposition!

This knocked Ahearn right out of the box. James "Ropes" O'Brien stepped in and began questioning Burns about how much money he'd been paid to testify. Burns was ready for him. In a matter-of-fact tone, he itemized the payments made by Ban Johnson, out of American League funds. They totaled $700, covering expenses he and his wife had incurred over a period of several months. He made it all sound very legitimate. After all, a workingman should not have to suffer financially for giving testimony for the State.

Max Lusker, attorney for gambler David Zelser, kept trying to shake Burn's identification of Zelser as "Bennett."

Q: Mr. Burns, when did you see Bennett first?

A: In the Ansonia Hotel in 1919.

Q: When last?

A: About a week ago, I saw his back in Chicago. He was about two hundred yards away.

Q: You have a good memory, have you? You are able to remember a man after two years' time?

It was a specious question, for it ignored all the times Burns had seen him during the Series.

A: I can remember faces.

Q: Backs, too, I suppose?

Everybody laughed, including Burns.

A: I did, this man.

Q: By the way, where were you going to get your reward for fixing the Series?

A: The players, and also Attell.

Q: You were going to be paid by Attell?

A: Yes.

Q: You didn't think that was double-crossing, did you?

A: No.

Q: You were going to get a slice both ways, eh?

A: Sure.

Q: Did you tell the players?

A: No. It was none of their business.

Q: You were afraid you would lose it if you told them, weren't you?

Burns refused to answer.

Lusker was then followed by the acrid, Defense Attorney Ben Short. He forced Burns to admit that one of the reasons he was testifying against the defendants was because they double-crossed him.

Q: You told Gandil you would spill the beans if they didn't come through with your share, didn't you?

A: That's right.

Q: The players double-crossed you, didn't they?

A: Yes.

Q: Well, you double-crossed them.

A: Not until they crossed me.

Q: Is that a reason for testifying?

A: One of them.

Q: Then it is not for the purity of baseball?

A: Well, they double-crossed me and I would have been the fall guy for the whole outfit.

The savage irony of this line of reasoning was not lost on Short. He exploited it for all he could get out of it. His voice rose to attack.

Q: If the players had *really* been crooked, you would have been satisfied! Do you think you are even with the boys now?

A: I am liable to be before I leave here!

The spectators laughed. Short snorted and stepped back. At this moment, he genuinely felt hatred for the witness.

"You don't like me much, do you, Bill?" Short's tone was full of contempt.

Burns was not one to relinquish the upper hand. "Sure I do, Ben. You're a smart fellow, and I wish we had someone like you at the head of this deal; we'd all be rich, now. . . ."

Short was followed by Thomas Nash, who tried to get Burns in a contradiction. He forced Burns to admit that he'd been mistaken when he said he had met the Sox players the evening before the first game, in the Sinton Hotel.

Q: Didn't you say you saw them before the first game?
A: I ain't saying.

Nash immediately turned to the Bench, declaring he would have the witness impeached as a perjurer. Burns got the message. He requested permission to change his testimony, admitting that he had made a mistake. He told the Judge he was just a "plain fella from Texas" and sometimes got a mite confused with all this lawyer talk. Judge Friend was amused, but granted permission. The Jury was instructed to note this change.

Burns was then allowed to leave the witness stand, his testimony and cross-examination finished. State's Attorney George Gorman was proud of him. Burns had been a magnificent witness. He had remained unshakable—with minor transgressions—in the face of a battery of high-powered attacks. His performance surprised those who had known him. Some were actually incredulous. The wiseacres among them said they hadn't thought that Sleepy Bill could stay awake long enough to put over such a big deal in the first place.

To Cicotte, who had known Burns over the years, his performance was baffling. He had never sensed that the drawling Texan was capable of anything like this. Burns could make a dozen mistakes, find himself in a manure pile of troubles, yet now he came up clean. Cicotte need slip only once, and they'd be cutting him up in pieces.

On the mound, Cicotte was king. Year after year, they hadn't come any better. Burns had been a sloppy, very mediocre, third-rate nothing. Was the difference all in the skill of the pitching arm? What changed the pattern when it really came to staying alive?

The answer to that was the answer to the whole story of Cicotte's life. He had grown up believing it was talent that made a man big. If you were good enough, and dedicated yourself, you could get to the top. Wasn't that enough of a reward? But when he got there, he had found out otherwise. They all fed off him, the men who ran the show and pulled the strings that kept it working. They used him and used him, and when they had used him up, they would dump him. In the few years he had been up, they had always praised him and made him feel like a hero to the people of America. But all the time they paid him peanuts. The newspapermen who came to watch him pitch and wrote stories about him made more money than he did. Meanwhile, Comiskey made a half million dollars a year on Cicotte's right arm.

Burns knew how to operate. So did Gandil. Cicotte didn't. That was the answer.

4

Having disposed of his star witnesses, State's Attorney George Gorman then advised the Court that the original copies of the signed confessions and immunity waivers had disappeared. His statement was delivered as if this had just been discovered, and the courtroom responded with a sense of shock. Gorman explained that he had never seen them, that they had been stolen before he had taken office. He did not know where they were or what had happened to them. His response to persistent questions was "Ask Arnold Rothstein, maybe he knows!"

However, he had no intention of letting their disappearance exclude them from being admissible. "We would like to have them, of course, but the hole they leave can easily be plugged up by the testimony of the Grand Jurors, the court stenographers, and others present when the statements were obtained."

Judge Friend was sympathetic. He had, of course, already covered the law on this problem. He ruled that unless the State could prove that the confessions (copies were available) were made voluntarily, they could not be entered into the trial.

The battle then began over the immunity waivers. If the players had signed waivers, then the court would accept their confessions as freely given.

Gorman's first big gun was former Assistant State's Attorney Hartley Replogle. He, too, did not know what had happened to the waivers. He recalled that just before Maclay Hoyne had left office, Hoyne had taken a large quantity of papers from the Grand Jury files, ostensibly to have them copied for his own uses. Replogle had called this breach of procedure to the attention of Judge Charles Mac-Donald who supposedly had the papers impounded. Replogle also recalled a statement by the newly appointed Commissioner Landis to the effect that if there was any suspicious business going on, he would take Federal action.

Replogle testified that the ballplayers had signed the waivers of immunity, without duress and without any offer of reward.

With that, the Court recessed until Monday.

The question of the disappearing Grand Jury papers dominated everybody's weekend. On Monday, July 25, the day opened with a statement that rocked everybody—especially Arnold Rothstein in New York. Its author was Ban Johnson:

"I charge that Arnold Rothstein paid $10,000 for the Grand Jury confessions of Cicotte, Jackson, and Williams. I charge that this money, brought to Chicago by a representative of Rothstein, went to an attaché of the State's Attorney's office under the Hoyne administration. I charge that after Rothstein had examined these confessions in New York City, and had found that the ballplayers had not involved him to the extent of criminal liability, he gave the documents to his friend, the managing editor of a New York newspaper. I charge that the editor offered these documents for sale broadcast throughout the country."

John Tyrrell, Attorney for the State, declared that the Grand Jury would be summoned to investigate. But he was firm in denying that Rothstein would be summoned as a witness at the trial.

It was a ringing challenge to Rothstein in New York. He cried out that he would sue Johnson for $250,000 for libel and defamation of character. Johnson, intractible as ever, barked back defiantly. "Rothstein can go ahead and sue anytime he wants!"

As it turned out, the gambler chose to ignore it all. It was said that he took the advice of his old mentor, Tammany Hall's Big Tim Sullivan: "Never sue. They might prove it!"

The ballplayers watched the battle rage around them. The potential benefits resulting from the stolen confessions and immunity waivers had been carefully explained to them: it would simplify the repudiation of those confessions and make it extremely difficult for the prosecution to get them admitted as evidence. If there were carbon copies (the attorneys knew there were), at least there were no signatures on them. Nor were the signed immunity waivers available; thus, there was no way for the State to prove their validity. In short, whoever stole those papers did the ballplayers a big favor.

It was all part of the strange alignment of forces that seemed to link them all together. First, Comiskey, and now, perhaps, Arnold Rothstein himself—suddenly wanting to play ball with the ballplayers.

However incredible it seemed to them, it was nonetheless extremely comforting. It gave them reason to believe they would win this victory. And that was all that really mattered to them.

The State continued to press for the right to use the confessions. The Judge decided to listen to what the players had to say in order to determine whether they had or hadn't signed immunity waivers. To do this, he dismissed the jury and permitted a private interrogation.

Cicotte was questioned by his lawyer, Ben Short: "Was any promise of immunity made to you?"

Cicotte repeated what had happened when he was brought to the State's Attorney's office by Alfred Austrian. He said he had signed something, but didn't know what it was.

Gorman: "Didn't Replogle tell you that what you said could be used against you, and read the waiver?"

Cicotte: "I don't remember. When I told Judge MacDonald I didn't know any more than I told him, he got sore and said, "What are you trying to do, bull me?" I told the Judge I wasn't worried because Replogle and Austrian had promised I would be taken care of. Then they took me to the washroom where they all talked some more. . . ."

Ben Short then put Joe Jackson in the chair. "Did they say anything to you about immunity?"

Jackson also told the Judge that Austrian had made vague promises that he would not be prosecuted.

Short: Did Austrian tell you that Cicotte had been taken care of and you would be, too?

Jackson: Yes. He said that after confessing I could go anywhere —all the way to the Portuguese Islands, the Judge said. Then they gave me two bailiffs to protect me, and I went out and got polluted.

Short: Were you drunk when you went before the Grand Jury?

Jackson: About half, I guess. I'd been boozing.

Short: Did Mr. Replogle tell you that you have to sign an immunity waiver and that you would later be held responsible criminally for what you told the jurors?

Jackson: He read a lot of stuff to to me. I don't know what it was.

Short: Didn't you read what you signed?

Jackson: No. They'd given me their promise. I'd've signed my death warrant if they asked me to.

In the afternoon, Judge Charles MacDonald was called to testify. He recounted his confrontations with the three confessors and denied that any of them had been deprived of their rights.

Following this, Judge Hugo Friend summoned the jury to return to the Court. He had decided that the confessions had been made voluntarily. They would be admissible as part of the State's case. The confessions, however, were to implicate the confessors only.

To Cicotte, this was a frightening omen. The Judge's decision was noised around the court building as another big victory for the prosecution. The inside talk, usually a reliable weathervane, had it that the three confessing ballplayers would be hardest hit in the verdict. Not only had they named themselves, but they were deeply enmeshed in the web as spun by Bill Burns. Except for Gandil, the other five were mentioned only in passing. . . .

As for the indicted gamblers, some were already making book that they would go free. Except for David Zelser (Bennett), there wasn't a thing on any of those on trial.

The State's Attorney was riding high with his pending victory. He still held Billy Maharg and Joe Gedeon on his bench, ready to go in at the end in case he needed them. If there was any weakness in the State's case, Judge Friend pointed it out that afternoon: "There is so little evidence against these men (Buck Weaver, Happy Felsch, and gambler Carl Zork) that I doubt if I would allow a verdict of guilty to stand if it were brought in. But as some evidence has been brought against them, I will not dismiss them unless the State is willing to *nolle prosse*."

George Gorman had no such intention.

On Wednesday, July 27, the defense put David Zelser on the stand. When questioned by his lawyer, Max Lusker, Zelser categorically denied he had even been mixed up in the scandal. No, he was not Bennett. He insisted he had never met Burns or Maharg. As for Arnold Rothstein, the man Burns had claimed he was working for, Zelser declared he had never even seen him.

When cross-examined, however, he nervously admitted he had bet huge sums on the Cincinnati Reds. At first he did not remember in what room he stayed while in Cincinnati, but when confronted with hotel records, his memory improved. As it turned out, he had not only lived in the same room with Attell, but had registered at the hotel for him! And this room, Tyrrell reminded the court, "is the same large sample room where Attell kept his money in cases and hidden under the mattress! It is the same room where the gamblers hatched their conspiracy, and to which Arnold Rothstein had a private wire from New York."

"Bedfellows," the prosecution reminded the Court, "are seldom coincidence."

"Irrelevant!" snapped the defense.

"Next witness," said the Judge.

He was Billy Maharg. He gave his age as forty-one, his address in Philadelphia; he said he had been raised on a farm, had been mixed up in the fight game as a middleweight, had played major-league ball in one game in Detroit and one game in Philadelphia with the Phillies.

"How come only one game?" Short wanted to know.

"Well, there was a player's strike in 1912——" Maharg explained.

"And you scabbed!" Short snapped at him.

Again, Short was a poor baseball historian. Maharg had been recruited into service so that the Detroit Tigers could put a team on the field to sustain their franchise. The regular players had refused to play, protesting Ban Johnson's highhanded action in suspending and firing Ty Cobb when he went into the stands after a heckling fan.

Questioned by George Gorman, Maharg was an articulate witness. He had told his story enough times to feel completely at home with it.

Q: It has been intimated by defense attorneys that you are a ballplayer named "Peaches" Graham. Is that correct?

A: No. I have never been anything but Billy Maharg. I know Graham, but I am not he.

Q: Do you know Bill Burns?

A: Yes, I've known him for ten years.

Q: Did you see him in September, 1919.

A: Yes, he was in New York and sent me a telegram to come to see him. He was going on a hunting trip. I met him at the Ansonia Hotel.

Maharg told how he failed to raise the money in Philadelphia, or when they met Rothstein in New York, and how, later, another telegram from Burns sent him hurrying to Cincinnati where Burns told him that Attell had gotten Rothstein to finance the deal.

Q: Did you see Attell that night? [After the first game.]

A: Yes. About 9:30. I asked him why Rothstein had finally come across. Attell said that he had reminded Rothstein that he had saved his life once in a shooting scrape, and finally Rothstein agreed. Attell said he was going to get the money, all right. I told him that it looked to me like he was lying. We made arrangements to meet him again at the Sinton the next day.

Like Burns, Maharg then identified Zelser as Bennett. Bennett had told him that the ballplayers could not get any money "because they had told all the gamblers in the East and West, and it was impossible to get any real money down!" Attell then told Maharg that Arnold Rothstein had $300,000 on the Series and when it was over, "they'd all get their money."

Maharg, like Burns, remained unshakable. His story was essentially the same as Burns,'s for they had shared the whole experience together. His auspices—Ban Johnson—were also the same. The sameness added a strong layer of testimony to the State's apparently already strong case.

But there was one more inning to play.

5

On the morning of July 28, the battery of defense attorneys seemed surprisingly confident as they filed into Court. Their eagerness to get going infected the courtroom. There was an air of expectancy as Judge Friend entered and the clerk called the Court to order.

Thomas Nash, for the defense, rose and called William "Kid" Gleason to the stand. Nash went immediately to the point.

Q: Mr. Gleason, will you tell the Court, when did you arrive in Cincinnati for the 1919 Series?

A: Tuesday morning, the day before the first game.

Q: Did you get to the ball park for practice?

A: I did, about ten o'clock.

Q: How long did you stay?

A: For about an hour and a half.

Q: Then if Burns said he saw the defendants in a room at the Sinton Hotel in the forenoon, he is not telling the truth?

Gorman rose quickly to object. Judge Friend sustained it. The witness was not qualified to determine that.

Nash rephrased the question.

Q: Well, these defendants could not have been in a room at the Sinton during the hours between ten and twelve that morning?

A: Not while they were practicing.

The spectators reacted. Burns had clearly testified about a meeting on that morning that was vital to the conspiracy. The question was, could this kind of testimony shake Burns's effectiveness as a witness? Could it really shake the entire structure of his story?

The State then cross-examined Gleason, trying to challenge his recollection of time. Gleason was forced to admit that he could not be absolutely certain just what time the players left the hotel for practice.

Nash rose again and asked Gleason what must have seemed to
many a startling question for the defense to ask:

Q: Mr. Gleason, I will ask, from your experience, have you
an opinion as to whether these defendants executed the plays during
the World Series to the best of their abilities?

Startling! Hadn't Gleason's feeling about this been clearly enough
indicated on numerous previous occasions? Hadn't he stated to Comiskey in no uncertain terms that he felt the Series was being sold out
by his boys? Hadn't he publicly berated Risberg and Cicotte and
Gandil in the lobby of the Sinton on the night after the first game?
Hadn't he, in the locker room after the fifth game in Chicago, even
accused them of selling out?

What defense attorney in his right mind would ask such a question of Kid Gleason?

Then, to compound the mystery, George Gorman leaped to his
feet. "Objection!" he cried out.

Even more startling. Why should the State wish to stop Gleason
from spilling his suspicions?

"Sustained!" Judge Friend ordered.

Gleason was followed by Ray Schalk.

Nash then repeated the questions he had asked Gleason and received the same answers.

Gorman challenged Schalk as he had Gleason. But he added a
telling point:

Q: On the evening of the second game, state whether you saw
the defendants together in a room at the Sinton.

A: I did.

The court buzzed with this admission. Gorman smiled. "That's
all, thank you," he said.

Ben Short approached the witness and made a desperate try to
cross him up.

Q: Captain Eddie Collins and some of the other players were
there, were they not?

Schalk stared at him coldly.

A: No.

Thomas Nash then asked Schalk that same, startling question:

Q: Mr. Schalk, in your opinion, did the defendants play the
1919 World Series to the fullest extent of their abilities?

Schalk, the man who had gone raging to Gleason that Williams had not been following signs, had deliberately thrown bad pitches. Schalk, the man who in his fury had grabbed Williams under the grandstand and worked him over with his fists. . . . Again how could the defense ask him for such an opinion?

And again, incredibly, Gorman shouted "Objection!"

The defense put Eddie Collins, Dickie Kerr, and Roy Wilkinson on the stand, repeated the same questions it had asked of Gleason and Schalk. They all gave the same answers and were promptly dismissed. Dickie Kerr was contemptuous of the whole affair. "I came nine hundred miles to tell this!"

Nash questioned the White Sox trainer, H. W. Stephenson.

Q: I'll ask you if you gave Swede Risberg any medicine on the evening before the first game.

A: I did. He complained of a cold on his chest.

Nash was laying it in for the jury to ponder: if the Swede had played badly that day, he was, after all, a sick man. . . .

The defense then made one final salvo at the bastions of Charles Comiskey's financial power. Ben Short put Harry Grabiner on the stand, and finally managed to get into the record of statistics of the Chicago White Sox gate receipts. In 1919: $521,175.75. In 1920, they almost doubled: $910,206.59. And 1920, he made clear, was the year after the defendants had allegedly conspired to destroy his equity!

There was an audible response from the jurors and spectators alike. With this, the final examination of witnesses was concluded. The summations would begin on the following day.

The ballplayers filed out of the courtroom elated that their defense attorneys had rallied with a fine closing day. There was plenty of the backslapping and excited jabbering that went with a sense of pending triumph. The inclusion of the 1920 receipts was said to be especially telling. Ben Short claimed there was no greater reaction by the jury to anything that preceded it during the entire testimony.

To the ballplayers, however, it seemed like a small thing. They had sat through five weeks in almost complete silence, unable to expose the real fabric of their lives as Comiskey's ballplayers. For that was the deal. Nobody was to testify. Not a word was to be spoken

against the great American pastime. The name of Charles A. Comiskey was to be kept holy. The ballplayers would keep silent in exchange for protection. They would sit out the trial and Baseball would
do what it could to shield them from the bite of the law.

And so it had gone. Nobody had spoken. Not even Gleason, not
even Schalk.

On the morning of July 29, the prosecution began its statement.
The first piece of oratory was delivered by Assistant State's Attorney,
Edward Prindeville:

"What more convincing proof do you want than the statements made by the ballplayers? Joe Jackson, Eddie Cicotte, and
Claude Williams sold out the American public for a paltry $20,000.
They collected the money, but they could not keep quiet. Their
consciences would not let them rest. When the scandal broke, they
sought out the State's Attorney's office and made their confessions
voluntarily. Cicotte told his story to Chief Justice MacDonald. Then
he told it to the Grand Jury. He was followed to the Grand Jury room
by Jackson and Williams. On evidence which they gave the jurors,
Bill Burns, the State's star witness, was indicted. They have called
Burns a squealer, but I tell you that he owes his connection in the
case to what these defendant ballplayers have confessed."

Short objected that Cicotte had not incriminated Burns. Judge
Friend sustained.

Prindeville continued: "This is an unusual case as it deals with a
class of men who are involved in the great national game which all
red-blooded men follow. This game, gentlemen, has been the subject of a crime. The public, the club owners, even the small boys on
the sandlots have been swindled. That is why these defendants are
charged with conspiracy.

"This conspiracy started when Eddie Cicotte told Burns in New
York that if the White Sox won the pennant there was something on
and he would let him in on it. All the way through you will find that
Cicotte's statements are corroborated by Burns and vice versa.

"Cicotte was advised of his rights, yet he told his story. He told
of the ten thousand dollars he got under his pillow. He told of meeting his pals and talking over the conspiracy details. He told of
watching while his companions filed one by one from the meeting

place so as not to raise suspicions of the honest players. Then what did this idol of the diamond do? He went home and took the ten thousand dollars from under his pillow. Of course he was uneasy!

"Then, the gamblers met again on the morning before the World Series began. The gamblers accepted the players' terms. It was agreed that Cicotte should lose the first game. Of course he lost. With ten thousand dollars in his pocket, how could you expect him to keep his balance and win. The weight would bear him down!"

The bailiff had to rap for order to quiet the laughter.

"Gentlemen, you will find that Burns was also corroborated in his testimony by Joe Jackson and Williams. Jackson tells you he got the five thousand dollars after the fourth game———"

O'Brien exploded. "I suppose that sharpened his batting average!"

"He certainly was batting 1000% when he got the $5,000!" Prindeville retorted. Then he continued: "Swede Risberg then tells you he had a cold. The only trouble with him was that he had an overdose of conspiracy in his hide. You recall the defendants said they could not win for Kerr because he was a busher. Abe Attell told them to win and they won! There is no pitcher on God's green earth who could have won that ball game if the defendants had not backed him up!

"I say, gentlemen, that the evidence shows that a swindle and a con game has been worked on the American people. The crime in this case warrants the most severe punishment of the law. This country is for sending criminals to the penitentiary whether they are idols of the baseball diamond or gangsters guilty of robbery with a gun. Unless the jury, by convicting the ballplayers in this trial, does its part to stamp out gambling that is corrupting baseball, I predict restrictive legislation for baseball such as has been enacted for boxing and horseracing.

"The State is asking in this case for a verdict of guilty with five years in the penitentiary and a fine of $2,000 for each defendant!"

He was followed by George Gorman with more of the same: ". . . The attorneys for the defense will ask for mercy. They point out that Lefty Williams got only five hundred dollars a month for his services. They charge that Charles Comiskey, the grand old man of baseball, is persecuting the players because he has tried to clean out rottenness in the national game. Gentlemen, Charles Comiskey wants to keep the game clean for the American public and I will tell you now that if the owners don't get busy when rottenness crops up, baseball won't last long.

"Comiskey gave these men a job. And here we find the defendants deliberately conspiring to injure and destroy his business. They have dragged the game through the mire and in their blunders deliberately fouled their own nest.

"There has been much poison injected into the case by the attorneys for the defense. They have attacked Bill Burns, the man who bared the conspiracy of their clients. They have hit at Billy Maharg, the man who corroborated him. They tell you these men lied. They call Burns an accomplice. By their own words they convict their own clients. If Burns is an accomplice, some crime must have been committed. If he has committed a crime with the defendants, then it is your duty to find them guilty. I tell you, at least three of their clients, Eddie Cicotte, Lefty Williams, and Joe Jackson have condemned themselves so badly that I don't see how you can acquit them. In his confession, Eddie Cicotte tells how the games were fixed. Then we have the spectacle of the public going to the game believing it was on the square. Thousands of men throughout the chilly hours of the night, crouched in line waiting for the opening of the first World Series game. All morning they waited, eating a sandwich, perhaps, never daring to leave their places for a moment. There they waited to see the great Cicotte pitch a ballgame. Gentlemen, they went to see a ballgame. But all they saw was a con game!"

The Court recessed for the weekend.

On Monday, August 1, the defense began its plea. As with the State, they were allowed ten hours to wrap up their case. Ben Short was the first to speak. He argued a strictly legal interpretation of the case:

". . . The State failed to establish criminal conspiracy. There may have been an agreement entered by the defendants to take the gamblers' money, but it has not been shown the players had any intention of defrauding the public or of bringing the game into ill repute. They believed any arrangement they may have made was a secret one and would, therefore, reflect no discredit on the national pastime or injure the business of their employer as it would never be detected!"

If this was less than a moral argument, Short at least had reminded the jury of the nature of the indictments.

A. Morgan Frumberg, attorney for the gamblers, followed with a big swing at the power behind the prosecution:

"Arnold Rothstein came here to Chicago during the Grand Jury investigation and immediately went to Alfred Austrian, the White Sox attorney. What bowing and scraping must have taken place when 'Arnold the Just,' the millionaire gambler, entered the sanctum of 'Alfred the Great.' By his own testimony, Mr. Austrian admits conducting the financier to the Grand Jury and bringing him back unindicted!"

Frumberg repeatedly asked the jury to ponder over why Rothstein had never been indicted when the State's own witness in the trial had named him as the financier! "Why was he not indicted? Why were Brown, Sullivan, Attell, and Chase allowed to escape? Why were these underpaid ballplayers, these penny-ante gamblers from Des Moines and St. Louis, who may have bet a few nickels on the World Series, brought here to be the goats in this case? Ask the powers in baseball. Ask Ban Johnson who pulled the strings in this case. Ask him who saved Arnold Rothstein!"

Later, Thomas Nash hammered it home: Rothstein was left out of the case at Johnson's instigation because he only wanted to get Comiskey by wrecking his ball club!

Ahearn followed by calling Burns and Maharg every name in the book. Liars, con men, fortune hunters, rattlesnakes. But the principal target remained Ban Johnson. "Ban Johnson was the directing genius of the prosecution. His hand runs like a scarlet thread through the whole prosecution. Johnson is boss. The czar of Russia never had more power over his subjects than Johnson has over the American League. He controlled the case. His money hired Burns and Maharg to dig up evidence. He sent Maharg on a wild-goose chase to Mexico to find Burns. The State's attorneys have no more control over the prosecution than a bat boy has over the direction of play in a World Series game.

"Maharg came to court as an auto worker, but he flashed enough diamonds on his fingers to buy a flock of autos. And Burns has been proved a liar in a score of instances. He said he talked to Gandil in Chicago after the second game. He lied. He said he talked to the ballplayers on the morning before the opening game. He lied. He makes me think of a drink of moonshine: It looks good, but when you drink it it gives you a stomachache!"

And that was it. A lot of words. Millions of words in a matter of weeks. All that was left was for the Judge to digest them and deliver his charge to the jury. The ballplayers realized that much depended on the manner in which this was done. A bunch of raw, green, unknowing athletes, they had inescapably picked up an education during the course of the trial. In the hallways of the Criminal Courts Building they discussed the testimony in speech that was colored by the jargon of their lawyers. Their emotions were keyed up in anticipation of the Judge's apparent friendliness. And when they finally heard his words in the early evening of August 2, they were quick to understand:

"The State must prove that it was the intent of the ballplayers and gamblers charged with conspiracy through the throwing of the World Series, to defraud the public and others, and not merely to throw ballgames!"

The ballplayers smiled. This charge was exactly what they'd been hoping for. It attached to the prosecution an extremely difficult burden of proof. And there had been nothing said during the trial that pertained to it. They could relax now, as the clerk read the nine charges solemnly to the jurors, and smile as the twelve good men filed into the jury room to begin deliberation. It was exactly 7:52 P.M.

Buck Weaver strolled down the long corridors with a celebrative cigar in his mouth and a grin on his boyish face. It was raining hard outside, and the halls were congested. He joined groups of idling spectators who were reluctant to go home for fear of missing the verdict.

"Good luck, Buck!" they called out to him.

Many thought the players would be acquitted, but there were also some old courthouse hands who did not. They warned Weaver you could never trust a jury to do what was expected. You never really knew what was going on in a juror's mind. But Weaver's spirits were soaring. Just two days before, he'd had a long talk with John McGraw of the New York Giants. McGraw had visited the trial to see John Heydler, or so it had been reported. The Giant manager, himself one of the great third basemen of his day, had made it clear that he wanted Weaver to play in New York.

There was no other way for Buck Weaver to look at the future. His past was clean. No matter what the implications of being on trial in this scandal, he felt that everybody knew he was clean. No one could even accuse him of taking a dirty dime or making a suspect play in the series. No one had tried. He was Buck Weaver, a man in love with baseball, and that's where he belonged.

To Joe Jackson, life in the big cities of America had been a tremendous ten-year experience. But he had never fully become accustomed to being away from home. The confusions of the trial had emphasized this to him—all these smart men endlessly pouring out big words he couldn't understand. For all the hot-shot clothes and snappy dressing he'd adopted, the vaudeville tours and dizzy spins with show girls in night spots, the all-night drinking, restaurant eating, spending money as if it were a burden to keep in his pocket—despite all this, these ten years were merely seasons away from South Carolina. It was enough for him to adjust to it as well as he did. It was always in his mind how he had never wanted to come North in the first place, back in 1909, and how he had fled that first train ride to Philadelphia in the middle of the night. Suddenly, it seemed natural that he should end up this way, in a court of law, on trial for being dishonest, with a judge and a jury and a few hundred spectators with neckties on.

They all stood around and waited. With each passing minute, they lost a little more of the glow of anticipated victory. What was taking that jury so long? Would there be a verdict that night? They found themselves talking in endless circles of repeated comments, trying to buoy themselves through the nervous wait with words of hope. They joked and tried to forget the trial. They talked baseball, especially about Babe Ruth and the new lively ball. A fan remembered a game last year when Ruth had hit a tremendous shot off Cicotte's fast ball, but it had blown foul. Cicotte had taken a new ball, thrown the Babe a knuckler, only to watch Ruth hit another, farther than the one before, and this time fair. Cicotte remembered and grinned. He said something about how he'd managed to keep Ruth from hitting more than one shot out of the park—each game.

Someone cornered Felsch and asked him if it was true that Jackson couldn't read or write. And Happy recalled a time when a fan came up to Joe as they were all going for a beer, and asked him to autograph a baseball. Joe took the ball and the kid's pen and said he'd meet Hap inside the tavern. Felsch claimed that he had four slow beers and that, when he came out, Jackson was still trying to write his name.

Then there were three loud knocks on the jury-room door, indicating that a verdict had been reached. It wasn't even ten o'clock! They hurried into the courtroom, which once again was jammed with several hundred spectators who had sweated through the hours just to be on hand for the finale.

But there would be another wait: Judge Friend had gone home to the Cooper Carlton Hotel. It would take a half hour or so for him to arrive.

"Gentlemen of the jury, have you reached a verdict?"

"We have, your Honor."

The Judge nodded. The Court tensed. Chief Clerk Edward Meyers was handed a slip of paper from the jury foreman. He read slowly. "We the jury find the defendant Claude Williams not guilty. . . ."

A roar went up in the courtroom; it was as if a pitcher had slipped a third strike passed Ty Cobb in the ninth inning. By the time the jury had read the complete list of acquittals, the courtroom was a bedlam of rousing cheers. The bailiffs kept pounding for order, until they saw Judge Friend smiling and waving at the ballplayers. Immediately, they abandoned any further efforts at austerity and joined in the jubilation. Hats sailed into the air, papers were torn up and thrown as confetti. The room was a scene of wild confusion unheard of in a court of law.

Cicotte leaped across the room and grabbed the juror William Barrett, the foreman. He shouted his thanks above the din. Jackson and Williams were close behind, pounding the jurors' backs. The jurors themselves joined in the cheering, then lifted the ballplayers to their shoulders, parading them around the room before a battery of popping flash bulbs. The spectators joined them, slapping the jurors' backs in congratulations and approval.

Weaver and Risberg grabbed each other by the arms and danced around. Felsch and Williams could not stop laughing. When Cicotte was asked to make a statement, he laughed, replied, "All I want to do is get home to Detroit. Talk? You say, talk? Not here, buddy. I talked once in this building—never again!"

Never again.

Risberg came by to join Cicotte, and the two rushed out to send telegrams to their wives.

Buck Weaver was all smiles. "I knew I'd be cleared. And I'm glad the public stood by me until the trial was over." Felsch played it lightly: "I never had anything to do with any so-called conspiracy." Defense Attorney Henry Berger said, "The verdict is a complete vindication of the most mistreated ballplayers in history." Gandil shook hands with everybody and bellowed a magnificent farewell message to the court: "I guess that'll learn Ban Johnson he can't frame an honest bunch of ballplayers!"

Only George Gorman and his staff were silent.

The ballplayers joined to celebrate their victory. They chose an Italian restaurant not far from the Criminal Courts Building, set up a huge dinner table in a private room, and began a night of eating and drinking. By some strange coincidence—or so it was reported—the twelve good men who had acquitted them were celebrating in like fashion in the adjoining room of that very same restaurant! The door between them was flung open and the party, now doubled, lasted through the balance of the night.

As the party broke up, the early morning newspapers were rolling off the Chicago presses. The front pages noted the official ending of the celebration. Judge Kenesaw Mountain Landis had issued a statement:

". . . Regardless of the verdict of juries, no player who throws a ball game, no player that undertakes or promises to throw a ballgame, no player that sits in conference with a bunch of crooked players and gamblers where the ways and means of throwing a game are discussed and does not promptly tell his club about it, will ever play professional baseball!"

6

The Inquiring Reporter of the Chicago *Tribune* went out into the streets and interviewed seven random Chicagoans. Did they believe the eight ballplayers should be reinstated? Five of them said they did. Meanwhile, a Southside petition was circulated, calling for the reinstatement of Buck Weaver. In one day, 14,000 fans signed it.

There were others who thought differently. The men in power were unanimous about it. The club owners feigned shock at the acquittal and trumpeted righteously: "These men must be barred from the national game at all hazards!" William "Kid" Gleason obediently shook his head: "If those boys are allowed to play organized ball again, then I am through with the game!" Ban Johnson pontificated: "The trial uncovered the greatest crime it was possible to commit in baseball. The fact that they were freed does not alter the conditions one iota or minimize the magnitude of the offense."

The respectable public press, meanwhile, heaped its righteous scorn on the workings of the law. The editor of Chicago's *Herald and Examiner* wrote: ". . . The law and the jury seem to say that the question in such a conspiracy is not what you do but what you can get away with. . . . This is a time of great issues, affecting profoundly the future of the country. A case like this might seem unimportant in comparison with disarmament, or world commerce, or the race problem, or prohibition. But at the bottom of every issue lies the national character. . . ."

The New York *Times* was angry and sardonic: "The Chicago White Sox are once more whiter than snow. A jury has said that they are not guilty, so that settles that. The Court instructed the jury to determine whether the defendants intended to defraud the public and others and not merely to throw ball games. To the lay mind, this sounds very much like asking whether the defendant intended to murder his victim or merely to cut his head off!"

As for the Illinois State's Attorney's office: "The case is closed!"

said Robert Crowe. "We will quash any remaining indictments." What he really meant was that there would be no further re-examination of the scandal by the Grand Jury, the matter of the stolen papers would be forgotten, and Arnold Rothstein would neither be summoned for questioning nor indicted, despite Ban Johnson's ringing accusation and George Gorman's pledge.

So, in the end, organized baseball won its battle. They had rescued the ballplayers from the clutches of the law, only to make victims of them on their own terms. Baseball, the club owners could boast, had cleaned its own house. "Regardless of the verdict of juries . . ." Judge Landis repeated for America to take note. It was a pronouncement that sent the status of the Commissioner of Baseball skyrocketing. Landis was hailed as a hero, a savior, a mighty power for the forces of honesty and clean sport. To Comiskey and the other owners, his effectiveness was not to be denied. If the public would respect the integrity of Kenesaw Mountain Landis and the dignity of his Commission, he was worth every penny of the $42,500 they were paying him.

So desperate had been their fears, it was even worth the risk of having created a potential threat to their own domination!

Baseball, then, was ready for a new era. If Landis was the image of its new purity, it was Babe Ruth who gave it excitement. In terms of dollars and cents—the measure of a magnate's mind—the great home-run slugger was worth a million.

VI | THE AFTERMATH

"Say they made a great ball club and let it go at that.
Say it all once, a score of long years after.
Then, let it go at that . . ."

Nelson Algren

1

> "Don't bring up Buck Weaver
> Or how he looked that last time you saw
> him
> Begging a reporter six months out of
> high school
> To clear his name so he could play again.
> 'I'll play for nothing, tell 'em. Just
> one season, tell 'em!' "
>
> *Nelson Algren*

Early in December, five months after his acquittal, Buck Weaver walked into the offices of Commissioner Landis. "Sit down, sit down!" The Judge was warm and friendly. He offered Weaver a chew of his special cut of tobacco. Weaver smiled: at least they had that in common. It relieved his nervousness and relaxed him. This was going to be a crucial hour for him.

To Buck Weaver, there was only one reality: he had played eight games in the 1919 World Series to the best of his great ability. He had not taken one dime of dirty money. He had stood trial and was acquitted of any crime. He was thirty-one years old and reputed to be the best third baseman in the game.

He was, above all, ready to play ball.

He proceeded to tell Landis how he'd been approached by Gandil back in 1919, how he was offered $10,000 to get in the fix. He'd just opened a drugstore with his brother and he needed cash, but he couldn't go through with a thing like that. Landis listened, told him that since he had knowledge of the fix, he should have done something to stop it. Weaver cringed. Talk? He couldn't have talked. It was not in him to talk. He'd thought about doing it, to protect himself, but those men were his friends. Besides, he explained, he never really knew which of them got any money from it. He never really knew if they actually went through with it. Nobody ever said anything. He hadn't known enough to talk, even if he'd wanted to!

Landis nodded with apparent sympathy, but would not give him an answer. He would review the case and write Weaver a letter with his decision.

There was no letter. Just a blunt statement to the press:

"Birds of a feather flock together. Men associating with gamblers and crooks could expect no leniency."

This was Landis's reply. Weaver choked on it and bided his time.

Like Jackson, Weaver had signed a three-year contract in 1920, calling for $7,500 a year. Having received no money in 1921, he sued for the balance of his contract. The case dragged on for four years, until in Federal Court, it was dismissed when it came to trial: Weaver's lawyers had failed to appear. To add substance to the defeat, he was ordered to pay court costs. Nevertheless, he continued to pursue the matter relentlessly. And finally, in 1924, he forced Comiskey into a settlement out of court. To Buck, it was more than the few thousand dollars he so sorely needed: it was a statement of Comiskey's admission of guilt.

Again, Weaver appealed for reinstatement. Landis's reply this time was another frustrating distortion of reality: ". . . On the trial of this case, Burns gave a detailed account of his meeting with the indicted men and arranging with them for the throwing of the World Series games. Weaver was present in the Court during the testimony of this witness who most specifically stated that Weaver was present at the conference, and yet the case went to the jury without any denial from Weaver from the witness stand. . . . If the incriminating evidence was false, the public had a right to Weaver's denial under oath."

The Commissioner made argument impossible. How could Weaver have denied anything if he was denied the right to take the stand? How could he have testified if the best defense for the group was a united silence? Did he not ask for a separate trial? Was it not denied him? Was he not told by Judge Friend himself that on the basis of the evidence presented there was no chance for his conviction? Must he be punished for all that, too?

Weaver spent the years running his drugstore. He could be found there jerking sodas or passing out cosmetics over the counter. He also spent a lot of time at the race track, playing the horses. By 1927, he realized that his desire to play ball could no longer be repressed. He announced he would play semipro ball with a local club. More than three hundred local owners, managers, and players voted unanimously to let him play. It was the first opportunity for Southside fans to see him in action after seven years. They turned out in the numbers. It was a moment of joy for Weaver—but it was not enough, nor was it the real thing. He lived constantly with a sense of his guilty status in the eyes of others, the stigma of banishment that marked him lousy. He avoided social events where prominent sporting people gathered because he did not wish to be the subject of either their sympathy or their contempt. He would pass his time with a group of friends playing pinochle in the back room of a saloon. He never drank or caroused. His wife was devoted to him and he to her. They had no children of their own, but raised two children of relatives.

As time passed, Weaver grew too old to play. Ray Schalk, another Southsider whom he saw around town over the years, became manager of the Sox. Red Faber, also of Weaver's neighborhood, ran a tavern and bowling alley outside of Chicago. Faber was the last of the 1919 aggregation, and retired in 1933. Weaver worked at the parimutuel windows of the race track. Later, he organized and managed a girl's softball team. But he wanted to get back into organized ball. He could coach rookies, as Gleason had done. He could coach at some college, as Schalk would do at Purdue University. If only Landis would reinstate him, he would again feel like an honorable man.

He appealed repeatedly, maybe a half-dozen times, always with the same result. When Landis was replaced by Happy Chandler in 1946, Weaver appealed to Chandler. He went to visit Judge Hugo Friend, who was convinced of his innocence. The Judge was sympathetic and wrote the Commissioner of his knowledge and opinion, reviewing the 1921 trial, recommending a special leniency in Weaver's case. But Chandler and his successor, Ford Frick, turned it down.

Thirty-five years passed and they were all the same. When James T. Farrell met Weaver he found, ". . . a thin, pale, gray man in his sixties. He dressed on the sporty side, and there were small red blotches on his face. He smiled easily and readily." The single, dominating thought on his mind was still to clear his name. More than anything else, he wanted that. He wanted to bring that to his now-ailing wife whom he took care of, and to his cronies with whom he played pinochle. . . .

Then, one cold, grim morning in January, 1956, Buck was walking down 71st Street on Chicago's Southside, on his way to an income-tax consultant. Suddenly, he writhed in pain and began to fall. He clutched at a picket fence to hold himself up. A man named John Spengler, a heating contractor, was driving by and saw him. He stopped to help, but before he could get to him, Weaver toppled over. Spengler called a policeman while passers-by gathered around. But it was too late. At the hospital, it was simply reported that Weaver had died, at sixty-six, of natural causes.

At the funeral, a man shook his head sadly and said, "I was just a kid in 1922, sitting in the stands at the White City Park where the Black Sox were playing a gang called the Southside All-Stars. Weaver sat down next to me. Risberg and Felsch came up and asked Buck to play. He waved them away. 'Nothing doing. I'll be back in the majors soon, and you guys will still be semipros.' "

He never made it.

2

In 1921, the White Sox finished in seventh place, but Dickie Kerr pitched his heart out and won nineteen games. Comiskey, however, had no rewards for this loyal little giant. If Kerr pitched out of the joy of playing ball, he also pitched for money. When he received Comiskey's contract for the 1922 season, he turned it back, as he had done in 1921. Only this time, he rebelled at what Harry Grabiner called a "compromise figure." Kerr ended up spending the summer around home, in Paris, Texas. Still pitching, but no longer in professional ball.

It was a classical case: if Kerr did not agree to Comiskey's terms, he could not play organized baseball—with any club, anywhere. The irony was that Kerr's pride and pluckiness, which had won those two

1919 World Series games for Comiskey, now served to deny Comiskey the use of those qualities. Kerr had measured his own value in dollars and cents and would not pitch for Comiskey for less. He would play semipro ball, no different, in effect, than the eight Black Sox. It seemed almost that his stand was a vindication of their sellout. In fact, in 1923, Judge Landis declared Kerr ineligible, since he had played against some of the expelled ballplayers and would have to serve a year's penance!

The loyal and disloyal . . . somehow Comiskey and Landis had thrown them all into the same pot together.

By 1923, William "Kid" Gleason became fully aware of how severe a blow he had suffered. He had tried to cover it up with toughness, to forget the old and build up the new. But memories of the betrayal smothered him. Too much had gone before. He had found and developed Cicotte and made him great. He had worked for long hours with Buck Weaver over the years and made him the best. He had begun to find in Risberg the qualities that would stir his great potential. The same with Lefty Williams. He could not escape from his memories. To Gleason, a ball club was more than a collection of ballplayers. It was a family, a thing of pride, a labor of the heart.

But now he had a seventh-place ball club and he was too tired to bring it up. He had been in baseball for thirty-five years, a tough, willful, determined man, and finally the toughness was gone. He went to the Old Roman and told him he was through. Comiskey argued with him, tried to keep him there. But there was no chance. Gleason was fifty-seven now, and they weren't calling him "Kid" any more. The quality of the man had changed since the sellout. They were calling him "Pop" Gleason, and he knew what was in his heart.

He went home to Philadelphia and shut himself off from his friends and the rest of the sporting world. He saw no one, ate little, too sunk in despair to want anything. For three years he suffered, sick and lonely and devoid of ambition. Connie Mack of the Philadelphia A's saw him in 1926, pale and emaciated, and with the fire gone from his eyes. He induced Gleason to come to work as a coach, the same job he had had almost twenty years before with Comiskey. Gleason went through the motions, as loyal to Mack as he had been to Comiskey, but the spirit was gone. In 1933, at the age of sixty-seven, Pop Gleason suffered a heart attack and died at home.

He had outlived Comiskey by two years.

The eight Black Sox fanned out over the vast expanse of America, but their lives ran in similar patterns. They all played semipro and outlaw baseball for a few years, then gradually settled into various occupations. Eddie Cicotte farmed outside of Detroit, later became a game warden for the state of Michigan. He raised his family in as much seclusion as he could manage. Lefty Williams remained in Chicago for a while, eking out a sparse living with his poolroom, then moved to Laguna Beach, California, where he managed a garden-nursery business. Swede Risberg worked in Minnesota at dairy farming, then moved west to northern California and later to a tavern on the Oregon border. Happy Felsch went home to Milwaukee, raised six children, who in turn gave him nine grandchildren. Happy opened up a tavern and smiled across the bar at the oiled-up wiseacres who tried to rile him with references to his past—until that, too, receded with the passing years. Chick Gandil returned to California with his wife and daughter, became a plumber, then retired to the beautiful spa country of the Napa Valley in northern California.

The one experience they had in common remained very much their own. Though they had almost no contact with each other over the decades that followed, they maintained a solid front of silence to the world. It was as if a pact existed between them and the forces that had brought them to it. It was a silence of shame and sorrow and futility. It was also a silence of fear, for the threats hanging over them made talking a doubly difficult adventure. But mostly, it was a story rooted in the bitterness and frustration of their lives. There seemed to be no way to talk of it that made sense to them, no way that would give some measure of understanding and, perhaps, vindication to their actions.

Once again, in Chicago, there was a moment of contact in 1927 at the near-sensational exposure of baseball corruption over the betting habits of Ty Cobb and Tris Speaker. Risberg saw a chance to awake the sleeping tiger of 1917 when the White Sox had been assessed $45 each to pay off Detroit. He blasted at the memory of it, told America in screaming headlines that a deal had been made to fix two con-secutive double headers with the Tigers, to help the Sox clinch the pennant—and this with the knowledge and endorsement of the White Sox management itself! Gandil came to Chicago from California to substantiate Risberg's account and embellish it with additional data. After all, it was he who'd been appointed paymaster. Thirty ballplayers were involved in an investigation that again threatened to rock the baseball world. In the end, Judge Landis dismissed the accusations, claiming he was not interested in matters that occurred before he came to power. But both Cobb and Speaker were shifted to other ball clubs. . . .

In New York, on August 8, 1921, a few days after the Black Sox trial had ended in Chicago, a small man with a handkerchief partially obscuring his face, walked up to a ticket window at the Polo Grounds and purchased a ticket. When he tried to pass through a turnstile, however, a detective named Cummings laid a heavy hand on his shoulder and prevented his entrance. The little man said his name was Joseph Wellar, but the detective knew better. This was Abe Attell and he was no longer welcome at the Polo Grounds.

Attell, forced to submit, retreated from 155th Street and started down Eighth Avenue. Stuck with his ticket, he found a man who wanted one and sold it to him. But he had not reckoned with Detective Cummings who had followed him and promptly had him arrested for speculating. (When asked why he was ejected from the Polo Grounds in the first place, Attell blandly said he'd had "an argument there about a year ago.")

Attell passed through the thorny 'twenties with nothing more than a few minor scratches. He was arrested for illegal possession and transportation of intoxicating whiskeys in Plattsburg, New York, in 1924; then again in 1925, for moving liquor from one speakeasy to another. In 1926, he was in trouble while owning a speakeasy on West 48th Street, and faced perjury charges as well as illegal operation. In 1929, he was arrested for ticket speculating outside a boxing arena in Long Island City.

Eventually, however, after Prohibition ended in 1933, he settled down to running a legal tavern, which became a successful hangout for the sporting crowd. His more illicit activities were forgotten with the revival of his history as a boxer. In time, to many, his link with the 1919 World Series fix seemed almost a myth. Attell, himself, encouraged that. In 1961, he made a public statement of his involvement, a kind of confession of his innocence. Perhaps, at the age of seventy-eight, he had come to believe it. He blamed it all on Arnold Rothstein, whom he called a liar and betrayer. He told how he had called him that to his face, right on the street in front of Lindy's restaurant in Times Square: " 'Rothstein,' I finished up, boiling with anger, 'you're gonna die with your shoes on!' "

Arnold Rothstein *was* shot during a poker game at the Park Central Hotel on 7th Avenue and 56th Street. The principal suspect was gambler George McManus. But the law never prosecuted, for no one would talk. Rothstein, himself, refused to name his assailant, even on his deathbed.

When the F.B.I. worked over Rothstein's files, they found papers revealing that William J. Kelly, "Sport" Sullivan's Boston attorney, had come into possession of four affidavits dealing with Rothstein's involvement in the 1919 World Series fix, including a reference to his payments of $80,000 to the ballplayers. These affidavits were signed by Abe Attell, William J. Fallon, Eugene McGee (Fallon's partner), and Joseph "Sport" Sullivan. The records showed that Rothstein had bought these affidavits from Kelly for $53,000. Kelly was later indicted for blackmail and was disbarred. Nobody seemed to remember that these six people had been partners in 1920 and 1921.

3

"Here, on another fall afternoon
A Carolina millhand the kids called
    Shoeless Joe
Pegged a runner out at the plate on his knees
From against the far left field stands
And never played again
Nor pegged another."

Nelson Algren

On June 28, 1922, two thousand baseball fans jammed into Hackensack (New Jersey) Oval for a Sunday game against Bogota. It was a bigger crowd than usual, for the rivalry of these two neighboring towns had sustained a special intensity over the years. There was a new ballplayer on the Hackensack nine, an event that always excited the local fans. He was a tall, rangy center fielder, a right-handed thrower and left-handed hitter. The name listed on the mimeographed score card was simply Joseph. They were ready to withhold any opinions until Joseph could show what he could do. They took their baseball seriously in Hackensack. And this was one game they especially wanted to win.

Joseph turned out to be a very special treat. He hit a tremendous double his first time up, then followed with a single, and finally a towering home run out of the park. He stole second, and even threw a man out at the plate, trying to score from second on a long single to center. Hackensack won in the ninth inning, 9–7.

It wasn't until after the game that somebody told the Bogota manager that this man Joseph looked just like Shoeless Joe Jackson.

The informant was right. Jackson had come north again in the spring, drawn to the baseball world and the money of New York's semipro circuit. Knowing the stigma attached to his name less than a year after the trial, he chose to remain anonymous, capitalizing not on his fame but purely on his talent. It was a feeble joke to think he could get away with anonymity.

The reaction of the Bogota club was typical. They insisted that the game be declared forfeit, even though there were no league standings. And they swore they would not compete again as long as Jackson remained with the club.

In New York City, sports promoter Eddie Phelon saw an opportunity to make a dollar. If there were clubs that refused to play against Jackson, there were others that would welcome the opportunity. Like the Scranton Miners, a new attraction with ballplayers who played with coal miners' lights on their caps. The thing to do was to come right out in the open and make the most of it. He would organize a new club around Jackson—and perhaps Weaver, too. He would call the club the "Big League Martyrs" and tour the greater New York semipro circuit. To effect this, he agreed to pay Jackson a salary that allegedly came close to $1,000 a week!

Phelon went further. To abet his investment, he launched a placard campaign in which petitions were to be passed out and displayed in every major-league ball park in the country, soliciting signatures of sympathetic fans to clear Jackson's name of taint, ". . . leaving the said Joe Jackson free to solicit without stigma, and practice in peace and without hindrance his honorable livelihood and calling before the world as a great artist in the game of baseball." Phelon had a gift for publicity and a flare for promotion. As far as Jackson was concerned, it was good for a month or so, and he received part of the money promised him.

The following year, he joined Cicotte and Risberg in an outlaw league in Louisiana. Cicotte pitched under the name of Moore. Jackson changed his again, this time to Johnson. He played thirty-five games and hit over .500 until his phenomenal power once again exposed him. The Bastrop (Louisiana) Club could boast of an incredible winning streak, having thrashed every club in the circuit.

During the winters, Jackson kept his Savannah valet business going. His wife, Katie, helped him run it. He tried to keep as busy as possible, but his life inescapably centered around his talent as a ballplayer. There was never a day when it did not come up in conversation.

In the fall of 1923, he heard of a Milwaukee attorney named Raymond J. Cannon who had gone to bat for Happy Felsch. Cannon was well equipped to handle the problems of ballplayers. It could be said that professional baseball had paid for his legal education. He had pitched in the Wisconsin-Illinois League during his college and law-school years and might have climbed to the majors if he had stuck with it. Unlike Charles Comiskey who chose baseball over bricks, Cannon chose books over baseball.

Out of his experience, Cannon became a maverick. He hated the bigness of the baseball business. He believed the contractual system by which ballplayers were controlled was in violation of a man's rights and of the Sherman Anti-Trust Law. In 1922, he began work on the formation of a players' union. "I found a spirit of discontent about many conditions . . . and every player I talked with regretted the fact that there was no real appeal. The only chance, they felt, was to unionize. Letters began to flood in on me from all over the big-league circuits and the idea simply developed automatically. It had nothing to do with the Black Sox . . . but their plight, whatever brought it

about, has started something which may be a factor in keeping baseball on the level in more ways than one."

Cannon made sense to Jackson. The man could talk baseball
problems and really understand what the issues were. Cannon was a
fighter, and loved it. He was quick to reveal the fact that he'd won
one hundred consecutive jury findings. Inside of an hour, he had
Jackson convinced he could recoup the two years' salary, $9,000 a
year, that Comiskey owed him on his three-year contract.

In 1924, Jackson filed suit for $18,000 back pay. Cannon opened
the case by charging fraud in Harry Grabiner's successful efforts to
get Jackson to sign that contract. He claimed that Jackson had been
deliberately misled because of his inability to read and write. Grabiner
had assured Jackson there was no mention of the ten-day clause, for
Jackson had specified that he would not sign such a contract. On the
supposition that this was an ironclad three-year contract, Jackson had
signed. This, he testified, was executed outside, on the hood of the
car, rather than inside the house after his wife had read it. Grabiner
denied this, testified that the opposite was true. It had all been fully
explained, he insisted, and Jackson's wife was seated in the living
room where he signed it.

Cannon had some choice descriptive words on the use of the ten-
day clause. A ballplayer "may sign a five-year contract, say, at $4,000
a year. He may develop into a sensation, and be a tremendous box-
office draw. But his salary is set. He takes it for all five years or he's
through. On the other hand, he may break a leg sliding into a base—
but the club is not bound in any way. Ten days later, he can be released, without further pay!" Cannon put Comiskey on the stand and
made him admit that this was a completely unfair practice.

But this, said Comiskey, was a different circumstance. After all,
it was Jackson who had failed to comply with his contract, not
Comiskey! Had he not sold out the World Series?

At once, Cannon snapped at him: "The law has tried my client
and acquitted him! Where, then, is any proof of guilt?"

Comiskey's attorney, George B. Hudnall, working for Alfred
Austrian, immediately referred to Jackson's confession before the
Grand Jury in 1920.

"What confession?" Cannon demanded.

Then, incredibly, the stolen confessions, missing since the winter

of 1920, suddenly reappeared in Hudnall's brief case! Cannon roared
indignantly: "How is it that these Grand Jury records are in *your*
hands?" Hudnall had not expected to be challenged. He paled, unable
to answer, and turned toward Comiskey for assistance. They exchanged glances, and Comiskey feebly replied, "I don't know."

"You don't know!" Cannon exclaimed.

Comiskey was ruffled. He shook his head and repeated his answer,
the only answer he could give. "I'm sorry, I don't know."

Cannon knew. He knew the whole story. How Rothstein, through
Fallon, had them lifted from the State's Attorney's office. He knew
that Austrian had represented Rothstein and had gotten the confessions from him. Whatever sum they had cost Rothstein to obtain, they
were present in this court to save Comiskey $18,000. Cannon could
smirk at this. "Birds of a feather flock together!" Judge Landis had
said, condemning Buck Weaver. This was all so neatly packaged.
Even Rothstein kept himself completely innocent in the eyes of the
law.

Well, let them, Cannon gauged the moment. It was enough to
question it. He had laid a suspicion for the jury to reckon with. Let
them take it as far as they wished. He knew full well he couldn't prove
anything anyway. This was a jury trial, and Cannon was a master at
handling juries.

He proceeded to hit the Comiskey defense hard. He got Henry
Brigham, foreman of the Cook County Grand Jury, to state that
Jackson, in his confession, had denied being in the conspiracy, and
had affirmed that he had tried to see Comiskey after the Series to tell
what he knew. Brigham also admitted that the Grand Jury had made
no investigation of Comiskey's conduct pertaining to the running
down of rumors after the 1919 Series.

When Alfred Austrian referred to John Hunter, the private detective hired by Comiskey to delve into the finances of the suspected
players, Cannon wanted to know why his findings were never made
public, or even revealed to the Grand Jury. And above all, why was
John Hunter never called to testify before that body? Why, in fact,
had the very mention of his name been held secret until this time?
What, specifically, had Hunter learned? Cannon wanted to know:
Hunter must have learned something!

Cannon hit hardest at Comiskey's duplicity in his repeated claim
to fighting for clean baseball. "This investigation after the World

Series was merely a subterfuge to fall back on in the event that the disloyalty of the ballplayers was later discovered! Comiskey accused Gandil of being a ringleader immediately after the Series was over, and notwithstanding that fact, he sent him a contract for the following year!

"If Comiskey intends to hold the confidence of the American public, he will have to refrain from highhanded methods of dealing with his players. The truth is, his Secretary, Harry Grabiner, tricked Jackson into signing this three-year contract, and slipped into it a ten-day clause. The contract itself, thusly forced on a ballplayer, is so grossly and obviously unfair that Comiskey himself must blush with shame at the signing of it!"

It all seemed to boil down to Harry Grabiner's fountain pen. Did Jackson sign the contract on the hood of the car—with Grabiner's pen—or did he sign it inside, in his wife's presence, with full knowledge of its content? Grabiner insisted that he did not even have a pen! A handwriting expert, brought in by Hudnall, testified that Jackson's signature was written on a flat, normal surface without awkwardness of position, using an ordinary steel pen slightly the worse for wear, and not a fountain pen. Cannon later found a rebuttal expert, W. W. Way, who was convinced that the signature *was* written with a fountain pen, and certainly not on a level surface!

On the following day, the jury retired to the sanctity of the jury room to determine its verdict. At the very moment when the bailiff turned the key in the door, locking them in, the Judge rapped for order and asked Jackson to the bench.

"Mr. Jackson, you are guilty of perjury, and I order you to be placed under arrest and fix your bail at five thousand dollars."

The legal question involved was an old one to this case: Jackson, according to the Judge, had signed a sworn confession of his complicity before the Grand Jury in 1920. He had now testified under oath of his innocence. Cannon, incensed by the situation, quickly arranged for bail.

The jury, meanwhile, was quick to arrive at a verdict. Jackson was awarded $16,711.04 as payment for the balance of his contract. It was another victory for Cannon. He called it a major victory for the abused ballplayers, a victory "so far-reaching as to bring about Jackson's ultimate return to organized baseball!"

Then, startlingly, Judge Gregory bitterly criticized the jury, and declared the entire case was based on Jackson's perjury. As a result, he set aside the verdict and dismissed the case!

Jackson ended up collecting only a small part of the $18,000. As with Weaver, his claim was settled out of court.

Jackson moved from Savannah in 1929 and brought his wife, Katie, back home with him to Greenville. They had no children of their own, but helped raise the son of one of Joe's brothers. In Greenville, he set up another dry-cleaning business and played semipro ball in the summers. He started to gain weight, and by the time he was forty, he had put on 35 pounds. His hair turned gray and his movements slowed down. At 220 pounds, he could no longer run and steal bases, but he never stopped hitting. At the age of forty-four, he was still the terror of every pitcher he faced. His manner became gentle and soft-spoken in the easy surroundings of his home town. He was said to make "better money pressing pants than he ever made playing big-league ball." To the local folk, he remained a hero, well liked and highly respected. He was never without their support, and the dignity of his talent never seemed to dwindle.

When he spoke of his past, he always insisted on his innocence in the 1919 fix. His denials took on an increased fervor—and, perhaps, exaggeration—as the years went by. There were always friendly people to listen, and no one to challenge him. "I ain't ever asked Judge Landis for reinstatement [though others did for him]. I don't suppose he'd give it to me if I did, but I believe I could get back in there right now. If I couldn't lead my club in hitting, I'd work without pay!"

In 1933, Greenville decided to put their club back in organized baseball. A franchise was opened up to them, and they offered Jackson the job of playing-manager. Judge Landis maintained his rigidity. "There are not, and cannot be, two standards of eligibility . . . one for the major leagues, and one for the minors."

The stigma remained. Jackson, like Weaver, grew old under its pale. He spent the declining years of his life running a liquor store in town. Ty Cobb told of a last meeting with him. Cobb, past his own prime and then a heavy drinker, was passing through Greenville and stopped in at Jackson's to buy a fifth of bourbon. These two great rivals talked to each other like total strangers, exchanging the usual banter of a merchant and a customer. Cobb, flustered at this, finally said, "Don't you know me, Joe?"

Jackson nodded sadly. "Sure—I know you, Ty. I just didn't think anyone I used to know up there wanted to recognize me again. . . ."

In his sixties, Jackson's heart began to fail. He had three coronary attacks, but managed to survive them. In 1951, a movement began to clear his name. A national television show invited him to New York to appear, a testimonial to his former greatness. He looked forward to this with tremendous pleasure.

But a few weeks before he was to appear, he suffered his last heart attack. He died on December 5, 1951, at the age of sixty-three. His funeral was well attended by his friends in Greenville. Senator Burnet Maybank of South Carolina wired condolences to his widow. So did Charles Albert Comiskey, grandson of the deceased White Sox owner.

"Do not be remembering the most natural man ever to
　　wear spiked shoes.
The canniest fielder and the longest hitter,
Who squatted on his heels
In a uniform muddied at the knees,
Till the bleacher shadows grew long behind him.
Who went along with Chick and Buck and Happy
Because they treated him so friendly-like,
Hardly like Yankees at all.
With Williams because Lefty was from the South too.
And with Risberg because the Swede was such a hard guy.
Who made an X for his name and couldn't argue with
　　Comiskey's sleepers.
But who could pick a line drive out of the air ten feet
　　outside the foul line
And rifle anything home from anywhere in the park.

For Shoeless Joe is gone, long gone,
A long yellow grass-blade between his teeth
And the bleacher shadows behind him. . . ."

Nelson Algren

INDEX